The Evolution of Film

For Sarah Turner

The Evolution of Film

Rethinking Film Studies

JANET HARBORD

polity

First published in 2007 by Polity Press

Polity Press
65 Bridge Street
Cambridge CB2 1UR, UK

Polity Press
350 Main Street
Malden, MA 02148, USA

ISBN-10: 0-7456-3473-7
ISBN-13: 978-07456-3473-9
ISBN-10: 0-7456-3476-1 (pb)
ISBN-13: 978-07456-3476-0 (pb)

A catalogue record for this book is available from the British Library.

Typeset in 11 on 13pt Bembo
by Servis Filmsetting Ltd, Manchester
Printed and bound in Great Britain by MPG Books Ltd, Bodmin, Cornwall

The publisher has used its best endeavours to ensure that the URLs for external websites referred to in this book are correct and active at the time of going to press. However, the publisher has no responsibility for the websites and can make no guarantee that a site will remain live or that the content is or will remain appropriate.

Every effort has been made to trace all copyright holders, but if any have been inadvertently overlooked the publishers will be pleased to include any necessary credits in any subsequent reprint or edition.

For further information on Polity, visit our website: www.polity.co.uk

Cinema, the way you say music.

Marguerite Duras, *Green Eyes*

There is no film. Cinema is dead. No more films are possible. If you wish, we can move on to a discussion.

Guy Debord, *Howls for Sade* soundtrack

Writing, I wanted to touch the depth of these problems. And having given myself this occupation, I fell asleep.

Georges Bataille, *The Unfinished System of Nonknowledge*

Contents

Acknowledgements

I would like to acknowledge a number of people, some of whom contributed in indirect ways, and others who are all too aware of the project of this book: Asu Aksoy, Tony Dowmunt, Julian Henriques, Mike Hoolboom, Grace McGrew, Angela McRobbie, David Morley, Patricia Pisters, Kevin Robins, Robert Smith, Gareth Stanton, Nelly Voorhuis and Richard Witts. Debts of a greater kind go to Jan Campbell for ongoing comradeship and the sharing of ideas, Sebastian Olma for stepping into the breach early on, Chris Berry for his knowledge of East Asian film and generosity with his personal archive, Kay Dickinson for rigorous readings of inertia and Palestinian film, Rachel O. Moore for arriving at Goldsmiths when she did and enlivening my thoughts on inertia and fatigue, among many other things, and Lynda Dyson for inspiring conversations about where and what film is, and for her provocative comments on cultural translation in particular. I would like to express a deep gratitude to Angela Kreeger whose insight and patience has indelibly marked my approach to intellectual life, and more besides.

My experience of the affectual in film and in life has been greatly extended by living with a film-maker and artist, Sarah Turner. This book is dedicated to her, my fellow traveller across planes extending well beyond this project, and the person who never fails to animate me, in the best of ways.

The author and publishers are grateful to the following for permission to quote from copyright works:

AK Press for the book epigraph taken from the *Howls for Sade* soundtrack by Guy Debord, from *Guy Debord: Complete Cinematic Works: Script, Stills, Documents*, translated by Ken Knabb, AK Press, Oakland, CA, www.akpress.org;

Columbia University Press for the book epigraph taken from Marguerite Duras, *Green Eyes*, translated by Carol Barko, Columbia University Press, New York, 1990;

Mike Hoolboom (director and writer) for the epigraph to chapter 5 taken from his film *Imitations of Life* (2003).

Introduction

A truism of our times is that film is not what it used to be. This truism may be elaborated in the following ways. Film is no longer spatially demarcated in the institutional sites of cinemas, but ubiquitous; in Francesco Casetti's words, 'It no longer has its own place, because it is everywhere, or at least everywhere that we are dealing with aesthetics and communication' (1999: 316). A second elaboration is that the designation 'film' refers to multiple and proliferating objects; again, Casetti, 'it is a fictional full length movie, but also an experimental work, an amateur's 8-millimeter production, an ethnographic documentary, a teaching tool, an author's test run'. A third paradoxical point is that the proliferating objects may in fact be the same object, that film has become mixed with and into other cultural forms. Victor Burgin suggests, 'Film studies must now confront as heterogeneous an "object" as that which confounds photography and television studies – in fact it is largely the same object' (2004: 9). A subsidiary note to this point is that technological convergence has disarmingly blurred the distinction between modes of dissemination and cultural forms: both television and the computer are associated with specific practices of production, aesthetic features and technologies, yet they are also transmitters of other cultural forms such as film. Fourth, the material properties of film, which once provided a definition of the medium and distinction from other media, are no longer a foundational category of classification. The property of celluloid is now combined or existing in tandem with the properties of the digital in the production of what we recognize as film.

The effects of such transformations, considered together, produce a disorientation, perhaps a momentary vertigo, for film studies.[1] To push disorientation further, the critical landscape and modes of enquiry that film studies has honed over the decades in its formation as a discipline have themselves run aground in the ill-defined context of globalization. Structuralism now appears to refer us to a system of oppositional differences and ideological persuasions long since gone. As Perry Anderson (2004) notes, the binaries that distinguished east from west, communism from capitalism, market economy from state economy, have disintegrated, memorably transmitted around the world as a falling wall, a student in front of a tank, a stock market in despair. And where poststructuralism afforded a practice of identifying the ruptures, ellipses and contradictions inherent to cultural works, cultural objects now arrive accompanied by their own mechanisms of dislocation and deconstruction. A DVD discloses the processes of film production, a computer game reveals the structure of narrative. A staple of film studies method, a linguistically inflected semiotics, now struggles with the distinction of different types of language embedded in media forms. Reflecting on the intellectual mutations in his own critical practice as a film scholar, David Rodowick writes, 'Contemporary electronic media were giving rise to hybrid and mutant forms that semiology was ill equipped to understand' (2001: x). The opposition of word and image, the relation between signifier and signified, the status of the index, cease to explicate what it is we do with or want to understand from our dealings with film. In short, the intellectual traditions and methods of a discipline determined three decades ago have come to acquire an emptiness, 'as if they constituted the rituals of a faith in which we no longer quite believe' (Flaxman, 2000: 7).

There are various responses to, or less consciously effects of, the transformations of both film and theory. In the paradigm of response (rather than effect) is an identification of theory itself as a problem (Bordwell and Carroll, 1996) and a call to disengage film analysis from what are presented as systems of thought that overwhelm the subject of film. A related though distinct trajectory is the science of cognitivism, which constructs critical practice as a form of conversation between the film and the theorist, the emphasis falling on the ability of the film to speak (rather than being spoken for by theory). A slower-burning effect of transformations in film and theory, or a simultaneous emergence, has been the renaissance in film historicism. If the present moment is characterized by definitional crisis for film, it raises questions of how and when film came into being, or rather, how and when a consensus developed about what a film is. The excavations of film historians reveal that film has for the duration of its existence been a recalcitrant object. Film scholarship has concerned itself with the identification of moments in which stability occurred, transformation slowed and film was consolidated by the formalized rituals of the cinema. Charles Musser and Tom Gunning's work on the standardization of early film exhibition provides an example of the moment in which the multiple ways of exhibiting and experiencing film are reduced and consolidated (Musser, 1990; Gunning, 1991b). With the shift of power from the film exhibitor to the distributor, according to Gunning (1991b), the heterogeneous elements of the film programme, its combination of multiple idioms, the deployment of side-barkers as local interpreters, and the narrative structure of film, all come under a pressure of standardization. The heterogeneous is effectively written out of the situation of exhibition in a move towards a homogeneous viewing experience reproducible in any socio-geographical context. Similarly, the advent of sound, according to Michael Chanan (1980), produced a thickening of film's significatory qualities, yet it tied film to a mode of enunciation at once explicatory and uniform.

Another dimension of the standardization of film as the practice of cinema-going is the social function that cinema provided, and which in turn consolidated cinema as a significant cultural practice. Miriam Hansen's work on the potential for cinema to provide a public sphere for migrants otherwise excluded from public forms of address in the early part of the twentieth century, reveals the dynamism between commercial consolidation and public use (Hansen, 1991). The standardization of cinematic time as of recognizable intensity and duration is described by Mary Ann Doane as a particular, and peculiar, consolidation of disparate strands of anxiety constituting modernity. In her work, cinema is seen to bridge the tensions of a statistical organization of the social, and an appetite for the contingent, that which exceeds expectation and control. The contingent, according to Doane, is the singularity of the instant, that which surprises and ruptures, and it is cinema's task to both generate such singularities and to make them legible to a general public.[2] 'The project of the cinema in modernity is that of endowing the singular with significance without relinquishing singularity', she argues, going on to make a claim on the present, 'That project is not necessarily abandoned with the emergence of even newer technologies of representation' (2002: 208).

If contingency is a particular attribute of the cinematic form, it is also a feature of the technological development of film and cinema. In addition to histories of film as a form, another type of history has emerged in recent years, concerned with film's relationship to other technologies. Jonathan Crary's work on perception and observation situates the naturalized mode of spectatorship in a longer *durée*, where practices of looking at images are connected to a range of instruments preceding the cinema. A range of proto-cinematic optical instruments, according to Crary, de-linked perspective from a stable position, or rather, objects refused to remain still: 'The very absence of referentiality is the ground on which new instrumental techniques will construct for an observer a new "real" world' (1991: 91). Friedrich Kittler's examination of the relationships between media forms that are also storage systems of a recorded moment, draws attention to the materiality of media, insisting on chemical and technological properties as elements to be considered. Kittler's focus on the unstable chemical formation of film, a process more akin to magic in its potency and instability, leads to the less obvious sites of strata formation where film became legitimized and consolidated as a medium for recording: 'the system of possible deceptions of the eye had to be converted from a type of knowledge specific to illusionists and magicians (such as Houdini) to one shared by physiologists and engineers' (1986: 119). Such histories not only uncover specific knowledges about film's genesis and development, but potentially transform our understanding of film as a 'pure' media. Its hybrid state, caught somewhere between the demands of witnessing (film as record and representation of nature), and its ability to deceive and imaginatively inspire (film as attraction), is more complex yet than the well-worn opposition between Lumière and Méliès.

As this selection of historiographic examples illustrates, history is always written from the shifting and invested perspective of the present moment. The translator's introduction to Kittler's *Gramophone, Film, Typewriter* (1986) states, 'The media of the present influence how we think about the media of the past or, for that matter, those of the future' (1999: xii). Film historiography provides not so much a reconstruction and uncovery of events as a reflection of our current fascinations and intellectual concerns. How did film become film, and at what point did it acquire the coherence of the institutional form of cinema, are questions very much of our time. They are questions fuelled, albeit implicitly, by a desire to comprehend and model change. That change rebounds from the past as a messy, arbitrary and inconsistent process, in equal measure to moments of consolidation and discovery, reflects the complex ways in which transformation is currently thought. Here, the cross-fertilization of disciplines comes into play in the tracing of genealogies of thought about film. In returning to questions of what film is and how it came to be (questions of ontology) as historical analysis, it becomes clear that film has always eluded categorical definition. In place of a definitive answer from the past, what comes into view is the nature of thought at that time, the time of early film, refracted through the present. Just as film has been detached from a logic of objective observation, film theory as historical enterprise has come to be seen as a double framing of the past from the present.

Film historiography also echoes the current mix of disciplinary influences that characterize work in the field in the contemporary. As many commentators have noted, the paradigm in which film emerged in the era of modernity is influenced by discourses of science, of physics, biology and chemistry, as well as the more familiar disciplines of the social sciences. There are two imports from science that have a critical impact on the formation of cinema, according to Doane. The first is the Second Law of Thermodynamics, a law of entropy stating that 'the mechanism that creates heat also dissipates heat, and this dissipation . . . is unrecoverable' (Charney, 1998: 15). The Second Law of Thermodynamics, writes Doane, 'engendered a conceptualization of time as the tightness of a direction, an inexorable and irreversible linearity', producing a reification of time as 'standardized, stabilized, and rationalized' (2002: 4–5). The conceptual framework impacts on the development of film, as the demand to create stable units of duration (the cinema programme), arranged in a linear fashion (the singular direction of the film moving through the gate of the projector). In addition, Doane argues, and in tension with the influence of physics, was the impact of evolutionary theory. Darwin's concept of natural selection 'was instrumental to the diffusion across a range of disciplines of the epistemological centrality of chance'. The notion of an 'aberration' occurring in the chain of reproduction, which then becomes a consolidated part of the 'species', reveals the contingent forces of change which appropriate matter in order to become. That film is always, in a sense, a hybrid, that all transformation is imagined through a kaleidoscope of disciplinary influence, is evident early on. In addition to the discourses of physics and evolutionary biology, early film was often described through a semi-mystical discourse of the inexplicable: that is, types of magic.

These multiple influences are evident in the eloquent writings of the film-maker and writer Jean Epstein: 'Raymond Lulle never knew a finer powder for projection and emotion. All volumes are displaced and reach flashpoint. Life recruits atoms, molecular movement is as sensual as the hips of a woman or young man. The hills harden like muscles. The universe is on edge. The philosopher's light. The atmosphere is heavy with love. I am looking' (1981:16). Epstein's poetic rendition of cinematic effect combines the chemical qualities of powder, and the flashpoint of magic, with atoms and molecular movement. This associative imagining that crosses science and art is common also to the writings of Kracauer ('the tremendous energies accumulated in the microscopic configurations of matter' (1960: 51)), Benjamin and Eisenstein.

The present paradigm in which we find ourselves attempting to think the transformations of film is also inflected by scientific discourses, of genetics, physics and calculus. In the writings of Prigogine and Stengers (1984, 1997), Latour (1993), Massumi (2002) and De Landa (1999, 2000), to name but a few influential thinkers, the interface of science and social science has been productively worked. Prigogine and Stengers' *Order out of Chaos* (1984) provides the model for this work, positing the evolution of both science and philosophy as 'open systems' that endlessly dialogue with the cultural environment, effecting change and in turn being marked by the exchange. The suggestiveness of the title sets in play the familiar dynamics of order and chaos. Yet this is not a model of a mastery of chaos through the imposition of knowledge, but a description of a new 'poised' system that surfs the fragile crest between chaos and order. The schematic reference to the work here can do no justice to the ideas, but the influence of this work is far-reaching, felt in the following ways. First, the concept of change, which has been dominated by models of social construction in film and media studies (change imposed from the outside), is turned upside down. Change is seen to be immanent to matter itself, is dependent on the particular combination of properties of matter and their mutual interference. Second, the direction of change is not predictable but possible, giving rise to a mode of thinking that 'poses an unpredictable futurity rather than anticipating outcomes – call that kind of thought *operative reason, as opposed to instrumental reason*' (Massumi, 2002: 110). Third, nature and culture are not opposed, with nature as the discovered term and culture as immanent (self-defining). Such a tradition of thought 'overlooks the simultaneous birth of "non-humanity" – things, or objects, or beasts', therefore it overlooks the multidirectional relations between these things (Latour, 1992: 13).

All of these points have a direct bearing on how we conceive of the present changes to film, posing a volatile and multi-directional process of change, and alerting us to the status of film as an object with which we enter a choreography of being. The model of change here is non-linear, dynamic, yielding a sense of innovation as both open and structured, and it is a model that can be seen to describe the context in which film exists and to affect the transformations of film as a thing. Digital film is at once an object, an affectual experience, an idea/memory, a system of code, and transferable data. The impact of other, scientific paradigms of thought have already occurred in the object itself; we have yet to see if film studies may make use of them. If we were to do so, our concept of the nature of film, of its ongoing impermanence and transformation, of its 'agency' as it travels to create networks and correspondences, of its reconceptualization of our sense of time and space, and our practice in film studies, would be changed. If, in Epstein's words, we are looking.

Midday–midnight

At the end of the second of his two books on film, *The Time-Image*, Deleuze returns to the question of theory and film: 'The usefulness of theoretical books on cinema has been called into question', adding wistfully in parenthesis '(especially today, because the times are not right)' (1985: 280). At the end of his ambitious feat of a project, concerned with writing the historical transformations of cinema and the critical importance that cinema has for thought, Deleuze glances momentarily towards the context of reception only to find, ironically, that the times are not right. Is the time right, we might enquire now, to reflect on what we do as well as what film is? If the project is conceived as a bolstering of the historical importance of film and cinema, the answer would undoubtedly be negative. An undertaking of this kind would know the answer in advance of the question. What such a project would repress is the opportunity afforded by changes in film to challenge the commonplace assumptions of both film, and film's ability to transform thought.

The chapters in this book attempt to work in this direction. The first chapter, 'One hundred years of film theory', marks the centenary of film theory as well as cinema. It is not, however, a glossing of a century of work. The title is in part a parody of the current obsession with creating compendiums of culture, which both reduce and exclude the rich variety of any history. It is also a reference to the two cinema books by Deleuze which provide, despite Deleuze's own denial of intent on the opening pages, a short history of cinema. This chapter examines the concept of theory in film studies, its maverick affects according to some commentators, and its potency and possibility according to others. The argument here derives from Deleuze's proposition that a sustained meditation on film and film theory illuminates the relation between image and thought. If the modus operandi in thought is conceptual, the mode of film is affectual. Importantly, both concept and affect are open systems, exchanging information and experience.

What Deleuze both encourages and demonstrates in the cinema books is the creation – that is, the invention – of concepts for the study of film. Whilst I am critical of the emphasis that Deleuze gives to time at the expense of space in these works, his invitation to invent is a productive one. In the light of this discussion, what is called for is the invention of new categories of classification for film, and new paradigms to organize analytical study. These are critical concerns in the present context when the idea of genre describes only the well-worn categories of large-scale film production, and the burgeoning film culture external to this system travels under the eponym 'world cinema'. Whilst systems of classification and taxonomy are always contingent enterprises, suited to the needs at hand as well as sensitive to the differences between objects, film studies is now poised to reorganize its field. This task is of course, in the work of many scholars, already underway.

The second chapter examines what we understand by the term 'Hollywood'. Once a staple of film studies curricula, Hollywood has now lost its defining power as an analytical category. Whilst there is an acknowledged golden age of Hollywood film, the subsequent transformations to this system of production have found little consensus. It is suggested here that Hollywood's last decade was the 1990s, a consideration that is staged in three transformations. First, Hollywood is no longer defined by the production of film. Second, Hollywood no longer generates the majority of its income through cinema attendance. Third, film as a celluloid form looks certain to be eclipsed by digital stock, with Eastman Kodak announcing the suspension of the production of celluloid film by 2010. In light of these changes, this chapter explores the types of film produced by whatever we still think of as 'Hollywood' in recent years, examining the preponderance of remakes (of film and television series), adaptations of books, comics and computer games, and reversionings of existing films. Hollywood's recycling of a history of media texts is productive of a mythical and internally sealed form of film culture, a virtual sphere where comic-book characters acquire a life that adapts over time and across texts. And whilst Hollywood extends its interests across media forms and geographical terrain, the management of copyright emerges as a critical form of virtual control.

The third chapter, 'Assemblage: editing space-time', begins an exploration of film's relationship to space and contingency, a continuing theme through the remaining chapters. The concept of montage has a lengthy history in film studies, regarded by some as the defining quality of film, placed oppositionally to the duration and depth of the shot. Montage has been the subject of particular political investments in the effects of film (for example, Eisenstein), and in the relationship between image and thought. The description of film as a visceral shock in early scholarship owes much to the practices of cutting and splicing, the juxtaposition of scale, subject and location. The trajectory of debate on montage has, however, taken the cutting of time as the significant factor for critical thought. Time, through montage, has become elastic, sculptural and eroticized. My interest here is to examine the ways in which recent film has used montage to sculpt space, to create 'unthought' relations between spaces, to produce correspondences between what are commonly regarded as incommensurate systems. Thus, Haneke's film *Code Unknown* moves jarringly between Paris, Africa and the Balkans, in an editing style that forges new connections.

'The limits of translation: transnational film', explores a way of reading film as transnational: that is, in contrast to the paradigm of the national and the dialogue of inter-national culture, transnational moves through networks that are productive of spatial relations. The chapter explores current conceptualizations and experience of space through the revised paradigm of anthropology: in particular, the work of Marc Augé. Augé claims that we are living in the condition of supermodernity, characterized by an excess of spatial and temporal referents: globalization effects an interconnectivity that works along both axes. Within this, he distinguishes non-place, the anonymous functional spaces of ATM lobbies, international hotels and airports, and place, the historic signifiers of local identity. Augé's gift in this work is to describe the affectual experience of diverse spaces, and the collapse of spatial binaries: the near and the far, the familiar and the foreign. These concepts are explored and extended in relation to two films, *Chungking Express* and *Tropical Malady*, where filmic space is a complex production. In summary form, there are three characteristics. Filmic space defies an originary cultural space. The 'here' of the film is mediated by the 'elsewhere' through a range of cultural references. Second, space is composed of images and media forms as much as a built environment. And third, many films contain an acknowledgement of their alterity within the text itself, an acknowledged 'foreignness' that prefigures and confronts its perceived 'foreignness' to be met in its journeys of circulation.

The fifth chapter, 'Innocent monsters: film and other media', examines the contingent nature of film's evolution as it comes into contact with other types of textual matter, and explores our inceasingly contingent engagements with it. The chapter reconfigures the story of the melancholic decline of cinema as an escape story; film is now on the loose, turning up in unexpected places and formats. In examining various encounters with film in diverse places and in different technological versions, its singularity is marked by its affectual appeal. That is, in a so-called information age, characterized by excessive flows of news stories and data, film remains something of an anomaly, a potent experience that defies an evaluation in terms of its utility. Film, poised between its objchood and an illusion, retains the alterity of the non-human world. In its affectual workings, its lasting trace is an imprint of the possible connections between the human and non-human worlds which decentre human autonomy.

In the final chapter, the concept of energy is mooted as a possible way of classifying film. Inertia is a state of being that is critically unfashionable, with social theory gravitating towards cultures and works that appear to be characterized by intensity. Yet inertia enables a framing of a particular kind of film, where mobility (of the narrative progression, of character development, and camera-work) is curtailed. In *Uzak* and *Divine Intervention*, various modes of inactivity reframe our fascination with the 'moving' image: movement, and mobility, have a range of registers. That these films describe a form of experience that is characteristic of particular socio-political contexts makes their sense of energy all the more significant.

Finally, a note on method. There is not one particular theoretical figure whose ideas are systematically worked through the chapters. There are, rather, a range of influential thinkers, from Deleuze to Derrida, Foucault, Augé, Latour and Massumi, whose concepts resonate with a particular force in the present moment. It is true that Deleuze is a weighty influence here, and indeed, the impact of his thought (along with Felix Guattari) on the current intellectual landscape is far-reaching. It is also a feature of the book that many of the ideas are drawn from conceptual frameworks external to the discipline of film studies, from philosophy, anthropology and visual culture. This is neither a flag-waving for interdisciplinarity nor a critique of film studies, but rather an effect of the cross-fertilization of thought in moments that we might conceive as periods of accelerated transformation. Thought, as Deleuze reminds us, comes from the outside, with all of its messy crossings, exchanges and infections.

Similarly, the recurring intellectual questions of the book are not intended to impose systematic order or to constitute a coherent field. They are ideas that have arisen in many publications and conference forums, that appear insistent, compelling and open to elaboration. These may be summarized in the following way. First, the potent relation between film and thought is moving in new directions, a relation in which each term moves against and transforms the other. Second, film has the facility to bring about situations of cultural encounter which resist the staged effects of commodification. Film underscores the possibilities and limits of cultural translation, of the ways in which cultures become recognizable to each other, or conversely remain incommensurate, insistent on difference. Third, the affectual appeal of film, its ability to capture and leave an imprint upon us, marks out its anomolous qualities in an era of abstract global information flows. Fourth, film's curious form as an illusion and (increasingly as we encounter it) an object, directs our attention to the life-forms of the non-human world. In Bruno Latour's terms, the hierarchy established centuries ago which divided the human from the non-human is an act of purification that dispels the agency of things (Latour, 1993). To become modern, Latour suggests, is to decentre the authoritative distinctions between the human and the life-world of things, and to recognize the hybridity of existence. To bring this idea to bear on film, whose institutional inauguration in cinema is deeply enmeshed with concepts of the modern, is a fertile crossing indeed.

The films selected for attention here are largely drawn from the ill-defined category of work that circulates under the heading of 'world cinema'. That this term is a classification in need of revision and a more subtle and imaginative inflection is a premiss of the book. The impulse to include certain films above others is not a result of selecting texts that are amenable to a pre-arranged set of ideas. Rather, they are films that have set in motion particular chains of thought. They are also the result of my own contexts of encounter with the partly arbitrary, partly structured circuits that film travels within Europe. Method is also marked by the contingent.

These ideas, and others, are expanded in what follows.

1

One hundred years of film theory

The preface to Foucault's book *The Order of Things* opens with laughter, laughter we are told that shattered 'all the familiar landmarks of my thought', that lasted some time and lingered as a prickly uneasiness. The text inspiring such revelry is 'a certain' Chinese encyclopaedia entry, cited by Borges, for the classification of animals. The entry is set out in the following way:

> animals are divided into (a) belonging to the Emperor, (b) embalmed, (c) tame, (d) sucking pigs, (e) sirens, (f) fabulous, (g) stray dogs, (h) included in the present classification, (i) frenzied, (j) innumerable, (k) drawn with a very fine camelhair brush, (l) *et cetera*, (m) having just broken the water pitcher, (n) that from a long way off look like flies. (Foucault, 1966: xvi)

What produces such enjoyment in Foucault is not the ridicule of another system of thought, but the 'stark impossibility of thinking *that*', the way in which such an unfamiliar taxonomy reveals in the reader the strict limits and confines of his own imagination. It is not simply the range of definitions of animals themselves, but the logical sequence in which they are presented by the alphabetical system of order, linking each to the other in a chain of meaning.

That 'a' should follow 'b' in a connected series, for Foucault, 'transgresses the boundaries of all imagination'.

In contemplating the contents pages of compendiums of film theory, we may be forgiven for responding with a similar hysteria, as enjoyable or otherwise. Film theory may be classified as (a) concerned with the long take, (b) a study of the corporation MGM, (c) the structural properties of the genre of horror, (d) an analysis of the optical image, (e) an application of Lacanian psychoanalytic theory, (f) Soviet montage. What is surprising is not that this range of work exists, but that it is undertaken in what we largely assume to be a unified discipline in film studies. The listing of the categories of classification implies a common terrain, a relationship between different approaches, a certain intellectual order. Yet, as Foucault persuades us in *The Order of Things*, the organizational systems through which we access objects are possibly arbitrary grids. In accounts of film studies as a discipline (in film studies readers and introductory texts) there are, however, two recurring paradigms for the telling of the story: place and time. Film scholarship concerned with specific places (national cinemas, corporations, audiences) and particular times (new waves, movements) are anchored by these traditional axioms. And yet any close inspection of this description reveals that one dimension constantly encroaches upon the other.

In Foucault's response to Borges' enumeration of the category of animal is the sense of a disturbance, a monstrousness. The monstrousness for Foucault lies in the destruction of a common ground upon which such definitions may meet, or in other words, the undoing of the category of animal paradoxically in the process of its classification. The implication of Foucault's reading, when applied to the context of film studies, is that a similar monstrosity may be afoot. How can film theory be each of these, and then again, how can it be all of these? The question posed in this way gives rise to the sense that film studies may have little or no common ground. The question of the coherence of film theory, of the relation between its component parts, is a question sublimated to the discipline's historical interrogation of what is cinema (famously asked by Bazin), and more recently the questions of where cinema may be found (Sontag), and what we can take film to be (Rodowick). In the wake of film's encounter with digital matter, the question of film's ontology is given a new urgency. The displaced matter of celluloid threatens our conceptions of film, and in turn reverberates this threat throughout the discipline. What, we are enquiring now, is film becoming? By implication, the following but less frequently asked question has to be, what is film studies to become?

The relation between film and theory is vexed and involves the dispute of boundaries, a warfare of inclusion and exclusion, underpinned by concepts of purity and pollution. If the emergence of the study of film appeared to follow the object, evolving from journalism to be designated as theory in the latter half of the twentieth century,[1] this particular pathway centred the film itself, rather than models of thought, at the heart of the enquiry. Yet if film studies emerges as a discrete discipline focused on its object in the second half of the twentieth century, this focus comes under pressure from the designation of film studies as a discipline. In the post-1968 moment of cultural critique, the study of film becomes incorporated into the paradigms of the social sciences. Film is subject to enquiry and application from Marxism, psychoanalysis and structuralism, universal pass-keys to unlock the apparent meaning of a film. Film is a text within an intellectual and political context, and the balance between these two terms is a source of conflict. The specificity of a film is lost to readings of 'film', and the charge of symptomatic texts, selected to demonstrate a theoretical apparatus serving a political project, is thrown down. The partial resolution of this struggle is the turn to reception as the site of negotiated readings, a return to particular texts as film cultures, thus holding together the relation between text and context. But film studies appears here to stray into areas of cultural studies and identity politics, to lose its grip on the specificity of film. Context appears to speak for film, and film becomes enmeshed in the reading of culture as a vehicle of social reproduction, or conversely as a site of resistance.

The recent centennial celebrations of cinema, launched at the moment in which digital culture appears to usher in a new era, provoke a crisis in this struggle. The skirmishes of intellectual approach appear to be eclipsed by the anxiety that the object itself is under threat. The mourning of cinema as an institution, a particular practice and experience, crystallizes the mix of nostalgia and futurology at work in the thinking about film. The most reductive representation of this debate is played out as a belief in the future of film versus the apocalypse of cinema. An alternative approach to film in this moment where film studies appears to teeter on the edge of existence is a turn to historical film study. In the work of Miriam Hansen (1991), Tom Gunning (1991b), Anne Friedberg (1993), Mary Ann Doane (2002) and Sean Cubitt (2004), film history is excavated to reveal analogies and connections with the present. Coupled with historical work on the evolution of technologies from Alfred Kittler and Jonathan Crary, the present is revealed through the past as a series of unlikely resonances and connections, history as helix, a spiral in which different moments echo across the circling form but never meet: to complete the circle this would suggest history as pure repetition.[2]

If the renaissance in film history has facilitated an opening on to conceptualizations of technological change, challenging and enriching comprehension of the digital environment, it has only indirectly addressed the status of theory within the field. One hundred years of cinema is also one hundred years of film discourse and we have yet to catch up with the tracing of where theory has been, and where its openings and energies reside. My aim in this chapter is precisely not to attempt to collate the range of work within the discipline over a hundred years, nor to summarize what might be considered its most prescient eras, movements or individual works, aims that would eviscerate rather than illuminate anything about the field. Rather my project here is to consider the relationships between the chapter's titular terms of film, theory and history in order to posit what it is, or what it might be, that we think we are doing with film and within film studies at this moment. These three terms are indelibly imbricated, tangled, intermeshed on the table before us. Any attempt to pick up one element immediately pulls at the contours of the other two. How to relate a history of film without conceptualizing what film is? How to articulate an idea of film without a philosophical foundation? And how to think, to move in thought in a culture of the visual without the presence of filmic images?

Tyrannical thought

The history of the discipline of film studies is not simply a legacy of different theories, but a history in which the place of theory itself has been challenged and refuted. That a notion of post-theory has been presented as the demarcation of a new era of critical study reveals the extent to which theory is regarded as exterior to the discipline, a polluting force to be excised at its most extreme (Bordwell and Carroll, 1996). The proposition of a post-theoretical film studies needs to be situated in the context against which it is in revolt, and that is the context of the dominance of semiotic theory and its method of textual analysis, rising in the postwar period in Anglo-American work to gain prominence in the 1970s and 1980s. The focus of semiotic interpretation pivoted in this period, twisting away from the structural position that language speaks us, and its analysis of film language as a revelation of the under-girding ideological formations, to the poststructural position that language retains a fundamental lack of coherence, revealed in paradoxes, slips and textual ruptures of meaning. Despite this pivotal shift of emphasis, both structuralist and poststructuralist accounts fetishize an interpretation of the text as the work to be done. Reception studies relocated the emphasis from the text towards context and a specific historical–cultural event of reading (Klinger, 1997), purporting what Janet Staiger has described as a historical explanation of interpretive acts. Yet the emphasis of reception studies remains on the act of interpretation, albeit through a pluralized range of interpretive frameworks. David Bordwell comments in exasperation: 'Any interpretive practice seeks to show that texts mean more than they seem to say. But one might ask, why does a text not say what it means?' (1989: 64–5).

The inference of Bordwell's statement is developed further in the work of *Post-theory: reconstructing film studies* (Bordwell and Carroll, 1996), where it is not simply interpretive theory that is to be laid to rest, but theory period, in a turn to the science of cognitivism. In a sense, Bordwell unwittingly reifies interpretative analysis by reading it as the manifestation of theory, as though there may be interpretive theoretical studies or no theory at all. Post-theory in one sense articulates a desire for less complexity in the study of film, a call for a clarification of objectives that recentres a notion of film analysis as a pragmatic, concrete activity cleaved from the contortions and distortions of theoretical investments. By a curious turn of positions, the theoretical paradigms that were once employed to reveal the ideological fault lines of a culture have themselves become the suspicious ideological underpinnings of the discipline, to be equally exposed and critiqued. Bordwell's polemic rightly points to the institutional regulation of critical accounts in its reward and promotion of certain readings and its exclusion of others, an effective delimitation of thought. Yet his position tacitly suggests that there is a naturalism to a type of formalist analysis that must go unchallenged. As Slavoj Žižek comments, post-theory suggests 'we can magically return to some kind of naiveté before things like the unconscious, the overdetermination of our lives by the decentred symbolic processes, and so forth became part of our theoretical awareness' (2001: 14). A less polemical refutation of structural analysis is found in the work of Stanley Cavell (1981) and Dudley Andrew (1984), where the potency of reading arrives as the result of an address of the text. In this scholarship, film is perceived to be the pedagogic partner, leading the critic into an awareness of its complexity.

Whether gentle or savage, the discourse of film studies bifurcates into oppositional camps where either position is known in advance: either text or context, formalist analysis or interpretive analysis, film or theory, must take priority. The extant schema of binary thought maps out the possibilities, yet the cartography ceases to serve us. As Gregory Flaxman notes:

> In recent years, film theory has more or less gone underground; the tenets of semiotics, psychoanalysis, and (Althusserian) Marxism are still called upon, but without the same conviction, as if they constituted the rituals of a faith in which we no longer quite believe. In their stead, historicism, spectator studies, cultural studies, and cognitivism have come to dominate the field. The result is a peculiar, and peculiarly fashionable, absence of debate – about what film is, about its difference from other arts, about its effect on thought, about the way its images can be distinguished – in which a set of traditional assumptions quietly cement themselves. (Flaxman, 2000: 7–8)

In the arranging of the landscape in such a way, the question of how thinking and film take place together, of how film affects thought and vice versa, is suspended. In the failure to move outside of a structural-poststructural paradigm and its related skirmishes, film studies has not only neglected the specificity of film's diverse forms of address, as some film scholars have claimed. It has also failed to engage with the changing formations of critical thought. In this context, to isolate theory as the problem and to oust it from the discipline is possibly the most hazardous gesture for the future of film studies.

One of the most influential thinkers of the new paradigm of critical thought is Gilles Deleuze, whose work has at times been labelled as constructivism, a reference to its capacity for invention. In Deleuze's expansive oeuvre, the philosophical paradigms of the twentieth century are recast, with recourse to a sublimated tradition of thinkers invoked as an alternative to the hermeneutical tradition (which assumes an always already given): in place of Husserl, Hegel and Heidegger are Bergson, Kant, Nietzsche, Leibniz and Spinoza, thinkers whose work has not been assimilated by traditional philosophy. Deleuze's method is to create, to make, to invent concepts any-which-way, in a project set to renew thought, to deterritorialize the familiar landscape in which thought moves. The process of renewal is not an isolated philosophical enterprise but one that reaches into and across other forms of 'thinking', as Deleuze would have it. Deleuze's thought is woven through literature, art, film and music, for artists, film-makers and musicians are also thinkers but in the creation of different forms. Where philosophers invent concepts, artists create percepts and affects through the specificity of their medium. Thinking for Deleuze is movement, the capacity to travel, to transform, to mutate, and movement is in itself a definition of being alive.

It is a curious situation then that Deleuze's two-volume work on cinema has had so little impact on the discipline of film studies. Stranger still, *The Movement-Image* (1983, English translation 1986) and *The Time-Image* (1985, English translation 1989) emerge at a moment when other intellectual paradigms in film studies are losing their explicatory force. Gregory Flaxman describes the Anglo-American context of reception as sceptical, in regard to both the philosophical source of the work and the scale of the books. Appropriated in piecemeal ways into film studies, Flaxman describes their fate as receiving 'initial intrigue', giving way to avoidance, 'the subtle labor of evasion', in film scholarship (2000: 2). Similarly, David Rodowick comments on the nature of challenge implicit to the cinema books, confronting film studies with its own systems of impasse. And yet, 'That much of the recent anglophone work on Deleuze and film is coming from writers who are approaching film theory from outside the field is symptomatic, then, of a certain inertia in film studies' (1997: xi). If Deleuze's challenge to film studies has until relatively recently gone unnoticed, it has produced the subsequent irony: whilst Deleuze demands thought to emerge from the outside, external to the borders of the familiar intellectual field, this has been played out with a literalism in film studies.[3]

In asking what it is that film does for us, and what we do with it, the question of the relationship of the moving image to thought is a critical concern. Deleuze, in the cinema books, prises this open for us and arranges the parts across the early and mid-century's cinematic forms. The mode of production is not a method; as Claire Colebrook notes of Deleuze's work in general, he refers to his process as intuition if he names it at all. But in the preface to the first cinema book, *The Movement-Image*, the description of the process appears as a taxonomy, a practice that resonates the work of Foucault. He states, 'This work is not a history of the cinema. It is a taxonomy, an attempt at the classification of images and signs' (p. xiv). Although the books are not strictly a history, they trace an emergence of diverse patterns in cinema and thought, from the movement image to the time image, movements pertaining to the first half of the century and the postwar period respectively. However, the emphasis that Deleuze places on time, which is dependent on the exclusion of space, falls short of adequately grasping the spatial mutation of thought in the latter part of the century. In the conceptualization of cinema and time, time becomes the indefatigable discovery that revitalizes thought. Space in turn is the conservative force, singularly appearing as the measurement of time, its empirical plodding other. One might ask here, why does space have to mean this for Deleuze? Indeed, in the work that follows closely on the heels of the cinema books, co-written with Felix Guattari, space re-emerges as a more vital pliable component and thinking tool. In *A Thousand Plateaus: capitalism and schizophrenia* (1987), space has become a geological form, both smooth and striated, revealed as multiform surfaces of planes, plateaus, strata. In this work, the geographical imagination is set alive, resonant with the way in which contemporary film and contemporary capitalism perform space for and through us.[4] This treatment of space does not contradict or displace Deleuze's thesis on time, but rather the spatial is allowed to come into its own with a complexity equal to the temporal. This is a shortcoming in the cinema books, a point to which I return later in the chapter, but first a consideration of the work of the cinema books themselves, which purport to offer that illusive and impossible thing, a short history of cinema.[5]

For Deleuze, philosophy, science and art in their mutual contamination reinvigorate each other, facilitating new means of expression in their cross-fertilization. In this context, the cinema holds a particular potency for thought as its fundamental blocks or units are movement and time. Both terms have great significance for philosophy, but in the context in which Deleuze is attempting a deterritorialization of thought, time is the concept that transforms and is transformed. In the tradition of philosophy that Deleuze is attempting to create a break from, various systems of thought have become manifest as an official knowledge, or truth. Deleuze's project is to expose these systems as judgements rather than universal tenets, and the cinema provides a way of doing this in its shaping of time. For 'time has always put the notion of truth into crisis' (1985: 130). The notion of time is a consistent project across both books, for the concept of time registers movement, change, becoming, and thus redescribes the philosophical postulation that ontology is an essence of being, a static conceptualization of self. Deleuze's formulation of time then enables a conceptualization of the self and the world as a series of energies rather than entities, subject to continuous variation. This is a critical concept that returns in relation to what we conceive of as film. For in Deleuze's philosophical reworking, whether we are talking about the self, place or objects such as film, these are not knowable, stable forms undergoing moments of intermittent or radical change. Rather, each of these components is (rather than is 'in') a process of constant transformation and differentiation, an emerging difference from itself as much as from other matter.

At its simplest, the main question driving the cinema books, according to Rodowick, is 'How does a sustained meditation on film and film theory illuminate the relation between image and thought?' (1997: 5). Cinema takes on a privileged position within this formulation as it deals in both time and movement, and Deleuze carves a distinction between two types of cinematic logic through these terms. Periodization is an effect of this analysis, as early and classical cinema (pre-Second World War) operates through signs and images that are of a different nature to postwar cinema.[6] In prewar classical cinema, time is traced through movement, therefore it posits an indirect relation to time. In *The Movement-Image*, Deleuze is reading the philosophy of Bergson through and with cinema. Here, the fascination with movement and time at the beginning of the twentieth century is widespread, with Bergson's work threading associations between philosophy, psychology and photography. Photographic attempts to capture movement are caught in a dilemma of the spatial and temporal. Whilst a relay of cameras records the process of a moving body, it is the record of a series of instants which construct movement as a series of spatial images. Thus time appears indirectly as the measure of a body across space. Within cinema, of course, this relay of 'snapshots' is spatialized again within the linear ribbon of the film strip, each frame set apart from but in sequential relation to another frame. The image of time that photographic studies and early cinema produce is indirect in the sense that it renders time spatial, and it forges time as a serial form.

The concept that Deleuze finds so fertile in Bergson's work is the temporal nature of thought, thought as movement. Bergson's 'open totality in movement' describes the process of thought as movement operating in two directions: a non-linear associative process, and a movement of integration and differentiation. The first form of thought moves in a lateral way to create associations and connections, whilst the second form of thought as movement distinguishes and arranges thought into sets or ensembles. As images of thought are organized into a conceptual whole, the set changes qualitatively, and this consciousness of a qualitative change is named as 'the whole of relations'. For Deleuze, movement is not the instant captured in the snapshot, but the interval between, the gap that facilitates the transition from sensation to integration. The cinema retains a privileged position amongst the arts in its presentation of movement; where literature and painting require the brain to effect movement from sensation, the movement of the cinema 'converts into potential what was only possibility' in other arts (Flaxman, 2000: 19). The movement of the cinema, which might be the movement of the camera as a shot, or the cutting together of images in editing, produces the qualitative change of sets. And this is the critical factor in this theory of sets: the set, in being open to change, is open to the 'whole of relations', a term for the unthought (images of the past or future) which exists outside of the set but to which the set is open. For Bergson, time is the open, that which is in constant transformation and becoming.

The cinema is a privileged art-form for unravelling the relation of thought to movement, as it provides a 'shock to thought'. In the specificity of the cinematic form, in the camera's roving eye which is not a human eye, perception is transformed from everyday acts of seeing. If vision is always a process of selection from an infinite range of perceptions, moderated by our own sense of the quotidian and that which 'fits' into our ordering of the world, the camera presents us with perception that is free from such constraints. Cinema's shock to thought, rather like that of Benjamin's conception of the edit, shakes the foundations of perception and provides new possibilities. Through this sensation, we are conscious not only of the framed image on the screen, but also the infinite possibilities (both extended time and space) outside of the screen. The movement of the image and the system of 'irrational cuts' manifest as the practice of editing, recompose the world as images that are incommensurate, disjoint and virtual. In this focus on the specificity of what Deleuze considers a 'new' art-form, movement and montage suggest the singularity of cinema, and through these forms, everyday perceptions are thrown out of joint. The ability to perceive movement as movement – that is, as a quality rather than a process, such as tracing the path of an object from one point to another opens up the world as a chaotic entity composed of different energies and qualities of movement. In such a way, cinema facilitates movement of thought, or opens up thought from the outside.

As early cinema evolves into a classical form, it increasingly imitates human perception. Practices of shot and reverse shot map out and predict a response, systems of editing gravitate towards continuity of cuts, matching cuts in time and space with preconceived visual or narrative themes. According to Deleuze, classical cinema stabilizes the image flux by creating logical connections and associations, a logic driven by narrative structure. In the theory of sets that has been noted, the shot builds and extends itself, and through montage the set is linked to another system of ensembles, thus enlarging the conception of movement. Whilst the classical cinema perfects this method through the development of a particular logic, a causal chain, the relation of movement to the cut pervades and obsesses all forms of cinema during this period. In the early parts of *The Movement-Image*, Deleuze considers the various strategies of montage in the work of the early American school (Griffiths), the Soviet school (Eisenstein and Vertov), the French school (Gance), and the German school in expressionism. 'The only generality about montage is that it puts the cinematographic image into a relationship with the whole; that is, with time conceived as the Open', Deleuze asserts, suggesting that montage might break open our relationship to time and enable us to see it as divergent durations. Yet he continues, 'In this way it gives an indirect image of time, simultaneously in the individual movement-image and in the whole of the film' (1983: 55). Montage remains an indirect rendition of time: time here appears or works through movement, and often through distinction (one set of shots is in contrast to another oppositional set). In each of these schools of montage, the practice of editing takes the rhythms and contrasts of movement, the differences imposed by cuts, as the ordering of images under a higher principle. Even in politically oppositional films, such as the work of Eisenstein, montage is subjected to the principle of the dialectical production of truth. Through contrasting images, a state of truth is produced as the third term, the outcome of the juxtaposition. Within classical cinema, this becomes an institutionalized set of rhythms and associations, a familiar practice. Cinema replicates our sensory-motor schema, or our quotidian perceptions and conceptions of time, movement and the connection of parts into an organic whole.

In this schematic version of Deleuze's cinema books, I want to highlight the tensions between the significance that Deleuze affords to montage, and the historical context mobilized in the gap between the two books. Here, the knotty relations between time, space and the principles of editing are set up as a historical rupture. The final chapter of *The Movement-Image* begins to identify a breach in the systems of logical connection that thread together classical (or oppositional) film up until this point, and we find Deleuze speculating on the reasons: the Second World War and its aftermath, the failure of the American Dream, the emergence of minorities and the challenge to unified perspectives. This is a crisis for Hollywood in particular and its configuration of film as genre (or 'its old genres' as it appears in the chapter, a term that signals the weary schemas of image production by this point). We are mindful of Deleuze's warning, that the cinema books are not a history of cinema.[7] Yet, as Jacques Rancière poses the question, 'how are we to think the relationship between a break internal to the art of images and the ruptures that affect history in general?' (2001: 108). In other words, is this a breach caused by an external context, or a distinction arising out of the images, or signs, themselves? If cinema is not a representational form, why does a war create a rupture in its process?

Rancière's answer, and critique of Deleuze, is that the crisis of classical cinema, presented at the end of the movement image in the figure of Hitchcock, is manifestly an allegorical reading of the films. That is, it is not the identity or nature of signs that is in crisis, but a rupture in thought: 'if Deleuze has to allegorize this rupture by means of emblems taken from the stories, isn't it because it cannot be identified as an actual difference between types of image?' (Rancière, 2001: 116). Where Deleuze reads Hitchcock as producing a crisis in the sign, Rancière reads a crisis staged as plot device. In *Vertigo*, for example, Rancière argues that Scottie's vertigo provides the opportunity for Hitchcock to present the spectacle of the character hanging from a gutter; Scottie's vertigo facilitates the theatrical in cinema. For Deleuze, Hitchcock's films retain a particular significance as a mode of cinema that begins to disintegrate the schema of action cinema. By paralysing his characters, the imposed stasis creates a chain of associations that are mental, pushing to the limits the normative sensory-motor schema and moving towards a

virtual image. What Rancière overlooks is the paranoid schema of
Hitchcock's work, whereby the internal perceptions of the characters are mixed up in the shots themselves with the *mise en scène*.
Thus, in *Marnie*, red becomes a danger because of the collapse of
internal and external 'realities', rather than simply being a plot
device. The act of perception and the status of the image as 'reality'
are troubled, and this disturbance is in itself a crisis that Deleuze
reads as paralysis, albeit a paralysis that concerns the plot. The
virtual, as the multiple possibilities of emergence from a situation,
comes into view. In so doing, the actual and virtual are articulated
ambiguously through the image, an ambiguity that is more fully
developed by Deleuze in the first chapter of *The Time-Image* in relation to Italian neo-realism. In contrast to Bazin's claims regarding
realism (1971), Deleuze posits neo-realism as a collapsing of the distinction between the external and internal, the subject and object.
In the images of this cinema, we are unsure of the status of what
we are seeing and hearing; despite the apparently 'real' locations,
there is no containing schema or guarantor that these situations or
settings have an existence outside of the image.

The distinction that Deleuze sets up in the juncture between the
two cinema books is then a distinction of types of signs and image
relations rather than a shift located in the historical context.
Deleuze's comments at the end of *The Movement-Image* concerning
historical shifts are in some ways a red herring, for the project is to
connect cinema not to a history external to itself, but to a movement intrinsic to the evolution of the cinematic form. As Alain
Ménil writes, the 'beyond' that figures the difference between the
movement image of *Cinema 1* and the time image of *Cinema 2*, 'is
not thinkable (or observable) until after the cinema has *exhausted* all
the possibilities of the movement image' (1999: 90). Deleuze's
concern is not with chronological time, but with stratified time, and
in this archaeology of the cinema, the time image has always existed
as a potential, a virtual relation to the image. The question remains
of how the time image takes its departure from the movement
image, or, to conceptualize it within the terms of the book, how
the time image realizes the potential of the cinematic form. This is
set out clearly as three distinctions almost halfway through *The Time-
Image*, in a chapter entitled 'The powers of the false'. Here Deleuze

elaborates on the distinction he is attempting to draw between the cinema of the movement image as an organic regime, and the time image as a crystalline regime. The first point concerns the release of the image from forms of schematic and logical certainty, where signs are identifiable as a mimicry of an external world. For the image to exist in itself, it is no longer subjected to representation (of a thing or a place), but becomes a purely optical or sensory experience (opsigns and sonsigns). The organic system of imaging describes the scene as if it were independent of the description, as if, for example, the scene existed independently of the image, exterior to it. In the crystalline description, the film 'creates and erases' the subject matter and setting: that is, the description becomes the thing itself rather than a representation of an independent object or scenario. This is a shift in which the properties of description – light, colour, tone, sound – take on a potency of their own, a potency that includes contradictory and conflicting sensations. The concept of the actual mutates as the virtual, a space of possibilities which are not imaginary or future, but a splaying out of the paths of possibility and the notion of time as multi-directional.

The second distinction between the organic and the crystalline system is the relation to the imaginary and the real. In the organic description, the boundary between them remains intact; even if film of this kind moves between dream states and conscious states, we are able to orientate ourselves. In the crystalline description, there are no arbiters to make this distinction: the two modes are 'combined in a circuit where the real and the imaginary, the actual and the virtual, chase after each other, exchange their roles and become indiscernible' (Deleuze, 1985: 127). The third characteristic of this difference between systems concerns the relationship of images to space. Deleuze's conception of filmic space is here closely linked to the causal drive of narrative, the chain of associations, actions, reversals, triumphs and resolutions that characterize classical narrative forms of cinema. Such actions for Deleuze are not temporal, although we might point out that they do engage the temporal in terms of suspense, flashback and the rhythms of a revelation of knowledge over a duration. For Deleuze, the organic description of space ties movement, and thus time, to its empirical form. Action is performed across space, by attaining goals, discovering blind alleys and taking detours, all of which read as a description of the classical quest narrative. By contrast, the crystalline relation to space scrambles coordinates, collapsing spatial references in a way that denies action its organizing function. Deleuze identifies an initial crisis of action in the cinema of neo-realism, in which seeing becomes paramount, vision as a witnessing rather than as an act of comprehension. The logic of the sensory-motor schema is collapsed in films in which space has lost the 'legal connections' of its ordering principles, peopled by characters 'who have become seers, [who] cannot or will not react' (Deleuze, 1983: 128).

The 'legal connections' which are lost in the cinema of the time image are posed here in spatial terms; space as a grid of references that mimic 'real' location in classical film have mutated into 'any space whatever', the lost, derelict sensibility of a postwar cinema. Yet in the elaboration of the time image, space becomes subordinate to time, pushed into a conservative position in order for time properly, for Deleuze, to do its work. In the chapter 'The powers of the false', the process is evident in a passage that gathers the various sensibilities of spatial deconstruction, only to denounce them. In this passage, in which Deleuze is describing the collapse of the sensory-motor schemata, or our normative paradigms of comprehension, the spatial is a key component. In order to present the fracturing of Euclidean space within the crystalline regime, Deleuze borrows from science a set of terminology: space is Riemanian, quantum, probabilistic, topographical. In the same passage, it is also crystalline, empty and amorphous. The textures, forms, qualities of space are, it seems, extensive in their variability and intensive in their affectual qualities. Yet Deleuze goes on to state: 'Now what characterizes these spaces is that their nature cannot be explained in a simply spatial way. They imply non-localizable relations. These are direct presentations of time. We no longer have an indirect image of time which derives from movement, but a direct time-image from which movement derives' (1985: 129).

Space needs to be explained in a non-spatial way, and that is in the terms of the temporal, to which the passage moves swiftly on. Yet why can space not exist in a paradigm as equally complex as time, and as its inseparable axis? Indeed, in the paradigms of science cited by Deleuze, space is attributed with these complex properties of bending, warping and folding, but the philosophical framework here appears *necessarily* to remove this complexity to make way for time. In the following paragraph, Deleuze delivers his punch line: 'If we take the history of thought, we see that time has always put the notion of truth into crisis' (1985: 130). In the history of thought, time is realized through movement as a becoming, not of a particular object or person, but as a quality in itself. Time is detached from the empirical foundation through which we perceive, entering a realm of the virtual (the idea of time detached from experience). In this sense, Deleuze finds in cinema a potent expression of time's virtual qualities, where perception is put back into the world as a slice into the fabric of infinite becoming. If we recall Deleuze's reading of Bergson, perception is similar to a screen grab of moving matter; it is cinema that allows us to recognize the endless movement of things, and thus of time itself in its infinite variability. Yet the cinematic form that Deleuze identifies as the 'properly cinematic' – that is, decoupage, framing and montage – is also a spatial realization. Indeed, in this context, the question of the separability of time and space is thrown into question by the cinematic form. For every cut, framing and recomposition is also spatial, and moreover, it is spatial in a way that renders concepts of space curiously unstable, folded and collapsed. To subordinate space to time omits this possibility of a recognition of the complexity of the specifically spatial form in cinema. An example is needed in order to unravel the relationship of space and time in cinematic form.

Beau Travail (Claire Denis, 1998) is ostensibly a film about the French Foreign Legion, yet its story does not offer a representation of people, place or motivation. It is loosely an adaptation of a book, yet as a film it reveals the specific differences of film from literature. The opening sequence begins to exemplify the difference. The opening images scan across a painting on what appears to be the surface of rock. The image is accompanied by a song of the legion, celebrating the values of heroism. It then moves to a scene of a nightclub in Africa, where a band of legionnaires move amongst and against the women dancing. The following shot is of a man in an office making a phone call. The next image is of a desert viewed through the constraints of a window of a moving vehicle. As the camera pulls back, the vehicle is seen to be a train; the camera settles momentarily on this scene but refuses to single out any one occupant. The next shots are images of the desert, a derelict tank, the wind moving across reeds in the sand, and finally falling on to an image of a shadow. The shape remains abstract until the camera pans right and we see a number of male bodies with upraised arms. Possibly the men are exercising, but the image is ambiguous here as the characters are stationary, eyes closed. The following shot is the surface of water with light moving across the undulations. A letter is superimposed over the top of the water and held as a layered image. We then see the same men sitting in a boat, swaying to the rhythmic movement of the sea. Finally a setting is located with the next sequence, which is subtitled 'Marseille', and opens with a man, Galoup, sitting at a desk outside an apartment.

Although Galoup is the writer of the text which provides the voice-over, a singular viewpoint is radically destabilized threefold: by its contrast to the abstract framing of the images, by the disjunctive editing formation and by the destabilization of sound and image. In a sense, this is a cinema of Pasolini's free indirect speech, an utterance without a speaker, a mechanical eye detached from a human body. Whilst the film mobilizes the most intimate of forms, the diary confession that retrospectively narrates events, the filmic language constantly undermines this perspective of a naturalized point of view. In a sense, the subject of the film, the French Foreign Legion, becomes a stage for this filmic relation between individual and collective identity, and between a fixed subjectivity and an abstract being as becoming. The opening sequence refuses to identify a location, a time or a central character. The camera is detached from point of view in its roaming movement, and the cutting together of the sequences refuses to identify a main character through whom we are witnessing these images. Indeed, *Beau Travail* replays this tension of expectation, and its erasure, repeatedly. Galoup may be the origin of the voice, which recurs in the film to add impressions, thoughts, asides. And yet the voice-over struggles to produce a narrative, a commentary on events that shapes them into a coherent and stable sequence. The point of view offered by the camera is constantly disconnecting from the voice through a dissociation of sound from image. The image fails to illustrate the

voice, roving across the textures of sand, light on the surface of
water, washing on a line, shot from below so that the stark blue sky
contrasts with the uniform green of the clothes. Here, everything
is in movement, and the framing of shots gives emphasis to textures
of smooth liquid reflection, peeling sun-baked paint, the soft oili-
ness of skin.

Subverting clichéd expectations of war films, predicated on
action, conflict and heroism, *Beau Travail* detaches activity from
any sense of purpose. In place of action, which has an aim and
an outcome, there is movement. Long sequences of the film com-
prise the camera following the routine of the men exercising. The
camera angles, framing and position transform military exercise into
a seemingly mystical ritual of embodiment. The fluidity of the
image, the strangeness of the shapes of the bodies as they stretch,
poise and contract, delivers a pattern of movement that appears to
peel away from the 'reality' of bodies. The human form becomes a
series of arching and falling shapes, acting in unison as a block of
movement. In these moments, the image is purely optical, a device
that allows us to experience imaging and perception. The dilemma
of the film in terms of narrative is produced with the arrival of a
new recruit, Sentain, whose seductiveness provokes jealousy in the
narrator, Galoup. Yet the voice-over fails to convince that a change
in the dynamic of the group is more than his hallucinatory or paranoid thoughts. The voice is narrated over sequences that leave
the interpretation of images in ambiguity. The evening sequence at
the club, we are told, was a marker of change and a harbinger of
things to come. Yet the images show the men taking turns to carry
two men through the streets, Sentain and another. The narration
becomes an oscillation between external and internal realities,
which appears at times to give shape to the images, and at other
moments to sit outside of their world.

The structure of the editing mixes the present with the past; the
present appears to be Marseille following Galoup's dismissal, and the
majority of the film a recalling of events. Yet the movement cuts
back and forth between space and times to the extent that it is
unclear whether the images are memories, dreams or projections.
But the spatial aspect of the film is critical for opening on to another
plane of time, that of a French colonial past in Africa. This past

surfaces in particular contexts where the strangeness of the legion is refracted through the observation of the group by Africans. 'We' are placed outside of the legion, and in an ongoing detachment of the shot from a consistent point of view, African life is inserted into the film in an arbitrary manner. Martine Beugnet reads this practice as an example of Deleuze's crystalline narration (of the time image), which condenses multiple temporal relations into one image: 'The fleeting image of the shepherdess that appears later on in the film for instance, although inserted between two shots of Galoup resting, remains disconnected, suspended (like a Deleuzian crystal image) between the virtual and the actual' (2004: 122). For Beugnet, the legion effects the static qualities of myth, a self-producing fantasy of a sameness over time, commenting that the 'sense of stasis that characterises the legion's life is thus ruptured by the resurfacing of fragments of other temporal and spatial planes'. Here, the spatial and temporal are imbricated, overlapping in their effect. The spatial co-existence of both Africans and the legion summons the temporal co-existence of the history of colonialism and the contemporary presence of the legion.

The sense of *foreignness* that is implied as trope through the Foreign Legion (foreign to whom?) resonates in the film, infecting a sense of subjectivity as foreign to itself, and indeed, refracting through the medium of film. In the final scene of the film, when Galoup appears alone in the space of the club and begins to dance, the manic, rapid display of movement is an eruption of a body in the emptiness of the space. It is the same club that has appeared throughout the film, with latticed mirrors, and in front of his own reflection Galoup dances. The moment closes the film, but in a space that appears outside of any narrative logic: is this the fantasy of himself and his potency, is it an expression of his release from the rigours of exercised control, or is it simply what a body can do?[8] The moment is affectual in that it is a disruption, an assault on any attempt to synthesize events causally. It resists meaning, and it is here that the strangeness, or indeed foreignness, of cinema as a medium that imposes itself on the viewing subject, emerges most fully. Somewhere between sensation and apprehension, in what Deleuze would call an interval, cinema can accelerate us into a space of that which is outside of thought.

The space-time image

The appeal to Deleuze's work is not offered as a definitive model for the study of film, involving the adoption of his vocabulary, concepts and framework. Rather, Deleuze in the cinema books sets certain ideas in motion, recasting the framework in which we come to think and experience (with) film. Deleuze's work is important for that which it clears away in our pathway to film, concepts and approaches that may have become obstacles and produced situations of impasse rather than enhancing our existence in and with film. His thought detaches us from the imperatives of regarding film through certain intellectual legacies. As David Rodowick comments, Deleuze 'unselfconsciously yet fundamentally redistributes the oppositions film theory has inherited from *Tel Quel* thought: realism/modernism, illusionism/materialism, continuity/discontinuity, identification/distance' (1997: xi). In this sense, the cinema books present the opportunity for a certain liberation from the baggage that film theory has accumulated. At the same time, his work casts the history of film theory in a new light, returning to a sense of the strangeness of film that prevailed in theoretical writing of the 1920s (for example, Jean Epstein, Rudolf Arnheim, Hans Richter). These writers, like Deleuze, were captured by the question of film's specificity, its difference from other art-forms, and by identifying its most assured mode of practice. But where, in earlier writing, the debate tended to settle into definitions of an ontology of the film (what can film be said to 'be'?), Deleuze enquires, what is it that film can do? In the cinema books, film is an active force, and in this sense, film is not fixed in one mode of being but is itself a process, always in a state of emergence.   .

This concept of film clears yet another obstacle in the pathway to thinking about film and its current transformations, and that is the obstacle of technology and its relation to change. To an extent, both film and media studies have remained under the sway of a social scientific model, social constructivism, which has polarized intellectual approaches to technology and change. Either technology is seen to be an external force imposing particular effects on the social sphere (techno-determinism), or technology is regarded as a social construct, obedient to the needs and demands of the context in/for which it was produced. Deleuzian thought shifts this binary structure by attributing film a sense of its own emergence, as matter, as a force changed by and changing within every encounter. In place of the stark oppositions of film as either active or compliant, it is recentred as a mobile process that changes according to its own imminent matter (the shift from celluloid to digital is a case in point), as well as through its relations with other actants. In a sense, one of the most powerful ideas in the cinema books is the decentring of the human being as the single site of agency; film's mechanical eye, its cutting of time and space, its scale of projection, all perform a different perception of the world that potentially transforms our conceptual practice.

In addition to the above two points, the cinema books prise open possibilities for thinking what it is we do in film studies. Perhaps most importantly here, the cinema books are the creation of a vocabulary of new terms and concepts, and an incitement for theoreticians to do the same.[9] This is the first point that I wish to emphasize about the spirit of enquiry. Deleuze in a sense authorizes the creativity of working with film; indeed, the practice of invention is more or less an imperative. The second point concerns the relationship of cinema to thought. What Deleuze's work offers is a new way of understanding thought and the image. In refusing to oppose thought (as the rational, masterful partner) and film (as the compliant or resistant serf), Deleuze identifies what is particular or peculiar to each but also sets them in relation. Thought is characterized by its creation of concepts, film by its production of affects and percepts. Common to each is the process of movement, a dynamism. Both film and theory, in their diverse ways, are remade in Deleuze's work as activity and emergence, and thus a particular uncertainty is built into the project. Uncertainty, experimentation and contingency (that film and thought will constantly reinvent themselves) are the markers of a type of grace as well as a life-force, whilst certainty, stasis and cliché line up on the side of death. The third point of emphasis concerns the film and time. The temporal, in Deleuze's hands, becomes a complex, multiform concept that the cinema breaks open for us. A fundamentally cinematic attribute, the sculpting of time in its various modes, cuts through conventional apprehensions of linearity, teleology and measurement, apprehensions which, for Deleuze, numb us to the possibilities of our own emergence in time.

Yet it is here, in the particular division of time from space, that I wish to depart from Deleuze's project, or to move it in another direction. In Deleuze's 'short' history of cinema, movement and time are identified as the specific qualities of film that appear in some ways as its singularity, the features that shock, inspire, affect and perplex audiences. The features of movement and time are, of course, foundational to our enduring fascination with the cinematic, features that are returned to and turned over by historiographers of film. But Deleuze's investment in the concept of time is motivated by a philosophical tradition in which time has traditionally been sublimated to space, whereby time has been tamed, civilized, made docile. The reinvigoration that Deleuze brings to the concept of time is startling, yet it is also dependent on a form of reprisal, a suppression of the spatial. For Deleuze, space has to be the empirical measure of time, the civilizing force that has commanded time for centuries. This reinvention of time at the expense of space in the cinema books denies us an understanding of the significance of space in the present moment, of the complex ways in which film is rearticulating space and our relationships to it.

One of the transformations of film in the present is, with the decline of cinema, its dispersal (rather than demise) across various locations. If we read this process as the demise of film, the context of the discussion remains in the realm of the temporal, as the historical trajectory of cinema, and the question of the spatial relocation of film is suspended. Yet film in many ways produces a sense of space as complex as time, a complexity that I will attempt to set out schematically. The first aspect concerns film's transient relocation, its movement out of an institution as the main site of encounter, and into various types of space – on transport systems such as planes, in public urban screens, in art galleries – and its new portability in personal audio-visual players. In this diffusion of film, it is a substance that is emitted, sent through a system, appearing in surprising places, or it is a medium that is mobile and can be carried with us. The effect of film in these other spaces is to provide a portal into another space and time, a portal that is experienced differently from the collective gathering of the cinema, where the presence of an audience responding is key to the cinematic ritual. In its relocation, film transforms space: here, in the station concourse or the back of a seat in a plane, space becomes a curious archive of other place and times. In the discourse of globalization, it has become commonplace to articulate space in a generalized sense as having been erased, shrunk and compressed. An analysis that traces the locations of film runs counter to the example of compression, suggesting that film produces space as depth, as the surface (of a building) shifts dimension and opens on to other space-times.

A second connected point concerns the framing of film in space-time as it circulates. Historically, film's 'release' into the world has been temporally staged, imaged as a number of 'windows' through which it passes; the window of theatrical release, television premier, satellite broadcast, video and DVD release. Increasingly, the temporal staging of film has been eroded, partly as a result of the failure of cinema to perform the role of a critical event. With the slackening of the temporal framing of film's circulation, the release of film has become a choice of types of viewing, with the combined effects of different technological interfaces and spatial locations creating the possibilities. Film does not possess the appeal of immediacy (an appeal that has migrated into other forms of audio-visual culture such as reality television and the streaming of news), but in this changing context, its auratic qualities distinguish its form. How and where film circulates shifts our conception of film's appeal, and conversely, the presence of film in various sites changes our experience of those spaces. Film actively produces familiar space in new ways.

The third aspect of film's spatiality concerns the production of types of space within the film itself. In film theory, the textual production of space attracts attention for its rendering of urban space as particularly 'realist'. Yet it is the affectual, rather than the realist register of film that is secreted largely through place. In *The Time-Image*, there is an increasing fascination with the spatial, for example, as it is put to work in the films of Antonioni. Deleuze comments that Antonioni's films develop in two directions, 'an astonishing development of the idle periods of everyday banality;

then, starting with *The Eclipse*, a treatment of limit-situations which pushes them to the point of dehumanised landscapes, of emptied spaces that might be seen as having absorbed characters and actions, retaining only a geophysical description, an abstract inventory of them' (1985: 5). Here, Deleuze provides a reading of spatiality that moves towards the uncanny affectual presence of a landscape which decentres the human, reducing characters to a faint 'inventory'. This is space as an affectual register in its own right, not simply as nature mirroring the emotional state of character. Filmic space produces an affectual register that is not simply a human projection: filmic space may be claustrophobic, agoraphobic, neurotic, eroticized. It is not simply location, a container or backdrop for action, but a creation of the mobile forces at work between the human and the non-human. Space is also produced through rhythm and repetition, through an exercise of energy that is manifest as intensity: for example, the eroticized surfaces of the desert in *Beau Travail*, or the agoraphobic apartment in *The Piano Teacher* (Michael Haneke). In an excavation of filmic space, its properties emerge as a corollary to time, as folded, pocketed, stretched and compressed.

The final aspect I want to draw attention to concerns film as an assemblage of elements, its cutting together of various spaces, and of sound and image. One of the central components of film, montage, is a spatial as well as temporal practice, and here film facilitates linkages between incommensurate and remote spaces, forging relations that are, until that moment, outside of thought. The creation of relations through montage presses on our naturalized sense of linkage and connection, reappropriating the contingency that early cinema so famously toyed with (Doane, 2002). In so doing, film can be seen to transform space into a verb, to practise a spacing, a recombination of spatial elements that allows space to be as amenable to crafting and putting into process as time. Here, space-time emerges as interleaved passages within film; the space of the desert in *Beau Travail*, which is butted up against scenes of domestic interiors of an African house, where the dislocation is of both elements. In the conventions of film theory, montage is set against duration of shot as its counterpart, converting montage into a practice of rhythm, yet its relational quality of joining shots is a critical component of film's work. The assemblage of parts can, of course, strive to attain continuity of space and time, but its more surprising potential is in the setting into relation space-times that struggle to find a connection. In so doing, film provides an experience of difference (cultural, social, ethnic), which is potentially incommensurate, without common ground. Arguably, one of the most critical tasks that film performs in the present moment is a question of how we thread together the differences that we come into contact with, or conversely, how social, cultural and ethnic differences are to be comprehended as beyond our own repertoire of experience, to remain precisely as difference.

These are merely examples of the ways in which space and film may be thought together to extend the remit of what we consider film studies to be about in a new century. What we become, after all, is not determined by what we have been. And if the transformations of the object of study fascinate and perplex the discipline, as film becomes a digitized flow and available to view through a mobile micro frame, it surely follows that film theory is open to such unexpected mutations. If concepts are creations, the possibilities for reclassifying, inventing contingent systems of order and analysis, is an open field. This process is, of course, underway within the discipline, in many areas of work. For example, in the work of Hamid Naficy, the reclassification of film outside of national boundaries gives rise to a new grouping and set of issues arising out of the particularity of this formation. Naficy approaches the decentring experience of globalization through the creation of a category of cinema produced by those who are forced to move through and across space. Naficy's classification for cinema of this kind as accented cinema emphasizes the traces of displacement as they register linguistically as a trope for 'outsider-ness'. He describes his project thus: 'My task here is to theorize this cinema's existence as an accented style that encompasses characteristics common to the works of differently situated film-makers involved in varied decentred social formations and cinematic practices across the globe – all of whom are presumed to share the fact of displacement and deterritorialization' (2001: 21). Within the category of accented cinema are three sub-categories: a cinema of exile, of diaspora and of ethnicity. Accented cinema is a form of classification that regroups film through a system that transgresses national boundaries, and in so

doing forges connections between films that have previously been
suppressed within a current organization of the field.

From another direction, Sean Cubitt provides a framework
for thinking film in its relation to the polarized axes of nature
and culture. Encyclopaedic in form, *The Cinema Effect* traces film's
curious history in both appropriating the 'natural' world as its own
and becoming a technological commodity. Cubitt writes: 'The
study of the cinema effect is a first step in identifying what it is
about human mediation that, to date, has left it grappling with
its separation from the natural as well as the technological' (2004:
360). Cubitt's reading elucidates certain stages through which film
culture has developed, arriving at a new set of classifications for
post-cinema: neoclassical film, oneiric film, revisionary film and
cosmopolitan film, to draw attention to but a few. Here, film is
written into a history of the fetish and the commodification of time
as a critical component in the production of the present. If Cubitt's
work has the epic quality of the cinema that he describes, Laura
Mulvey's focus is at the opposite end of the spectrum, at the
site where film becomes 'uncertain', a cinema of observation and
delay, a cinema unsure of its own footing as an indexical or affectual
medium (Mulvey, 2006). These works provide inventive ways of
managing the task in hand: that is, tracing the movement of film
as it slides out of paradigms of nation and genre, and mutates in
different directions.

The creative enterprise of classification, of both recognizing the
arbitrary nature of the foundation of our taxonomies in Foucault's
sense, and grasping the arbitrary as a chance for invention, impacts
on how we respond to, experience and think film. For the order of
things sets in place new relations, reveals correspondences and contradictions, and at best, sets thought moving in unexpected directions. The evolution of film is also the evolution of film theory, a
project of addition that enhances what we know of film rather than
a subtracting critique of its effects. Films may be innumerable, fab-
ulous, stray dogs or drawn with a very fine camelhair brush. They
may no longer belong to the Emperor but, having just broken the
water pitcher (of cinema), they are becoming *et cetera*.

2

Hollywood's last decade

In *Mulholland Drive* (David Lynch, 2002), Hollywood appears as the sinister and beguiling backdrop to the film. Hollywood is not exactly the subject or context here (although Mulholland Drive is a specific citation of a Hollywood place name), but the free-floating referent, the infamous neon sign on the hill, the strange attractor. In typical Lynchian disjunction, Hollywood plays out as both dream and nightmare, a recall of an earlier historic romanticism about film, and its inverse, a dream so thoroughly contaminated by corruption that the two stories struggle to correspond. This is the Lynchian thematic, reproduced across an oeuvre of films as a constant slippage between conscious and unconscious modes of being, romance and violence, not so much plot and sub-plot as constant reversal and inversion. Hollywood as the producer of dreams has become an archetypal dream in itself, a site of memory, nostalgia and longing, more than a tangible institution or historical mode of production.

The contradictory affectual principles put into play in Lynch's films recall the question posed by Jane Gaines, of whether the spliced dream/factory can work, or whether it is always a pair splitting apart.[1] Yet Lynch's use of Hollywood is evocative not simply for its combining of diametrically opposed sensibilities, in particular an oscillation between innocence and corruption, but for its invocation of a filmic era long gone. In Lynch's films, the specific temporal reference is the late 1940s and 1950s, a period of heightened melodrama and psychic subtexts.[2] The epoch is appropriated by Lynch to create a context where a Judy Garland naivety brushes up against Janet Leigh's nightmare in the shower. Yet the frisson of this collision is created in part by the retrospective framing of the world of film. Lynch invokes a Hollywood that has all but disappeared. There are reasons to believe that Hollywood's last decade was the 1990s, a decade in which the experience of film-going, the economy of the industry and the ontology of film transmute into new formations. This claim rests on three aspects of change. First, Hollywood (the logo of a corporate empire) no longer primarily produces film. Its productive remit has extended horizontally and vertically into the production of related products, a versioning of narrative across diverse media, connected and supported by an industry of promotion and distribution. Second, the theatrical experience of film, the cinematic context, is no longer central to revenue production. Whilst the media event of theatrical release remains the most visible and public experience of film, its purpose is to promote the first version of a product spread laterally across a range of objects, sites and practices. Cinema, economically, has become displaced as the critical focus, repositioned by ancillary objects and interests. Third, the materiality of film, the form of acetate ('celluloid' is a commercial label rather than a strictly descriptive term), is increasingly replaced by digital materials incorporated into various stages of production. Whilst film production in the present is characterized by a thoroughly hybrid mixing of digital and celluloid forms, Eastman Kodak's announcement that it intends to suspend celluloid production by 2010 provides a cut-off point for the period of transition. Thus, these three critical transitions shatter what we have known, and think we understand, of Hollywood film.

This analysis provides three key measures of change, yet these factors cease to retain such clarity when considered together. Each measure inevitably impacts on the other two, and takes us into a tautological sorting of relations if we are to abide by the conventional methods of film studies: the analysis of production, textual interpretation and the study of modes of viewing. Such methods may complicate rather than illuminate the situation, or at least give rise to a further set of questions. If film is no longer the primary object, how is it changed by its relationship to a new paradigm of objects (is it the starting point of a chain of associations or merely an advertisement)? Has narrative form become increasingly significant in the need to generate a thematic coherence for a disparate array of objects and practices, and is this question to be focused on the film itself or the film and its ancillary texts? If the cinematic viewing of film both complements and competes within this paradigm, what distinguishes it from other viewing experiences? If its distinctiveness is to be identified in its scale as spectacle, invoking bodily affect, why is film increasingly viewed in the diminished scale of the television or computer screen?

These questions constitute various areas of research in current paradigms of film studies. My intention here is not to sketch a reproduction of the debates, but to develop the theme of retrospection, a backward view of 'Hollywood' as it retreats historically but is simultaneously brought alive in the present. In a sense, Lynch's invocation of a filmic past provides a paradigm for the larger project of contemporary, high-budget film production. It is a paradigm in which the past resonates in the present in the form of remakes, adaptations and cross-media appropriations. The modes and sources of nostalgic return are multiple, but the desire is singular: to constitute the past in the present. Animated figures are made to adapt to the modern world in the attribution of an ongoing life-span (Batman's continual return), characters of television series are given new life as martial arts experts (*Charlie's Angels*, *Mission Impossible*), and the filmic past is 'remastered' as digital event (*King Kong*). If film studies struggles with the historiography of its field of study, contemporary Hollywood production is about the same business, albeit to different ends.

Eternal recurrence

Consider for a moment, in terms of memory and return, the highest-grossing Hollywood films of the past five years. There are certain films that reproduce the mythic past, stories that are known from a historical moment: *Gladiator, The Patriot, Ice Age, Pirates of the Caribbean, Bruce Almighty, Pearl Harbor, Jurassic Park III, Atlantis: The Lost Empire, Dinosaur.* A second sub-category are films reproducing television series, largely from the 1960s and 1970s: *Charlie's Angels, Mission Impossible, The Hulk, Scooby-Doo.* A third selection is derived from comics (and in some cases, television series): *Spider-Man, X-Men, Men in Black, Dr Suess' Cat in the Hat, Dr Seuss' How the Grinch Stole Christmas.* There are film versions of computer games: *Lara Croft Tomb Raider, Spy Kids 3D: Game Over.* Then there are films that remake earlier films: *Jungle Book, The Italian Job, Dr Doolittle 2, Planet of the Apes.* A substantial element of the list is the sequel film, extending the narrative over time, in some cases decades: *Nutty Professor II: The Klumps, Toy Story 2, Hannibal, Rush Hour 2, American Pie 2, The Matrix Reloaded, The Matrix Revolutions, Bad Boys 2, Kill Bill Vol. 2, Bayside Shakedown 2, Legally Blonde 2, Scary Movie 3, Die Another Day, X2: X-Men United, Terminator 3: Rise of the Machines, Star Wars Episode II – Attack of the Clones.* And films dependent on books: *The Beach, The Hours, Seabiscuit;* or on books creating a mythic past, and often produced as a series of films: *Harry Potter, Lord of the Rings, Dr Doolittle.*

This cross-section of Hollywood film illustrates not simply that film is no longer central to revenue production or the primary product. The dependency of film on other texts is specifically a temporal relation, a return to earlier historical moments, former experiences replayed, remembered. To take the first category of films set out above, the events recalled are those of a mythic past, a set of shared yet culturally unspecific stories (pirates, dinosaurs), stories that play to Hollywood's narrative structures of quest, obstacles and triumph over adversity. The slippage between mythic and 'real' stories, of for example *Jurassic Park* and *Gladiator*, slides history into the realm of historiography, a realm where the textuality is more pronounced than an historical 'real'. Yet the categories retaining a greater historical specificity are the second and third, of remakes of earlier film, televisual and comic texts, recalling the period from the 1950s to the 1970s. The reincarnation and extension of *Scooby-Doo* is this time round played as a genre inviting the knowing and sophisticated reading of an adult who remembers the 'original', and the child audience new to the text. But what is significant about this period in Hollywood's history, as is evident in the discussion of the demise of the classical system above, is that these were the televisual texts that signalled the fall of Hollywood's dominance. This is an intertextual cannibalism whereby what were formerly the domestic texts of a competitive medium have now become the content of high-budget cinema. It is not only that film has moved to television, but television has moved into film.

The argument here centres around two possible interpretations of Hollywood's relation to other media. It could be argued that, in insisting on a filmic version of a televisual text, Hollywood is asserting the ongoing difference of film from other media, that film is precisely not the same experience as reading a book or watching television. Indeed, film's differentiation from other media has long characterized its identity, as Gunning reminds us, recalling a situation a century ago, 'Curiously, when film began to define its own aesthetic identity in the teens and twenties, the extreme variety of its origins most often was reduced to a differentiation from theatre' (Gunning, 2000: 327). An alternative argument would propose that Hollywood has necessarily incorporated the differences between media in order to thread together diverse media experiences and disparate platforms of delivery. Thus the future of film is secured precisely through its relation to other media forms which signal the film text as one optional experience. Indeed, the demise of the temporal management of film as a spectacular release, trailed by advertisements, unveiled in premieres and finally released simultaneously across national space, suggests a new type of equivalence between media forms. The question then becomes one of definition, of whether film is a central text with ancillary products in other media forms, or whether film is simply a media platform in a multimedia environment, an environment characterized by the circulation of narrative through various cultural and technological channels.

Narrative has become central to the understanding of large budget film as the deployment of a known structure, and one through which historical events are replayed. Yet, if we are to consider the significance of narrative not only within the film text, but across its ancillary texts, it emerges as a key spatial as well as historical connector. Here, the polarization of film and historical narrative versus new

media spatial radicalism is broken down; Hollywood film is both nar-
ratively driven and a multimedia platform. Sean Cubitt explores the
place of narrative in multimedia, arguing that, common to many
accounts of new media, the non-linear model of the database provides the exemplary structure, whilst narrative has become marginal
(Cubitt, 2002). Employing the space-time axis, Cubitt follows
Manovich's lead in arguing that new media demonstrate a movement
away from temporality towards a spatialized culture. New media
detach information from temporal frameworks and linear models
associated with narrative, and move it towards spatial configurations
of screen surfaces (the layering of the computer interface), and search
engines moving across the spatial plane. In this context, argues
Cubitt, new media require narrative to retain a coherence, an invocation of connectivity across a fragmented assortment of screens,
texts, bits and parts. Narrative holds the potential to reintroduce time
into a culture temporally adrift, disconnected. In applying this argument to large-scale film production, it is possible to demonstrate that
narrative creates connection, rather than ideological coherence,
across texts.

Although Cubitt regards marginal cultural production as the site
of narrative's reintroduction, I would argue that it is an essential
component of film as a multi-media product. Yet, narrative is both
spatial and temporal: it is at once a critical spatial connection of the
various components (toys, games, DVDs), and a temporal structure
of story and character. Its familiarity facilitates exit points, or sites
of departure, into parallel pathways or scenarios. Pared down to key
sequences and three act structures, stories of triumph over adversity and defeat of opposition, narrative here testifies to the template
of Proppian narratology. *Charlie's Angels*, for example, stages familiar characters in a sequence of obstacles to be overcome, mysteries
to solve, adversity countered in the bodily spectacle of combat. It
takes us sideways geographically in encompassing the martial arts
sequences of the fight, a staging that allows combat to remain
embodied, a personal experiential combat unlike the technologi-
cally mediated battles of war film. And it takes us back in time. The
repositioning of narrative here shifts the debate away, first, from
the narrative-anti-narrative binary of popular versus avant-garde
film, and secondly, from the narrative versus spectacle opposition.

In asking what it is that narrative does in relation to film, it needs to be seen as a labour that is made to work across texts as well as within a text.

If film is increasingly dependent on historical narratives from various media forms, it in effect knits together the interrelations of television, film, computer games and so on as a shared history. There are stories and versions of stories, but all comply with a notion of kinship rather than competition, a collective evolution. This evolutionary model also moves sideways into territory, gathering together spatially distant and dislocated sites (public–private, urban–suburban, global–fragmented) through the family of stories. Yet, Dick Hebdige argues that the dispersion and extension of Disney-like narrative into other areas of life (rather than other media forms) has a disturbing resonance. In an article that extends the implications of a 'nostalgic return' to a wider socio-political context, 'Dis-gnosis: Disney and the re-tooling of knowledge, art, culture, life etc.', Hebdige argues that the Disneyfication of culture extends beyond the film text, characterizing a way of life, a mode of being, a global politics (Hebdige, 2003). Lost in childhood nostalgia, Disney returns to a past of narratives predicated on innocence, connoted by 'noble savagery, primitive simplicity, pre-lapsarian bliss and oneness with the world, impeccable awe and spiritual wonderment, openness to encounter and child-like purity' (2003: 157). For Hebdige, Disney stands in for the corporate cultural takeover of socio-psychic life. Yet this innocence is fabricated, a simulated unknowingness and openness, dis-gnosis as neither ignorance nor innocence but a wilful posturing of purity. Dis-gnosis facilitates a position whereby otherness is without context; history has not happened.

In Hebdige's account, this was not always so. The potency of animation as 'a line that went around the world' in its original unruly moment of filmic becoming has been chastised and made compliant to the predictable shapes and contours of known stories. It is a reading shared and given extensive treatment in Esther Leslie's *Hollywood Flatlands*, where the transition has a date: 'The idealized world moulded in Disney's fairy-tale reels made graphic the suppression of revolutionary hopes for social transformation in the 1930s and 1940s' (2002: vi). The idea of animation, of unthought conjunctions (the animal and human), the redistribution of life across forms (objects), of the curious, malleable playfulness of shapes and designs, gives way in the inter-war years to a standardized format. It is a loss of imaginary possibility in which hierarchies of distinction resurface: as Leslie elegantly describes it, 'Man is divided from nature, from others and in himself. He is disconnected. His spine is straightening and stiffening. Man is walking upright' (2002: 250).[3]

For Hebdige, the triumph of a specific, delimited version of Disney is fundamentally a regression, a refusal to live in the present and a convenient return to a mythified past. And the implications of the delimited Disney are not simply confined to the cinema and its related texts, but extend to the 'surburbanization of the global imaginary, the Taylorization of leisure, compliance with the overall mission . . . something close to "disenstrangement" – the domestication of all otherness, the subtraction of risk from pleasure' (2003: 152). Disney is a form of memory-wiping, an amnesia in the face of a conflicted and violent twentieth century, and a refusal of other experiences of the present. Disney is at once its material manifestation, in theme parks, holiday worlds, shopping malls (all types of self-enclosed world), and a psychic reality spread across the globe: a banal mythification of existence as 'magical', 'innocent' and 'fun'. This is a world in which all affectual relations are held in quotation marks as a recognition that each response is stage-managed. In a Baudrillard-inflected account, Disney has become the world, and the world has become Disney.

The instituting of an historical amnesia through film is an idea mapped out by Fredric Jameson as part of his explication of postmodernism, some fifteen years ago (1991). In Jameson's argument, however, the terms are reversed. It is not that 'postmodern' film relishes the return to particular eras, but that within designated texts, the specific markers of history are erased. In Jameson's example, the *mise en scène* is characterized by a bland, generic aesthetic that mixes certain styles to produce a temporally unlocatable film.[4] In the present, however, the return to particular periods is specifically referenced, the titles of the remakes precisely pulling on the historical referent for resonance. What is occurring here is of a different order to the postmodern. The current recycling as nostalgic return performs another production: the idea of progress. The past is alive but more perfectly rendered. The marketing and reviewing, for example, of the remake of the 1933 film *King Kong* (Peter Jackson, 2005) precisely mined this seam. The legacy of film history was acknowledged in references to the original; comparisons were drawn. Yet its acclaim moved in two directions: the film took us back to the past effectively, and it also improved upon it. The spectacular digital animation of both the creature and a 1930s city of New York feature as more 'real' than in the original. The return facilitates both a retelling of cinematic history, literally as a remake, and the telling of history teleologically as technological and aesthetic progress.

Hunting and gathering: copyright

If the centenary of cinema has brought a reflexive turn to film studies, the industry is not exempt from responding to its historical status. A century of cinema is the production of an archive of work, an economic and material resource. The archive as a material and figural form lends itself to the illustration of Hollywood's shift from production to an orchestration of its resources. The archive is a treasure house of the cinematic past, yet in a context in which media nostalgia is profitable, the safeguarding of resources becomes a critical labour. If the archive presents control along one axis, of the historical, copyright moves laterally in its control of film as it moves in space. In the context of a digital dissemination of film and its related products, a virtual control of their circulation and use becomes paramount. For the demise of cinema has also issued a freedom to film as a travelling property, a liberty that is double edged. As the next stage of Hollywood's development as a corporation, the virtual control of products through copyright has become a major facet of the industry; clearly, it is not a separate feature that follows production, but a component of production contributing to 'creative' decisions.

Whilst Hollywood is an umbrella corporate brand for the few major film producers globally, its infrastructure, processes and range of products have undergone a fragmentation. Hollywood is no longer centred as a location or characterized by a linear production process; its production is subcontracted largely to a network of specialized contractors. The product itself, we have noted, is now one of many objects produced, and its mode of dissemination is multiplatform. Copyright is recognized increasingly as a critical aspect of control by creating enclosures (technological encryption and circumscribed distribution), and limiting exposures. Yet, it is the *virtual* nature of copyright that articulates most clearly the paradigm shift from a centred mode of production to a dispersed form. Scott Lash describes the transition from Fordist to post-Fordist production as the tracing of the centre of power: 'Power in the manufacturing age was attached to property as the mechanical means of production. In the information age it is attached to intellectual property' (Lash, 2002: 3). The control of objects is conducted through the control of information about them and their uses. Copyright law rearticulates our relation to objects in circulation.

Historically, copyright is one of three forms of law dealing with intellectual property, along with patent law and trademark law. Developed in the eighteenth century in Europe, copyright brought into being the relations between objects, creators and audiences. In endowing the creator with proprietary rights, the attribution of copyright was, in part, the manufacturing of the subject of authorship, positing an original source to works and rights of control over the duplication and dissemination of the text (Lury, 1993). Both author and text emerge as 'original' in a context in which the printing press, a mechanism of duplication, threatens to disturb the notion of a single origin or source. Yet, there are two important points to elucidate here in a discussion of copyright. The first concerns an understanding of the law of a performative injunction concerning rights, a weighing of individual against public rights in ownership and use of objects. This is particularly pertinent in the USA where, as Haraway (2000) notes, concepts of copyright law depend on notions of rights and citizenship inscribed in the American constitution. The constitutional right of the individual to ownership – indeed, the subject's becoming citizen through the notion of ownership – facilitates the discourse of law based on a notion of individual ownership. The law of copyright protects not the idea but the manifestation of the idea, not the concept but the object. Where patent law protects the process of innovation, copyright law constitutes an original object, and creative subject, with rights over reproduction. The juridical regime of knowledge weighs public rights against individual rights, where certain forms of reproduction are perceived to be acceptable if the original does not suffer debasement or detrimental effect (Miller, et al., 2001: 122). Within this paradigm a set of tensions is in play. On one hand, the encouragement and facilitation of creativity, regarded as a public good and requiring financial return as an incentive, is upheld. Thus authors and artists are secured in a system that recognizes their labour. And in opposition to this, weigh the rights of the public to access and use the products of labour with a degree of creativity. This exercise of copyright law, locating originality in the text rather than the idea, distinguishes between public forms of knowledge and culture – for example, generic forms – and private manifestations of an idea in a particular object.

The second noteworthy point is that copyright, as an exercise of law, is a shifting framework of authority and definition. The history of the protection of Hollywood production is characterized by an increasing move in copyright from individual to corporate ownership: in effect, a shift from copyright to trademark law. Within this transition is the legal establishment of corporate identity, rather than individuals, as the source of originality. Yet, this is not without its contradictions. Can the corporate body take on the mantle and safeguarding of creativity? Can film provide specificity and originality from such a dispersed origin? As Rosemary Coombe argues, the shift from copyright to trademark law involves a transformation of the temporal registration of control: 'Unlike human authors or celebrity personas, the corporation may live forever, and its embodied identity in the trademark form shares its potential immortality and, if assigned, will survive even the corporate demise' (Coombe, 1998: 61). Where copyright expires after a period of time, implying that a work becomes public property as it is embedded in social life, trademark law enforces a boundary that distinguishes a product indefinitely. There is simultaneously a shift of priority here, from the product or text itself as the valuable object, to the value of the object under the sign of the corporation, as part of a series of productions rather than a free-standing object.

The shift in ownership of copyright marks a transition in expectation of the product, and a changed definition of the object protected. As the corporation emerges as proprietor, and the guarantor of standards of product, the law of trademark becomes the more relevant legal protection. In a less than subtle inversion, the shift from copyright to trademark law marks a transition from the legal protection of an original text or object, to the protection of a sign which stands for the reproduction of an experience. Thus, as Jane Gaines notes, the legal framework of trademark law is a reconfiguration of public expectation. According to Gaines, trademark guarantees 'that the buyer could expect, from the source behind the goods, the same values and qualities received with the last purchase' (Gaines, 2000: 592). The expectation of culture as it is inscribed in law has mutated from the protection of an original creation (the mark of difference), to the protection of the customer's right to expect the same (the mark of similitude). Yet, once again, the legal framework has shifted around the subject of its protection. Aoki comments:

> the old rationale of preventing consumer confusion over competing market goods has yielded to the current rationale of protecting from 'dilution' or 'misappropriation' the integrity of a set of positive meanings which have been 'created' by the trademark owner's investment. This recent conception of a trademark as property imports 'author reasoning' into trademark law. The trademark owner is viewed as a 'quasi-author' who 'creates' a particular set of meanings attached to a mark by investing time, labor, and money, thereby justifying expansive rights in a mark. (quoted in Coombe, 1998: 61)

What is being protected under trademark law is something less tangible than a film text or an object in circulation and its particular features. The matter constituted here, legally, as valuable is experience: trademark represents an identifiable sign in a world overrun with signs and symbols, and connects the sign with a reproducible form of experience. Where copyright represented, to some extent, an indexical relation to the world, in that it constituted a material object as an original source, trademark operates in the virtual world of experience. Thus, trademark law articulates a coherence between products from the same source, drawing a relation between films and other objects, and a coherence between objects produced over a broad period of time. The dispersed nature of film production and the proliferation of the film narrative into multiple objects is recentralized by the stabilizing force of corporate identity, manifest in the sign. The corporate logo condenses, sediments and appropriates meaning acquired over time. The brand both coheres and extracts meaning from a range of objects (Lury, 2004).

The legal infrastructure of Hollywood media is an integral part of the production of objects, rather than an external framework in which media objects exist. Rosemary Coombe argues that the field of intellectual property law is a field of cultural politics, whereby the law acts performatively (Coombe, 1998). For Coombe, trademark law harnesses the generative forces of signification accrued socially, and allocates them to the corporate domain: the use of law here has a spatial dimension, creating 'a private enclosure of the public domain of ideas, images and information' (1998: 53). There are two related implications of this curtailment of freedom. The first implication is that creativity is ascribed to the corporate body and removed from the individual or collective: the use of trademarked products in everyday contexts involves their appropriation and resignification, yet this is potentially an infringement of the trademark. Second, signs are not inherently meaningful, but acquire value and meaning over time. In disallowing the appropriation and resignification of signs in everyday use, trademark law attempts to fix the meaning of signs. Frozen in time, the logo imposes itself as repetition, a return of the past, an emphatic reiteration of a consistent meaning: the paramount logo informs us that we will experience the accumulated wealth of a century of production, in effect a repeat experience. Caught in this paradox of providing the same, but different, the trademark attempts to stave off dissonance and dilution, wards off an erosion of its magic against those who might attempt to usurp its meaning or steal from it. Yet, in offering the same, the trademark resists change, difference and the movement of time.

This brings me to the final point of the discussion of how Hollywood reconstitutes itself, through its management of the axes of space and time. The production of media artefacts by corporations now identified collectively as Hollywood operates under a threat of dispersion in two parts: a spatial dispersion characteristic of global production and dissemination, and a technological dispersion of narrative across media formats. The effects of spatial and technological dispersion are ameliorated by two strategies of control: the use of archive material, in effect creating an historical density to the products, and second, with recourse to a legal infrastructure that recognizes and protects the virtual value of the corporation as trademark. The description of Hollywood's operations becomes less a definable centre of production, and more a field of tensions that are managed as forces of dispersion and control. A spatial 'thinning' of materials across territories and media formats is balanced through a thickening of historical materials and the signification of the brand. If we reconsider the definition of Hollywood in light of this discussion, in place of a dominant imaginary is a collection of parts in tension. For Hollywood to maintain coherence across media and space, its defining qualities need to be emphatically presented and reiterated. Hollywood's turn to fictive histories, to its own archive, is a particular response or, more conceptually, a strategy.

The archive of media texts is the site where the legal discourses of ownership and brand value, on the one hand, and content, on the other, are brought into view in the same moment. The construction of the archive, a process of collecting objects and establishing rights, is also a process of selection, taxonomy and ordering. It is both material and virtual. It is a material institution, with its own processes of preservation, as Paolo Cherchi Usai has demonstrated (2001). It is also a virtual archive of ownership rights, facilitating and debarring access. The privatization of the archive allows certain uses, repeats, adaptations, controlling the public use and circulation of past media. The archive has become a staple of cable and satellite television, repackaged as the consumption of 'classic' forms of culture. Historical film and television texts are replayed, looped into thematic strands, canonized in popular poles. Yet, the dependency of contemporary film culture on such an archive is rarely commented on.

The archive is a critical response to the effects of cultural dispersion, displacement and proliferation. In creating an enclosure, an archive posits not only propriety, but also coherence: an archive is a collection and an ordering of objects according to its own internal logic (a practice of taxonomy reflected on by Benjamin in relation to the recreation of his library). The archive is in part a response to the proliferation of objects (here film, but any object that is situated within an archive undergoes the same transformation of meaning into a coherent series). An archive simultaneously constructs value through its practice of enclosure: objects become unavailable, scarce, protected, and also located, recognizable. Here, digital technology presents a double effect. For, on the one hand, digitalization provides the fantasy of a mechanism of storage that is infinite. The expanded capacity of digitalization to compress information, and to index materials in various formats of cross-referencing, enables the archive to expand its boundaries and to organize its field.[5] On the other hand, digitalization has developed the platforms of delivery and exchange that have facilitated an increase in the circulation and accessibility of objects. The tension played out through digital technology replicates the larger tension in Hollywood film culture, of dispersion and gathering.

But in addition to the effects of enclosure, the archive creates a relationship to the past that is full of promise. The archive is the fantasy of storage and preservation as memory, an expanded virtual memory residing like the cultural unconscious in the cool vaults (and the digital equivalent) of corporations. Derrida, in *Archive Fever* (1995), reads the dual seductions of the archive as a passion for collection and a deathly repetition. The term 'fever' resonates; it is both desire and malady, a desire for finitude and a malady manifest in repetition: on our way towards death, an ending, we keep going back to start again.[6] If we consider for a moment the range of highest-grossing films of recent years, this description fits them well. Paradoxically, the digital age facilitates this curious manoeuvre of offering a future so new that we are left marvelling in its wake, and at the same time we are endlessly going back. The archive fulfils both fantasies; there is an end (the archive as a filmic mortuary), and the possibility that return (to the past) is viable.

The archive as an imaginary works with the virtual effect of copyright, fabricating an authenticity that is situated in the corporate body rather than in individual film texts. In the *idea* of the film archive, control is not an association; rather, the archive is the comfortable fantasy of enclosure as the protection of our relationship to the past, a past that is vulnerable and valuable, an origin of childhood fantasies preserved. And whilst an archive purports to protect a collective history, the enclosure of its system is importantly the insurance of value. That there exists a fundamental antagonism between the concept of the archive as the storage of original artefacts, and film as a reproducible media, is noted by Mary Ann Doane: 'The archival object is singular; it must exist at only one place at any one time. Hence, archival desire is an attempt to halt the vertiginous movement of mechanical and electronic reproduction' (Doane, 2002: 222). Despite the reproductive capacities of film, in the legal discourse of rights and use (in effect, the collapse of a distinction between use and exchange value) an 'original' is established. Is the archive also, perhaps, a new production of film's auratic qualities?

Hollywood's academic profile

If we agree with the assessment that the film industry we recognized by the name of Hollywood demised in the last decade, what, we might ask, does this mean for film studies? For film studies, as a recently established subject, had much invested in the value of Hollywood in the discipline's moment of institutional legitimation. Hollywood film provided a canon of psychologically and aesthetically complex works, in response to which film studies honed a particular type of approach to the text, employing semiotics, psychoanalysis and an Althussarian ideological critique. This at least defined the Anglo-American tradition of film scholarship in the 1960s and 1970s, and has continued into the present as a memorable foundational moment. Hollywood also appeared to provide a discrete era of film production where industrial practices were stabilized as narrative form, assured in their effectiveness, and importantly amenable to a mode of analysis that established the language of cinema. To a significant extent Hollywood, as it was constituted by the discipline as an object of study, obligingly provided an object as complex (aesthetically, psychologically, technically) as the cultural texts of other disciplines.

The range of work that has appeared in relation to Hollywood, including responses to and developments of earlier analyses, cross-cultural perspectives, intertextual genre and performance studies, constitutes an ongoing thickening and dispute of what we understand by Hollywood. Whilst acknowledging the eclecticism of this work, I want to pick out two strands of debate that appear to have a particular investment in Hollywood. The first of these approaches was derived from an intellectual project that D. N. Rodowick names 'political modernism'. These approaches were definitively part of an intellectual movement in the 1960s and 1970s which sought to explicate the importance of culture in the reproduction of social relations, and consequently to cite culture as a field in which those relations could be challenged. Drawing on Althusser's model of ideological interpellation, culture became the named site of an ideological force field, where the implicit socio-historical beliefs of a culture could be structurally located and its effects, as the production of subject positions, imagined. The particular importance of film in this context was twofold. Film as a visual culture working through a complex set of unconscious processes (of identification, objectification, projection, fetishization), facilitated a mode of analysis where interpellation could literally, as it were, be seen in operation, where the naturalized positions of a culture could be teased out. The hierarchical arrangement of bodies in relation to the camera, the framing of subjects, the attribution of subject mobility, to name a few, provided a dramatic and dynamic playing out of social relations.

If this form of intellectual critique grasped authoritatively the workings of a particular form of visual popular culture, it gave rise to other questions, of what kinds of alternative practice were either desirable or in evidence. This set of questions mobilized the tradition of political modernism, an intellectual and artistic critique of dominant representational forms, drawing into a loose grouping analytical and practice-based enquiry. The potent range of influences forming this nexus were drawing on the modernist art practice at the turn of the century, a Brechtian-inspired critique of realist representation from practices of theatre, and a materialist analysis that met with structuralism. The significance of the central platform of Hollywood in the history of film studies was also its simultaneous production of alternative versions of film, as a practice and an analytical category. In a sense, Hollywood cannot be detached from its 'others'. Yet, it was not only Hollywood, but the socio-political context that moved the parameters, perhaps the foundations, of this paradigm. In a reflective account of transformations in the discipline and context, Laura Mulvey has written:

> The decline of this 'radical aspiration' lies across the 1980s, confused and disorientated by economic and political changes on a national and international scale. It was then that forces associated with conservative capitalism captured the dynamic of the new . . . Marxism has used 'history' intellectually to ground its sense of destiny, a dynamic movement forwards that would be both inevitable and just. This teleological confidence has moved into crisis. (2004: 152)

The sense of disorientation is both historically located and continuing, an ongoing crisis of the project of a left-inspired intellectual tradition. If Marxism found in dominant film culture, the locus of which was Hollywood, a set of norms to take leave of, neo-liberal capitalism has dismantled both terms: Marxism and Hollywood. Critically, what I want to hold on to here is the sense of Hollywood in relation to its others, that Hollywood provided a stable paradigm to work with, and equally to work against.

The second imaginative capture of Hollywood as an object of study focuses, conversely, on the system's consistency. The question of the definition and duration of Hollywood has a critical history in another tradition, that of American historical film scholarship. The desire to identify exactly when Hollywood was classical, to demarcate it as a period and a set of properties might be seen as a pre-figuring of an anxiety about what exactly film is, and when in history it attained the status as 'classical'. The most coherent and encompassing account of this period of film-making has been Bordwell, Staiger and Thompson's *The Classical Hollywood Cinema* (1985),[7] and consequent publications. This mode of historical scholarship employed by Bordwell et al. situates film as a paradigm within which the various facets of film-making are connected and mutually influencing. The material, technical, aesthetic and socio-political dimensions of film and film-making are drawn into a relation in which, during the classical era, a certain harmony and correspondence between terms is evident, producing the classical continuity system. Christopher Williams, in a lucid account of the term 'classic' in film studies, condenses the features of the classical Hollywood paradigm thus: 'It involves storytelling, unity, realism, naturalism, emotional appeal, decorum, proportion, harmony, rule-governed but self-effacing craftsmanship and "mainstream"-ness. The cement of these qualities is continuity . . . the 180 degree rule, the shot/reverse shot pattern, the eye line match and match on action' (Williams, 2000: 213). In the fetishistic emphasis on continuity between elements, the desire to prove the paradigm of the 'classical' becomes, according to Williams, an obsessive thematic, of exaggerated importance. It is as though difference must be repressed: 'Nothing is allowed seriously to qualify it', argues Williams. 'Differences between genres and studios, variations in the uses of lighting and colour, and differing uses of the long take and depth of field are all briefly glanced at before being crushed into uniformity' (p. 213). The investment in classical continuity film is at the same time an investment in a particular mode of analysis that appears to endure across time. Or does it?

What is curious about the Bordwell, Staiger and Thompson paradigm is that it appears at once to elevate the formal success of Hollywood film above other less 'effective' cinemas, and yet simultaneously to insist on its reductive form. The analysis traces the process of stabilization of film production, a sedimentation of various components of practice into a particular aesthetic model, characterized by proportion and formal harmony. Such stabilization, according to the authors, is dependent on the refinement of a studio system of production as a type of assembly line, an efficient and structured mode of assembly conditioned by wider proscriptive forces such as the Production Code. It is possible to surmise that the use of the term 'classical' is well advised, that classicism here is suggestive of an aesthetic standard comparative with other 'classical' art-forms (painting, literature, music). It is this a-historical dimension of the term 'classical' that Miriam Hansen (2000) regards as being at odds with the fundamentally modern appeal of cinema: 'I am interested in the anachronism involved in asserting the priority of stylistic principles modelled on seventeenth-century and eighteenth-century neo-classicism when we are dealing with a cultural formation that was, after all, perceived as the incarnation of *the modern*', she writes. She elaborates the dimensions of the modern as the experience of radically new modes of apprehension and social relations, 'drastic changes in social, sexual and gender relations, in the material fabric of everyday life, in the organisation of sensory perception and experience' (2000: 337). Ironically then, the desire to identify a classical Hollywood system and mode of analysis worked against the medium's very particular modern sensibility.

The unrelenting desire for a consistent reading and method of analysis for the study of Hollywood is evident in Bordwell, Staiger and Thompson's attempt to persuade that the model of *The Classical Hollywood Cinema* extended into the 1960s, and possibly beyond. If the unity of classical Hollywood has been tentatively (or otherwise) challenged by a prominent historical turn in film scholarship, the notion of a classicism continuing into the late twentieth century has been widely disputed. The ruptures of the Paramount decrees, the advent of television as a competing force, the proliferation of leisure activities and the decline of cinema attendance, and the emergence of a new American cinema widely influenced by European cinema, are presented as counter-arguments to the notion that classicism continued beyond the 1940s. In summary then, these two strands of particular engagement with Hollywood produced two types of momentum. One, in political modernism, was a drive towards change, a diversity of practice against which Hollywood was the standard bearer of conformity. The other was a drive for continuity and consistency, a return to the past to enable its repetition into the future. In this sense, two main motivations in the study of Hollywood bring us back to Derrida's contradictory demands that are apparent in the archive.

The contradictory accounts of Hollywood, its periodization, its effects and its (in)consistency, mark the failure of consensus and are, perhaps, a sign of the discipline's maturity. Historical accounts of the classical age of cinema are also historical accounts of the legitimization of a discipline, and here it becomes evident that any accession to the status of a coherent field is beset with dangers as well as pleasures. The status that film studies acquires as a discipline is simultaneously the emergence of debate about what constitutes the field, of what is prominent and subsidiary, how the narrative of the discipline works to contain contradiction, and to manage the constant process of boundary enforcement. Any account of Hollywood is implicated in this process. A further complication to the difficulty already evident in the historical narration of an emergent discipline is the disruption of the category of 'history' itself. Writing in 2000, Vivian Sobchack notes, 'Today, however, our interests in the field (let alone our circumscription of it) have complicated our notions of both "film" and "history"' (Sobchack, 2000: 301). An effect of the new historicism is by nature to excavate diversity in the historical field, to identify contradictory movements and practices that contradict the standard account. The textuality of historiography, as a reflexive process producing interleaving moments and jagged edges, disturbs 'history' as much as it consolidates its importance as a method of enquiry. Again, Vivian Sobchack's reflection on the differences between earlier film scholarship and the present:

> Today, however, the question of film history is much more vexed than it was mid-century when the infant discipline of film studies was first attempting to legitimate both itself as an academic enterprise and the cinema as an aesthetic (and secondarily historical) form worthy of serious scholarly attention. Indeed, until the late 1970s and early 1980s, film history seemed sure of what its 'proper' object was, where its focus should be, what events and people were important enough to be deemed fit as historical subjects. (Sobchack, 2000: 300)

In Sobchack's reading, there is the identification of the cycle of a discipline, a sense of its maturity taking its leave from its emergence, an 'infant' discipline. Yet there is also an implication that a broader transformation in our experience of history has left its mark, one gestured to by Laura Mulvey, as having unravelled in unexpected ways.

Sobchack's reference to a 'proper' object of study moves the account to another place. For film studies, the relationship to the category of history is complicated by the ontology of the medium itself as a recording device, and of course its changing matter as digital form. As Tom Gunning remarks, 'This centennial marks not only the first century of film history, but also the first century of history captured by motion pictures' (2000: 318). Film is at once a fictional artefact and a visual record of time. Thus historiography in film studies is forced to address, or indeed is made a critical inter-locutor of, the limits of historical 'truth'. There occurs a doubling of analytical reflexivity, in that the history of film is opened to con-testation and revision, whilst also the nature of representation and recording is the subject of study. Whilst all historical accounts are engaged with processes of inscription and recording, and the context of their occurrence, film overly signals the process of inscription in its apparent 'acquisition' of the temporal. Film is history and it is also not history, but artefactual, constructed and reduced from the ephemerality of experience. Gunning is critical of the utopian promise of the film archive to provide an account of a past: 'the proliferation of moving images threatens . . . to destroy rather than preserve memory, substituting widely circulated institu-tional images for the most personal resources of imagistic recall'. The all-too-often consequence, for Gunning, is 'the recycled dis-cards of the all-too-familiar'. This comment circles back to con-temporary Hollywood, and its preponderance for recycling its own authorized history.

If the three demarcations of the end of Hollywood signal a crisis within the industry, it is also a crisis for film studies. The dispersion of the film into various ancillary objects and texts, across a range of viewing locations, and its translations into a different material form in the digital, threaten not only the coherence of Hollywood, but the foundations of a discipline forged three decades ago in its rela-tion to classical Hollywood. The instability of Hollywood is refracted throughout conferences and publications attempting to grasp the changes at hand as either the death of cinema as a collec-tively experienced event, or the demise of celluloid as an aesthetic form. Critical to both Hollywood as an industry and film studies as a discipline is the relation to history, its recall and re-memory in both Hollywood product and film theory textbooks. History, it seems, is snapping at our heels. Catherine Russell summarizes the predicaments neatly:

> Is there an original object of study, if film history has entered such a state of flux? In Benjamin's terms, we may be said to be working with

'allegories of cinema'. Translated into the digital language of new media, torn from its original theatrical context, cinema recedes to something awaiting redemption. This is the task of today's historian and archivist, whose work is of course aided by those very technologies that threaten the existence of the object. (2004: 83)

Russell's elegiac return to Benjamin's formulation, that there are allegories of cinema, is prescient, striking at a possible figural conceptualization of the medium. And yet, we might wonder in the space of the same sentence, if cinema has ever appeared more than momentarily as 'solid', knowable, fixed? In other words, has the conception of cinema, with Hollywood as a privileged component of the field, forced a coherence and stability on to a set of practices, arrangements and experiences that were always unruly? If we take Miriam Hansen's reading of Hollywood to heart, there is a greater instability to Hollywood than the discipline has been keen to recognize. The system that is so reliably reproduced in textbooks, and popular memory, as a golden age, is in her view fleeting and temporary. Might film studies be dealing with the rigid effects of its own institutional becoming? Could it be that the demands for disciplinary coherence impose a reductive framework, where only certain eras, practices and ideas can be pulled into focus, whilst others are out of view? Has the filmic metaphor locked film studies into a narrow conceptualization of what can be in the frame? And to exhaust the analogy, should we no longer be concerned with a distinct definitional focus, but be prepared instead to move from frame to frame, to see, as it were, where film will take us?

The implication of following rather than directing is a practice already demonstrated in much film scholarship, across many planes. The fascination with film's technological legacies, for example, breaks out of a linear model and escapes into specific hollows and folds. To take a familiar example, Jonathan Crary's tracing of observation has reconfigured a paradigm of spectatorship as observation tooled through a range of optical instruments (1991, 1999). And cinema's relationship to various technologies of inscription and communication has surfaced through Friedrich Kittler's historical investigation. As E. Ann Kaplan writes, turning around the question from one of how to impose boundaries to one of linkages: 'Given

this convergence, we have an opportunity to demonstrate the connections among various media rather than focusing on differences',
reversing the interrogation of medium specificity. She continues,
'Friedrich Kittler's research years ago initiated interest in ways technologies develop out of each other, with new ones piggybacking, as
it were, on old ones, so that traces of the old remain and are carried
forward in new modes' (2004: 86). In Kittler's work we also discover
earlier moments of cultural disruption from another perspective, in
film's impact on the hegemony of the printed word.

If technology provides this sideways, tangential following of a
trace, it is a practice with a spatial dimension, the potential and
necessity to move into dialogue and discussion of other forms of
cinema. Robert Stam conceives of a relation between technological developments and the production of spatial relations; both
audio-visual technologies and cultural specificity are 'multichron-
otopic', mixing spatial and temporal indicators. Thus, the trace of
other cinemas is not located in an 'other' culture in its historical and
spatial singularity, but in its complexity as a culture produced by its
historical relations with 'elsewhere'. It is a question, then, of how
the markers of 'here' and 'there', 'now' and 'then' are placed. The
argument that has long since been the mantle of film analysis, that
the technologies of 'form' cannot be separated from content,
returns here in discussions of the 'new'. In a discussion of the
hybrid characteristics of Brazilian cinema, for example, Stam
writes, 'The multi-track nature of audio-visual media enables them
to orchestrate multiple, even contradictory, histories, temporalities,
and perspectives' (2003: 38).

Film studies may be in the process of becoming more polyphonic, so that what the discipline designates is less an orchestrated
set of subjects and more a tapestry of relations, more a process than
a method.[8] That this makes it less authoritative and centred is a
reality, but one that has been in the post for some time (in both
senses). The discourses of poststructuralism and all of the other
'posts' needed to come home to roost at some point. Film studies
may no longer be able to rely on the film text alone as the object
of study, but may have to allow the object and discipline to be
undone by its 'supplements' (an idea that returns in chapter 5 in a
discussion of film's relation to other media). In other words, what

may appear as marginal interests and approaches in film studies may surface to decentre the authority of the discipline as it has been founded. For the dual function of the supplement is to provide an addition to that which exists, and simultaneously, by the admission that a discipline can be added to, it reveals a lack in the original form. In short, the supplement suggests an indeterminacy between what is considered internal and external to an object or field. Film studies may benefit from the supplementary methods of cultural geography, visual culture, anthropology and new media theory, at the least, to operate in a way that is open to the possibility of unknown outcomes and connections. Such a move risks dilution and decentring. Yet it also offers the possibility of associative, rhizomatic thinking which deterritorializes and reterritorializes, a process so far colonized by multinational capitalism.

3

Assemblage: editing space-time

In a short essay, 'Observations on the sequence shot', Pasolini opens with a discussion of the 16mm film of the shooting of Kennedy, made by a spectator (Zapruder) in the crowd. He writes: 'In the possible film on the death of Kennedy all the other visual angles are missing: from that of Kennedy himself, to that of Jacqueline, from that of the assassin who was shooting, to that of his accomplices, from that of others present who were located at more fortunate vantage points, to that of the police escort, etc.' (1972: 233).

Here, in this moment of *verité*, of the most live of events whose liveness is guaranteed by a recorded death (the unexpected shooting of a President), the immediacy is somehow lost. The status of film as a recording device is simply lacking in presence, in affect. In its re-presentation of a critical moment, both shockingly visceral and historically monumental, it transpires that film is lack-lustre. We can play the film backwards and forwards, or over and over, repetition as our impoverished tool. Or, in the contemporary with video and digital technology, we can accelerate into the image in an attempt to solicit greater detail, yet every effort to do so is scuppered by the material matter of film itself. As a light-based chemically reactive substance shot in these conditions, subjection of the film to enlargement dissolves the image to texture: an event becomes an abstract pattern, a multitude of swimming grain. Yet the lack for Pasolini in this primary documentary material is not detail but subject positions, a lack of editing, of the cutting together of various subjective perspectives. Pasolini considers the situation again, and arguing against himself, he speculates that to multiply the present numerically would not be enough, for the result would be 'each of those presents postulating the relativity of the other'. Additional viewpoints signify proliferation without an elaboration of meaning. What is needed is co-ordination, the establishment of relationships rather than simple juxtaposition, to '*render the present past*'. Pasolini's retrospective ordering, which he aligns with death as the only point at which the randomness of life can be given coherence, is the practice of editing, the site of postproduction as the construction of meaning.

Pasolini could not have known that his words were to be literalized by a film-maker some years later in a high-budget rendition of all the possible presents of that moment and prior to it, milled through the machine of a commonplace conspiracy theory. This, one might deduce, is not exactly what he had in mind. Yet, in this discussion of the Kennedy film, a single, linear recording of an event, the central tenets of film and much of film theory are set out. The power of the recorded moment is what entices, yet this material is devoid of presence without the cut, the splice and the restitching of fabric. In a discussion of the emergence of film from photography written in a considerably earlier moment, Siegfried Kracauer has already stated, 'Of all the technical properties of film the most general and indispensable is editing' (1960: 29). Kracauer's reserve in speaking about the craft of film-making is palpable in the prefix 'technical', yet editing is nonetheless film's accession to its status precisely as film.

This chapter argues that editing is central to the ways in which we understand film historically, and that a particular axis of editing, engaging with the spatial, has become more pronounced in contemporary film. It is not only editing itself as a 'technical' practice, as Kracauer would have it, that is at stake, but the shifting theoretical terrain in which editing is made sense of, itself patched into debates about time, space, language and meaning. The proposition here is that editing in the present moment emphasizes the axis of space. Space, of course, is never separable from time, the one is articulated through the other: space in the account that follows is imbricated in the temporal frame of simultaneity. The critical significance of what occurs in different seemingly unconnected spaces in film is dependent on the sense of each running at the same time. In so doing, the conundrum of much contemporary film-making is the burden of storytelling in a world in which complexity is too great to calculate. Where in earlier film, and in the present practice of continuity editing in large-budget film, editing is an injection of suspense, anticipation, anxiety and ultimately closure, the present effects of editing are more ambivalent: correspondence moves up against disjunction, connection against dislocation, communication against incomprehension. The emphasis is on the relationality of spaces as separate pockets of being, unfolding across territory rather than through time. In so doing, many films of the present depart from the conventional premiss of film's structural property, as a time-based medium.

In order to make the argument for an historical difference or specificity, it is necessary to return, briefly, to accounts of editing in prior periods and trace the contours of thinking and practice. In early cinema we find the relation of film to time a central fascination. Embedded in the social transformations and concurrent anxieties of the age, cinema becomes the performative medium of differently textured moments, with editing as the assured sculpting of the temporal in the forging of a standard narrative form. At a later stage, and in a different context, in Russian cinema of the 1930s, editing becomes paramount to debates about the structural properties of film. Drawing threads between political context and the signifying potential of the image, the gaseous term 'editing' is made more specific through the French term *montage*: placing emphasis on the composite and contrasting properties of editing, Eisenstein's montage is first and foremost a fracturing of the order of meaning (Eisenstein, 1924). The investment that Eisenstein places in montage is perhaps the largest historically, perhaps unsurprisingly in a global context in which culture, and film in particular, was recruited in the reification of fascism. The third moment referenced here is that of postwar film-making when neo-realism again returned to questions of documentation, location and veracity. Bazin's work is well known for its defence of the long shot, and editing becomes reframed in a paradigm in which duration and *mis en scène* are the valuable assets.

The scope of this chapter limits discussion to a fitful coverage of film history, moments where editing becomes a site of inquiry for both film-makers and theorists, indeed, where there is often an imbrication of these positions. The concern here is to trace the paradigms in which editing has been worked, intellectually and aesthetically, and to draw out the present divergence from that work. It is not the case that editing in the contemporary presents a particular break, nor can current forms of editing be claimed for a radical politics of any kind. Rather, the argument here is that the landscape in which editing is currently thought and practised is a territory in which we find a very different sense of political possibility, one where the coherence of narrative is lost and the dialectic no longer in place. The films discussed here are European works from independent cinema and remix event cinema, where the framing perspective and the connections to 'elsewhere' become, through the trope of editing, the subject of the films. In these films, editing is primarily a crafting of spatial relations, cleaving open questions of how, in an historical moment in which time is thoroughly traversed and collapsed by technologies of communication, connective relations are forged.

Editing as a temporal art

If we understand a central fascination of early film as being rooted in the act of documentation, the practice of editing opens a further temporal possibility, in the words of Tarkovsky (1986), of sculpting time. Whilst the recording of time bears the logic of linearity as the celluloid strip moves through the camera, frame by frame corresponding to the clock's hands, the edit dissolves that process. In cutting up film, time becomes elastic and relative (Eisenstein, 1924), malleable and fragmented. Writing about the emergence of cinematic time, Mary Ann Doane impresses the significance of editing for an understanding not only of film and time, but of modernity: 'For general cultural theorists such as Walter Benjamin and Siegfried Kracauer, the cut was the incarnation of temporality in film, and it constituted the formal response to the restructuring of time in modernity' (2002: 184). The relationship of cinema to modernity has, in recent scholarship, been fully and richly excavated. What emerges from this work is a correspondence at the end of the nineteenth century between newly structured sensibilities of time. At its most extreme, these sensibilities form a dialectic between rationalized and ephemeral time. The emergence of a rationalized, measurable time (regulated through industrial work patterns, standardized in the establishment of Greenwich mean time), arguably produced a subjective liquid sense of time, leaking out of formal grids imposed on the body and psyche. Perhaps best characterized by Proust's meditation in *Remembrance of Things Past*, the subjective temporal is a palimpsest of memory and sensation, of waking and dreaming states. Indeed, the hybrid state of semi-consciousness, caught between the lure of sleep and the terrors of insomnia, colours much writing of this period and beyond, culminating in a form of existential fatigue (Charney, 1998; Moore, 2000). By 1921, Jean Epstein would wearily declare the state of the world thus: 'We are all erudite and professional scholars of fatigue, neurasthenic esthetes' (1921/1984: 192–3).[1]

If modernity spells fatigue in its relentless movement between a rationalized socio-political system and a psychic ephemerality of fragments that surface and loom, the cinema can be seen as a cultural corollary to this dynamic. For entering the cinematic experience is also entering the twilight state of the dream-life (it was no coincidence that the surrealists championed cinema's irrational potential and affinities to the dream world). And editing, more than any other aspect of cinema, unleashed the contingent into filmic structure. Through editing, images take up a sense of an indeterminate and endlessly contingent relation. In mixing up the temporal logic of the recording, editing threatens to unravel the 'natural' relations between things. In creating juxtapositions of images, the effect was not only of temporal disjunction, but of contrasts of scale and space.[2] In Leo Charney's account, 'Not only hurtling from place to place through parallel editing but also jerking the viewer's attention from longer shots to medium shots to close-ups and back again,' he argues, 'film began to take its place as the demon child of the over stimulated modern environment' (1998: 85). This is the shock affect described famously by Benjamin, although in his account, it is both the camera and the edit that work to produce the defamiliarization of 'reality'; in a peculiar alchemy of scale and assemblage, 'reality' ceases to be a record of 'nature', but becomes the blue flower in a technological landscape, inverting the binary of nature/culture (1955: 226).

The dream-state of cinema, as a hybrid condition of various modes of un/consciousness, was of course to become challenged by the advent of sound (Chion, 1990). Sound, or more properly dialogue, anchored film in specific paradigms of meaning, eliminating the potential for imaginative association through the image. And the disjunctive possibilities of editing were not simply to remain a contingent interplay of images, in the spirit of Vertov, but to become part of a standardized film grammar. As Doane notes, in the early life of film, editing was part of an attempt to create a legible articulated time that precisely did not detract from the 'real time' of the shot. Doane focuses on three types of editing in early cinema, not as a taxonomy of editing practices, but as key instances of the use of editing to create a coherence to filmic time and space. The first of these is the use of editing to repeat a scene, presented first from one viewpoint and subsequently repeated from a second position. Editing here is used to flesh out the possibilities of perspective, of viewpoints that exist simultaneously, yet in doing so, it requires a replay of time: time and space struggle to gain a coherence in the registering of difference. The second is the chase, where editing subtends the logic of linear time. The chase presents a series of tableaux where characters cross the frame, or more often, moving from or towards the camera to extend screen time. Working to a logic of accumulation, the chase scene creates a sequence of events, although as Doane notes, the order of the shots is unimportant. Characters move through space, but more significantly, we are to understand the passing of time and, within this, the possibility of multiple outcomes.

The third editing practice furthers this invocation of suspense. In parallel editing, dramatic tension is created through the contrast of different viewpoints. In many ways, parallel editing displaces the temporal logic of film, creating a simultaneity that requires the spectator to insert herself into the relationship between images, to forge connections. In the cross-referencing of shots, there is a curious tension at work. An image, of course, has an implication for what follows, but what follows is also that which is occurring simultaneously. The parallel edit grants the spectator greater knowledge than the single version of an event, and introduces the emotions associated with drama, of anxiety, fear, anticipation. Editing to other situations is an addition, but it also introduces a gap, a rupture in the visible that gestures to a whole world of happenings occurring beyond the frame: the extensive 'outside' of the time and space of the scene. For Doane, the affect of parallel editing primarily belongs to time: 'Parallel editing successfully eroticizes time, injects it with desire, expectation, anticipation', she argues, emphasizing the insertive quality of editing. She goes on, '[parallel editing] displaces the spectatorial time of viewing by contributing to the construction of a "lived", imaginary temporality' (2002: 193). Here then, in the cut, film comes to acquire its own temporal logic, separate from the experience of lived time or the industrialized linearity of production time. Cinematic time is a peculiar hybrid. On the one hand, a rationalized progressive momentum leads, with a sense of narrative inevitability, to a secure outcome. On the other hand, time is open to rupture, surprise, contradiction and chance. Editing facilitates both of these temporal features, both in joining images into a coherent set of associations and outcomes, and in gesturing to other possibilities beyond the frame.

The critical emphasis given to time in the playfulness of early film, and explored extensively in film scholarship, articulates the complex and contradictory logics afforded to the temporal in the first half of the twentieth century. In novels, art and music, and in the widely influential theses of time put forward by Henri Bergson in *Time and Free Will* (1889), *Matter and Memory* (1896) and *Creative Evolution* (1907), time, matter and consciousness leak into one another and disappoint demands for linearity. Commodified, rationalized and standardized time are not allowed to settle into a stable formation, but are undercut by alternative renditions. Time appears a central concern in the writings of modernism, and it is a phenomenon that resists a reductive conceptualization, remaining open-ended. In film, the cut reproduces this complexity: time is a fabric of various textures, to be shaped, stretched, made plastic and fluid. Space appears less redolent, and potentially more troublesome. Doane again: 'The yoking together of non-contiguous spaces through parallel editing forced a certain denaturalization of the filmic discourse. It required the spectator to accept enormous leaps in space and to allow the disfiguration of continuous time, its expansion or contraction' (2002: 194).

The effect of parallel editing is to disfigure time – that is, to distort, to change the appearance of – whilst editing produces a radical disjunction in space, requiring a 'leap', an act of physical (here psychical) propulsion across gaps. For Gunning, the spatial disjunction of the edit in early film borrows from the logics of other 'new' technology of the period, such as the telephone and the telegraph, technologies that connect discontiguous space without travelling the distance (Gunning, 1991a). The combination of intimacy and distance common to other technologies resurfaces in the editing of filmic space.

If the project of modernity, and cinema within that, is seen to be the management of time, and the rendering visible of time as a pliable substance, space remains the sublimated term. It is a theoretical move that reproduces a psychic repression of the age of modernity: space is topographical, knowable through grids and structures, is a map of empire. Lacking the dynamism of time, space is the unthinkable, sublimated term, for to think space is to think difference, otherness, exteriority. Whilst time is located within a paradigm of memory, of individual interiority, of what has happened before and after but remaining within the same narrative, space is the external, returning in anthropological film as journeys of elsewhere, but safely disconnected from the here. The subversion of space is a radically different project within modernity from the subversion of time. Cutting up and splicing time requires a movement back and forth, but along the same line of subjectivity. Space, in contrast, requires a displacement, a landing elsewhere, on the territory of otherness, a logic that cannot be subsumed within the same subjective sensibility as time.

The attraction of montage

What occurs then to the radical disjunctions of space, to the 'leaps' in territory manifest in editing? In Soviet cinema of the 1920s and 1930s, space is reinvested with a dynamism of the cut in the work of Vertov, Pudovkin and Eisenstein. In Vertov's work, the cut is subsumed within a project of what cinema can be, a dislocation not only of spatial location but also of scale, movement and image density. Manovich, in a work that affords Vertov the mantle of predecessor to computer culture, argues that Vertov's frenetic montage in *Man with a Movie Camera* allows images to clash semantically rather than form a single universe' (2001: xix). Reading Vertov through Benjamin's account of prying objects from their shell, the scale of the image and the cut perform the theatre of spectacle and shock affect. Eisenstein's early work, and his essay, 'The montage of film attractions', draw attention to the differences between theatre and cinema. Whilst theatre retains an ability to excite through a liveness of the event and the power of performance, film retrieves that excitement through the ability to combine ingredients of any order to achieve new associations. The power of montage for Eisenstein begins with a desire to excite, in tension with a need to create 'conditioned reflexes' (1924/1988: 45). There is slack in the system here; Eisenstein wants, on one hand, to generate the unexpected through montage, and on the other, to produce a predictable outcome. The sequence of the slaughter of the bull and the striking workers in *Strike* illustrates both tendencies, a contrast of surprising opposites, and yet a planned association between the slaughter of men and animals. The sequence prises open the traditional realism of the diegetic world by introducing the bull and appears to open out the possibilities of interpretation. Yet the contrast clearly requires a metaphoric connection between human and animal.

In this movement between two different types of image, and two spaces, Eisenstein shifts film into a space of the figural (Rodowick, 2001). The image ceases to retain its indexical relation to the world, becomes a textured frame in conflict and contrast with those preceding and following the shot. Rodowick's reading of Eisenstein's practice borrows from Marie-Claire Ropars-Wuilleumier's work on filmic writing (1982). Ropars contends that Eisenstein's hiero-glyphic editing establishes a system of signification that is open-ended, the meaning undecidable, constantly on the move in the creation of possible combinations and signifying chains. Montage, in this account is a deconstructive practice, creating an instability that remains open in cinematic discourse.[3] Yet the spectrum of pos-sibility for montage, for what can be achieved through the cut and join of image sequences, becomes narrowed in Eisenstein's work (1988, 1991). By the late 1920s Eisenstein had committed to paper his thoughts on montage in an essay, 'The fourth dimension in cinema' (1988). Here, a taxonomy of montage is presented in five different types (metric, rhythmic, tonal, overtonal, intellectual), moving towards intellectual montage as the most sophisticated concept. For Eisenstein, intellectual montage moves cinema towards the status of language as images acquire the status of signs, able to convey ideas.

In the development of an idea of montage in both theory and practice, the ideological function of editing in Eisenstein's work came to dominate. The Marxist principle of dialectical materialism is clearly the model for Eisenstein's practice (culminating in Eisenstein's plans for an adaptation of *Capital*).[4] Each image put in relation to another, oppositional image, gives rise to a third term, a new image or thought association. As a dialectic, montage is able to achieve a radical break, and breakthrough in apprehension, in apprehending not only the image but the world. Paradoxically, whilst Eisenstein had in mind a liberatory process, the theory of dialectical materialism increasingly guiding his film practice was perceived to be a narrowing of possibility (of both practice and apprehension). 'In his youth, Eisenstein had been less idealistic-minded, less totalitarian', writes Kracauer (1960: 221). In a com-mentary on *October*, Vance Kepley writes, 'The spectator must trace out an elaborate set of associations and arrive at a logical conclusion about the emptiness of religion and nationalism' (1997: 43). The totalitarian edge becomes more evident as the intellec-tualization of montage moves towards completion as a project: citing Ropars' analysis, Rodowick writes, 'Eisenstein's ideas were more radical in practice than in theory' (2001: 95). What begins then as a practice of disjunction comes to subtend an ideological project rigidly written into, and possibly inhibiting, the process of film-making.

This gloss of Eisenstein's work, however, constricts the breadth of his project to a single frame of reference, of dialectical materialism and the openness of the figural image. Throughout his career, Eisenstein worked at the development of a language of cinema components that included animation, gestural acting and sound.[5] Indeed, for Vertov as for Eisenstein, sound created a further possibility for contrast and conflict, for dissonance, in the form of film.[6] Whilst Eisenstein provided a fierce critique of sound as a naturalization of the filmic diegesis, and in the specificity of language, a threat to the status of film as an international art, his ideas of sound as a counterpoint to the image further developed the dissonant possibilities of montage (Kahn, 1999). Signing 'The Statement of Sound' in 1928, along with Pudovkin and Alexandrov, Eisenstein argued against the use of sound to smooth over the ruptures of filmic conflict.[7] The attachment of sound to natural objects and persons would purport a form of realism undercut by montage. Proposing the opposite, a use of asynchronous sounds, Eisenstein wrote '*Only the contrapuntal use* of sound vis-à-vis the visual fragment of montage will open up new possibilities for the development and perfection of montage' (quoted in Kahn, 1999: 147). As Kahn notes, Eisenstein's practice of these ideas would not occur until *Bezhin Meadow* (1935–7), a more conservative practice than the statement foreshadowed, due perhaps to his inexperience in sound technology, an inexperience that had sanctioned 'a wish list freed from practicality' (1999: 147).

If, in Eisenstein's work, the practice of montage is rooted in an ideological position that constrains the potential openness of its operation, it is a practice that draws attention to the importance of 'difference' in discontinuity. Eisenstein's laboured attempts to work against the grain of an increasingly standardized continuity editing in Hollywood, kept spatial disjunction in play in the presentation of images from 'elsewhere'. In his work, it is not the temporal fragmentation that is of concern, but the figural contrast of the shot, dependent on a discontiguous rendering of space. Eisenstein's work was to set in motion, and produce as counter-effect, a debate about the value of the cut versus the long take. Connected by a similar concern with the ideological properties of a film ontology, neo-realism of the 1950s proposed an oppositional practice to montage, located in the long shot, a ruminating duration of a framing coupled with a depth within the field of vision. Space again is implicit to the long shot, in two ways. First, the depth of screen space, facilitated by specific lens technology of the period, opens up an image to reveal layers and fragments of objects. Depth of field in a sense reveals more than it shows, allowing the eye to travel across surfaces and into folds, to glean from the image more than is 'intended'. It allows an ambiguity of reading but one that is none the less figured within the terms of a greater comprehension. The perceptual model of depth becomes, in the critical debates that ensue, an epistemological model of depth; in allowing the specta-tor to perceive in depth, the result is a deeper apprehension of the image. Second, the duration of the shot signifies a form of realism dependent on space. The return to an indexical relation of the image to the world relies on location, spatial reality as empirical possibility, a unity of time and space.

For André Bazin, the emergence of neo-realism in cinema of the 1950s constituted a 'new period', 'a vast stirring of the geological bed of cinema', and 'everywhere up to a point there had been a revolution in the language of the screen' (1967: 33). Bazin's com-ments occur after a discussion of Orson Welles' *Citizen Kane*, but it is clear that this film is not to be taken as a singular achievement. Welles provides an illustration of one tendency in the development of cinematic form, whilst Visconti, Rossellini and De Sica repre-sent another. Whilst Bazin is delineating a new period of cinema, the new requires a thorough refutation of what has preceded. Early cinema for Bazin thoroughly explores and exploits the practice of montage, which has at its disposal 'a whole arsenal' to work with, and, significantly, 'impose[s] its interpretation of an event on the spectator' (1967: 25). By the coming of sound, such an arsenal is 'full'. The terminology here is of use, for the military metaphor conveys the quality of aggression that Bazin attributes to a cinema of montage. Far from Eisenstein's dialectical opening of sig-nification through juxtaposition of images, Bazin infers a pedantic and more thoroughly authoritarian practice which drives the spec-tator towards one interpretation. For Bazin, in contrast, the cinema of Welles and Rossellini opens up the image to greater ambiguity in the depth and duration of shot.

The oppositions are drawn up. The cut is an exploitative mechanism, a sort of bullying tactic, a fetishization of organization: montage, 'after all, is simply the ordering of images in time'. The long shot and depth of focus in contrast confers an openness on interpretation, a dream-like quality where the spectator is free to roam the frame, enjoying a relation with the image that is closer than 'in reality'. Bazin ties this perceptual freedom to a psychology of viewing which is more demanding and active, requiring the spectator to exercise 'a minimum of personal choice'. Welles may use superimposition in *Citizen Kane*, but these moments operate in contrast to the long takes, characterized by a static camera, a sequence of actions carried out by actors, and a clarity of focus that allows the spectator a perceptual, and thus interpretative, mobility. Where montage imposes a frenetic rhythm, a pace of visual phenomena that assaults the spectator, the practices of neo-realism allow a continuum of reality. Bridging the American context of Welles with the European movement of neo-realism, Bazin notes with approval, 'the dream of Zavattini is just to make a ninety-minute film of the life of a man to whom nothing ever happens' (1967: 33). Bazin kicks away from the earlier practices of film-making in order to establish the ground of the new: static shots versus frenzy, depth over surface, length over the fragment, the quotidian over the dramatic, interpretive perceptual freedom over directorial visual pedantry.

Given the critical stance that Bazin takes up in relation to editing as a manipulation of time and perception, we might expect the spatial axis to be brought into alignment with other oppositions. Yet, this is one opposition that is not brought into play. The long shot with its depth of focus is, fundamentally, time constituted differently, time as the quotidian. Such a regeneration returns cinema to an origin of narrative form, the real-time of action bearing testimony to the actual occurrence of events, in tandem with the detail of everyday life: depth of field is imbricated with time in a slow unfolding of a revelation. Cinema is capable 'once more of bringing together real time, in which things exist, along with the duration of the action, for which classical editing had insidiously substituted mental and abstract time' (1967: 34). Bazin harnesses two sides of cinematic form: the controlled organization of events through narrative, and the more arbitrary randomness of the world of objects and their meaning. The relationship of these two aspects of neo-realist film depend, for Bazin, on what the camera may reveal, unwittingly, through duration. The space of shot, the unfolding of action in space, remains unelaborated. Montage, 'after all, is simply the ordering of images in time'.

Undoubtedly neo-realism established its veracity through a displacement of film from studio to location, 'liberated' by the development of more mobile camera units and new techniques of manoeuvring the camera. Yet, whether the debate concerns montage or the long shot, time remains the fabric of cinema. The rendering of the temporal, as abstract, plastic, malleable, or as unfolding before the camera, effectively represses the spatial dimensions of the debate. Here, again, it is necessary to emphasize the inseparability of time and space, the impossibility of shifting one part of the axis without implication for the other. Yet space remains the unexplored dimension of the dualism. Whereas time remains relational, subject to effect from what occurs before or after a shot, space is imaged as a container, a static entity within which events take place (Marcus, 1994). In turning to contemporary film, the editing practices of assemblage (a term that requires some unpacking) trace a filmic relationship between time and space that is more thoroughly dependent on an understanding of how space is produced.

Tracing the code

I dislike this word [editing] and think the French expression 'montage' far more adequate and expressive, for it means 'assembly' and that is really what happens in editing.

Béla Balázs, *Theory of the Film*

What does it mean to think of editing a film as a process of assembly rather than a series of cuts? Or, another way of shaping the question, why do we focus on the aspect of cutting rather than joining?

In thinking of the cut as the main editorial trope, film is regarded as a temporal anomaly, a mystification of time which, under the aegis of modernism, maps on to a psychic reality of fractured time. This description of editing, I would argue, has come to dominate conceptualizations of film as time-based, of the temporal as the most significant aspect, and affect, of film. To think differently about editing is then to reconceptualize film and its fundamental components. Editing as assemblage, a bringing together of parts into unforeseen relations, requires us to think about film's spatial manipulations, as a fabric that threads itself across space linking atomized images and producing new lines of connection. In so doing, film becomes a fundamentally relational medium with each seemingly separate part (shot sequence) impacting on all that has gone before and that which comes after. In a sense, editing is not so much a clinical cutting, but an act of contagion, in Deleuze and Guattari's (1980) use of the term. Editing perhaps is a virus, spreading its dis-ease into each new part, a lateral movement of disturbance and connection.

If, in thinking of editing as assemblage, space moves to the fore, it is not in the sense of suppressing one part of the space-time axis by the other. In reinserting space into thought here, time is present, but increasingly folded into and articulated through space. This, in one sense, is an obvious point to make about the articulation of time through space. Yet it is a thought repeatedly submerged in earlier writing on film. Béla Balázs, writing in the first half of the twentieth century, approaches the relation between what he calls time effect and space effect in editing. Indeed, it appears that Balázs is about to unravel the ambiguity of cuts in time and space. The disjunction produced by a cut and a move to another location potentially disorientates the chain of signification, producing a momentary questioning of where and when 'we' are. The point here, in Balázs's reading, is however moving in another direction, as 'fact corroborated by every experience': 'the film inserts a lapse of time between two scenes by means of cutting in a scene enacted in a different place. The experience is that the farther away the site of the inserted scene is from the site of the scenes between which it is inserted, the more time we will feel to have elapsed' (1952: 122).

Balázs's reading of 'cutting' on one hand focuses on more than temporal disjunction (suspense, condensation), and brings space into the discussion. On the other hand, the interpretation of the effect of the cut is to sublimate space to time. Space becomes distance, which signifies the time necessary to travel. A cut to a distant location then falls back on to a realist logic of 'real' time journeys, space as the index of continuous time past rather than as a territory produced in the cut.[8] This claim also relies on us inhabiting a universe of recognition, a shared cartography of identifiable locations. Michael Haneke's film, *Code Unknown* (2000), works from a different assumption, that the present cartography of a film may create various concepts of alien territory.[9]

In *Code Unknown*, Michael Haneke offers a different rendering of space and time, whereby space is multiplied as different story locations, and time unfurls into a number of simultaneous presents. What is critical to *Code Unknown* is precisely the lack of a logic of continuity across space and the possibility of space as disorientating. The shape of the film begins with a centre, a street in Paris where several key characters appear, collision and conflict take place, and the stories spin off in different directions. A woman who is an actress runs into a boy, her partner's brother, who has escaped life on his father's farm. The boy throws his rubbish disrespectfully into the lap of a Romanian woman begging in a doorway. A young man witnesses this act and goes after the boy to insist on an apology to the woman. A fight breaks out, police arrive and arrest both the young man, who is of African descent, and the Romanian woman. The film opens then in Paris, the city most closely associated with modernist writings and sensibility, but its streets are not peopled by an anonymous distracted crowd. The continuous take of the street scene, with the camera tracking sideways, initially lulls us into a sense of the fluidity of the city, yet by the close of the sequence the characters have dispersed in different directions. Contemporary Paris is marked by diversity, by competing 'realities' and histories, immediately butting up against one another. And it is a centre implicitly connected to other spaces.

This scene appears near the beginning, yet the pre-title sequence provides a critical introduction to the logic of the film and its editorial project. A deaf child performs a mime to a group of children. The children guess at the meaning of the communication through what appears to be a reciprocal sign language. But the children's guesses are wrong. There are several attempts by the children to suggest an interpretation (of sadness, imprisonment, a bad conscience) but each time their ideas are refused. The shots on the performing child become closer, more tightly framed, until her sense of isolation is palpable: she is not understood, the signs offered cannot be shared. Importantly, this scene, which is returned to with equal failure of outcome at the close of the film, is only one of two places in the film where a cut occurs within a sequence. The other moment of cutting, following a conventional shot reverse shot pattern in a scene of rising tension, is in fact a film within the film, in which the actress has a role. For the remainder of the film, each scene is played as a single take. The pre-title sequence establishes the question of the film, of what occurs when communication is no longer possible, when codes are not shared, and in the meaning of the child's mime being withheld, the audience is placed in the position of not understanding, experiencing the frustration of not knowing the code.

The shape of the film, subtitled 'Incomplete tales of several journeys', fans out from the early street scene to a series of stories connected to each of these characters. The emphasis is not on drama but largely on the quotidian, the everyday routines and rhythms of life. In this way, the film is able to challenge a notion that there is a collective understanding of critical concepts: 'home', 'comfort', 'safety', 'luxury', 'opportunity' are terms that shift in reference between each story. 'Home' translates diversely as: the farm that the boy experiences as a prison, a building in process in a Romanian village, an African town, a claustrophobic Parisian apartment where the screams of a neighbouring child leak through the walls. Most problematically, home is a shifting concept for Georges, the war correspondent working in Kosovo, who returns to Paris to find himself dislocated from life there. Ultimately he has made 'home' the territory of conflict, extremity and survival elsewhere. Whilst the film travels to the different spaces of Africa and Romania, the war zone of Kosovo is represented by still images, the correspondent's own photographs. Again, the film reproduces for the audience what the characters perform. Georges cannot communicate the experience of elsewhere, its radical and violent difference. It is a failure of his own ability to express it through language, and a failure of the images to convey that experience. Later in the film, in a second voice-over of a letter from Georges, the description of the war is laid over images that he has shot, covertly, of passengers travelling the metro. The incommensurability of the 'here' and the 'there' is performed by this disjunction: the voice-over narrates life-threatening situations where failure of a common language between captive and prisoner almost costs him his life, whilst the image works through a series of expressionless faces.

The twenty-seven scenes that are assembled as the film are not cut together to produce a continuous sense of each. We have, as the subtitle indicates, incomplete tales, cut into mid-sentence. The beginning of each take is never the beginning of a piece of dialogue or action, but a midpoint. Equally, the scenes cut out before any form of resolution takes place. It can only be assumed here that the stories were constructed in this way, yet the fragmentary nature of each sequence draws attention to the process of assemblage. Just as space exists beyond the frame, time runs on outside of the sequence. Film only offers us edited fragments, pieces placed in relation to each other. Whilst editing is conventionally used to link scenes, to create continuity and increased comprehension, *Code Unknown* assembles fragments of stories without resolution. As the audience, we are made to experience the shift of each edit, from story to story, from place to place. The result is not a culmination of meaning, a building of significance within each story. Rather, the shift between stories replays the same trope. Miscommunication is the common element of each tale, and as the film progresses, the sense of a possible relationship between these disparate parts recedes. The stories do not connect to form a bigger whole, but remain shards, paths of flight away and towards each other yet failing to illuminate.

Place here comes to signify the particularity of each story. Distance is traversed with ease by the industries of travel and technology, yet the specific experience of each place presents an incommensurability of experience, an excessive difficulty. Kosovo cannot be translated into Parisian life. Equally, Romania is unknowable to people on the streets of Paris. Characters move geographically, travel between sites, but are unable to make the experience of one place make sense in another. Most starkly, this is the photographer's experience in moving between a war zone and a European capital. But it is also the case in the other stories. The woman from Romania who has made her money begging, and sends the cash 'home' to support the building of a family house, lies about her life in Paris. She tells a neighbour that she has been working as a teacher and has returned home because she missed her children. This obscures the brutality of a life of begging on the streets and her deportation, and keeps in play the fantasy of Paris as a centre of a 'civilized', benevolent culture. Similarly, the father of the African family travels to Africa, returning to what he perceives to be 'home'. The reasons for this return are not explicit, but there is the inference of a return to a mythological place of origin. The father drives his car off the ferry and into the streets of an African town, yet as he drives through the crowded streets he is sealed in, stuck in a capsule that isolates him from this environment. And in Paris, when the family discuss his journey, the youngest child asks where Africa is.

Haneke uses editing as a critical component of the language of cinema. Cutting and reconnecting images and sounds is a primary process, a language that implies an absence of continuity, but a legible absence. Indeed, since the cinema of Vertov, the cut is the notable foundation of cinema's aliveness, showing 'that cinematographic images on their own are just inert pieces of celluloid that can only be brought to life by the operation of montage that arranges them' (Rancière, 2001: 174). Yet Haneke's use of editing questions exactly what it is that these cinematographic images articulate, what language it is that they speak. Is cinema after all mute, able to cut but unable to join? The free association so famously associated with cinema stalls, falters in the face of a multitude of stories and images that will not cohere, will not add up to a sum greater than its parts. If film is a medium capable of translating the less than conscious dimensions of experience into an affectual language of inference, it also reveals a limit to translation: images, like cultures, retain a specificity that may not be reduced to an equivalence. Haneke does not seem to suggest that cinematic language can be otherwise. The only possibility of connection appears in the scenes of collective drumming, powerful scenes of a crowd facing the same way and acting in unison. The rhythmic code of drumming provides a mode of communication that is widely understood; the drummers are faultless in their collective action. These scenes, appearing towards the end of the film, raise the tension. For once the film has rhythm, a rhythm that the editing has worked against throughout. They are the only scenes that are allowed to play out, to reach a point that is consistent with a conclusion.

The logic of the film is one of addition rather than development as each sequence unravels a fragment of a story: each fragment is an 'and', a link that fails to set a relation other than as an accumulation of parts. Assembling ever more fragments, the logic of addition, of 'also', maintains an experience of disjuncture. Taken with the previous fragments, the sense of story is of an activity proliferating, yet each tale retains a difference, a refusal to be assimilated into or to illuminate the significance of other sequences. Difference, as specificity of place, is the product of this assemblage. From the early scene of the street in Paris, which is the space of overlap and apparent commonality between characters, the sequences unravel further from the cosmopolitan 'heartland' into the socio-political outposts. Where the shared environment of Paris has failed to generate a unified experience of city life, a failed public sphere if you will, this failure of communication is reproduced in the movement into other spaces. In constructing the sequences in this way, the expectation might be that characters return to a location identified as 'home'. What occurs is a more thorough dislocation of identity, and a growing incoherence to the stories that the characters themselves tell: the deliberate misrepresentation of experience 'elsewhere' becomes an accumulating feature of the several tales. In the so-called connected infrastructure of globalization, the result is not an homogenization of experience but its opposite: a reinscription of difference and incommensurability. Whilst space is increasingly threaded together and distance compressed in faster modes of travel and communication, space refuses to surrender its peculiar specificity.

The style of editing then employs addition, as the film moves sideways into other spaces, as an assemblage of fragments. Yet there is also a method of withholding deployed by Haneke in the framing and duration of scenes. In choosing to avoid the shot–reverse shot sequence, Haneke adopts the long or medium shot, retaining a distance from the subjects in front of the camera. They are held at arm's length, as it were, a technique that utilizes space as distance.

'We' do not have the privileged access to expressive emotion enabled by the close-up, but are held to a perspective that emphasizes the space between characters.[10] The negotiation of that space is critical. In a scene in which the actress, Ann, returns to her apartment to find her lover has returned from Kosovo, the choreography of the scene plays out the dynamic of the relationship. Ann stands at the door, a greeting is offered across the space. Only when the telephone rings does she move towards him, a movement towards an other (the telephone) which coincidently places her in proximity to Georges. The telephone cuts out, she replaces the receiver and only then is proximity explored. It is awkward, reticent, fearful, and the sequence ends. Yet Haneke's use of the long shot, both as framing device and duration, is markedly different from the effects of neo-realism. Where Bazin locates the ambivalence of the scene in the spectator's ability to rove the frame visually, in *Code Unknown* it is the use of space within the frame rather than the detail of its *mise en scène* that is made to signify. This method of shot reproduces the question of how to negotiate space as difference, or difference as space.

To underscore this use of framing and editing technique, and its difference from conventional techniques, Haneke inserts a film within the film. The actress is shown at two auditions, in the shooting of a film in an empty apartment, and in a postproduction studio working on additional dialogue for the soundtrack. In this last sequence, the audience experience the film as though it were another sequence; it is only when the camera pulls back that we recognize the context: the film is projected in a studio in front of the actors. The sequence from the film within the film is set in a swimming pool where a couple playfully cavort in the water. Their exchange is edited in a fast shot–reverse shot sequence to the rhythm of the banter between them. The next shot is of a boy climbing on to a wall, the street a long way below, and back to the characters' reactions. The sequence creates a powerful contrast to the editing of the rest of *Code Unknown*, and the refusal of proximity and cutting. Here, in the film within the film, the devices of editing appear precisely as manipulative techniques, structuring intimacy and identification with each character, and facilitating an ease, and 'naturalness', of communication between characters. In the pool sequence, the two main characters communicate an emotional sequence of affection, desire and fear with accuracy and ease. In this 'fictional' context that Haneke has underscored, editing is precisely an activity of connection, and the mobile position of perspective as it moves between the characters fabricates a sense that point of view is expressive, visible and clear. Continuity editing transforms communication into a transparent activity, where each act of expression is a conscious articulation of self and received in the same spirit. In varying the syntax of editing across the film, Haneke provokes the question of code, of what we are familiar with and what we are alienated by; this applies to codes of intimate relationships, cultural signifiers and the language of film.

If editing, as an assemblage of sequences from different dislocated places, foregrounds space, it is not as a given territory or container of action, but as the product of interaction, travel and encounter. Space is produced as the distance between characters within scenes, and as the difference between cultures measured through transportation. In contrast to the claim by Balázs that a radical shift in location signifies a lengthy elapse, in *Code Unknown* the cutting between places is suggestive of a simultaneity of events. The effect is not to produce the tension and suspense of parallel editing, but to pose the question, what if there are many presents? How can we conceive of difference on such a scale? Whilst 'worlds' are strung together through technologies, transport and images, there is no logic to their relationship, and no ease of translation. Editing as assemblage does not mirror the 'real' world, but takes the shape, isomorphically, of the complex relational linkages that purportedly connect difference, whilst differences remain too many and too complex to be gathered into a coherent sequence.

Postproduction

In the introduction to Kracauer's *Theory of Film*, Miriam Hansen comments on the historical importance of the concept of the indexicality of film, and its contemporary demotion: 'Digital technologies such as computer enhancement, imaging, and editing have shifted the balance increasingly toward the postproduction phase, thus further diminishing the traces of photographic, indexical contingency in the final product' (1997: viii). The work of editing, unlike enhancement, does not concern the distinction between what has been recorded and what has been simulated, but it does transform the concept of film from another direction. For, if the balance of production as a site of meaning shifts towards postproduction, the idea that the meaning of an image lies within its own frame becomes disputable, or put into crisis. In the process of editing, sequences of images are put into relation with each other, and it is the relation, as a type of hinge between one shot and the next, that fires signification.[11] The emergence of what, in the sphere of art criticism, Nicolas Bourriaud has termed 'relational art' resonates for film also. The timing of its emergence as a critical and creative tool tells us something perhaps of what we are demanding from culture, more than it tells us of the materials themselves. Its most generalized conceptualization of art practice posits the following: given a ubiquitous circulation of images and objects, disembedded from contexts of production or sites of meaning, ubiquity is redeemed by their being gathered into a meaningful assemblage of new cross-references. Relational art, and the importance of the montage process of film, announces the possibility of relations, or in the case of Haneke's film, the need to recognize the absence of relations of commensurability.

For Bourriaud, relational art is a contemporary practice, 'taking as its theoretical horizon the realm of human interactions and its social context, rather than the assertion of an independent and *private* symbolic space' (1998: 14). Assembling different parts does not so much impose a unity of coherence on the work, but discloses the possibilities of setting in relation. Whilst *Relational Aesthetics* describes a type of practice, in bricolage, that has a recognizable evolution in the gallery, Bourriaud's subsequent work borrows its title from film, *Postproduction* (2000). Arguably, this text exposes the currency of the concept of assemblage across the spheres of art, film and music production. And yet there are differences between these modes of cultural production that we would be mindful to address. The category of the relational provides a loose gathering of ideas that unsettle, in useful ways, the conventional framework of comprehending film production, and which are different from those of art production. The emphasis on filmic postproduction disturbs the historico-industrial model, which appears to prioritize the 'shoot' as the creative centre of meaning; indeed, the prefix 'post' infers that production is that which has already happened. This observation may, of course, be accorded in part to the journalistic and theoretical interest in stories of production and performance, an attunement to the unofficial knowledge of production which foregrounds the shoot as the moment of 'making'. To focus on postproduction also divests us of the linear model of planning and authorial intentionality, a model that constructs film-making as a type of production-line of an author's work. In postproduction, the materiality of the film recovers some agency, as matter that is unruly, surprising and unknowable as it is constituted relationally, as shot next to shot, and sound and image. 'Cinema', writes Giorgio Agamben, 'will now be made on the basis of images from cinema' (2002: 315).

To take postproduction as a site of enquiry, it is necessary to situate a spectrum of filmic practice within which different processes are evident. At one end is the model of script development, where the substantial architecture and detail of the film is worked in advance. The shoot follows the map of the script, and the materials of the edit are assembled within the contingency of the editing room. At the other end of the spectrum is the appropriation of filmic materials from given sources, from archives, found footage and amateur works, a process that relies on the bricolage model of the ready-made object. Like Christian Boltanski's biscuit tins and newspaper cuttings, the materials exist in the world and are brought into new relationships in postproduction; thus production becomes an activity of gleaning and assembling. Between these two poles of extremity, a diversity of practice exists. Towards the script-based end of the spectrum *Code Unknown* is located. Despite the foregrounding of the process of editing, the film operates a model known in advance. Within the film, postproduction becomes a type of trope, a figurative presence in the film enacted through unexpected cuts, shifts of location and unexpected entry and exit points to scenes. The assemblage of the film creates a discomfort in the jarring of cuts, in the incomplete nature of knowledge and in the refusal to provide a 'bigger picture' within which the components make sense.

Haneke's film provides us with a knowledge that is local, blind as it moves from frame to frame. And the scenes of filmic production within the film, the scene of additional dialogue for example, reveal the labour of producing a filmic language that is legible.

Where *Code Unknown* enacts the editing practices of postproduction visibly within the film (or as the experience of the film),[12] at the other end of the spectrum is a mode of practice that sutures diverse materials into a semi-coherent unity. In Bill Morrison's *Decasia* (2002), images are gathered from a large number of archives and melded into a feature-length film. The images that Morrison selects are those of film where states of decay are evident. The nitrate-based materials struggle to register through marks that seem elemental; the images appear to be burnt or swimming in water. The gleaning of images was determined by the conflict between decay and decomposition of the materials, and the grandiose subject matter of the film. Morrison states: 'I was clearly drawn to those images where there was a dialogue between the image and the film stock it was printed on . . . examples of man defying his own mortality as in religious acts, or death-defying or heroic acts. The deterioration of the film seemed to belie the images portrayed on it' (Morrison, 2002).

Decasia registers a double sense of the temporal, in the stock itself and in the subject matter of the film. In the images of nuns leading children into what appears to be a school in a colonial outpost of European empire, the austere uniform of the women contrasts with the smiling faces of the children filing past the camera. The images leap, jump and flicker in the gate, attempting to jump across time but also hauntingly disintegrating before the eyes. Morrison's work in postproduction is in fact a production, a production that comes after film-making but with a century in between the shooting and assembling of the materials. Whilst *Decasia* has been received predominantly as an elegy to cinema, its energy of connection poses more difficult questions of 'our' relation to this earlier time, to this history out of which the present has uncoiled. The film stutters and starts in its attempts to reconnect us to other historical moments, but it also reaches out across space, into the heart of empire, an occidental framing of the world. The fragments and sequences of the film are held together by the logic of an occidental vision, moving from one location to another, leaping across cultures and continents, but connected by this thread of an identifiable perspective. A dervish pivots on the screen, arms outstretched, skirts flying outwards in a feat of balanced velocity, one of the many images of a cinema fascinated with the 'exotic', with alterity as a particularly bodily manifestation. It is a production that could only appear as a unified work from this temporal distance. *Decasia* is a baroque reminder of the real and imaginary links between cinema and travel, and cinema and alterity, which have been there since its inception.

At the furthest end of a spectrum of postproduction, beyond *Decasia* and archival work, is the practice of film remixing as an event. Here, the practices of music sampling and remix performance are applied to film, with, for example, Paul D. Miller's performance of a live mix of *Birth of a Nation*.[13] Miller writes, in *Rhythm Science*, of his use of Griffith's films as a double appropriation. Griffith is cited by Miller as the founder of the Hollywood cinematic form in his construction of narrative through the edit. Parallel actions occurring simultaneously and parallel actions occurring in separate temporal frames, in the case of *Birth of a Nation*, provide a model from which music was to evolve in sampling and cutting. The second appropriation in the remix is a stealing back of the film from its usage 'as a recruitment film for the Ku Klux Klan' (2004: 84). In Miller's live remix, the images are deployed to function with music, cut into to develop certain rhythms and associations, using repetition and loops. Miller's practice echoes the drumming scenes in *Code Unknown*; the question of which rhythms connect us provides a language of momentary collectivity. The transience of the event has another dimension. The version of the film produced at the event is a one-off remake, a concept that confuses the designations of 'remake' and 'original'. In one sense the film by Griffith is the obvious original, in the sense of a source material, but simultaneously, the film produced at the event takes on that mantle as a version that cannot be reproduced. Film staged as an event then refers originality to a moment of 'liveness' rather than recording. Film comes full circle but not quite connecting: it is a/live, moving medium that is also a recording.

Half way through *The Time-Image*, Deleuze remarks, 'How strange the great declarations, of Eisenstein, of Gance, ring today; we put them to one side like declarations worthy of a museum, all the hopes put into cinema, art of the masses and new thought' (1985: 164). Deleuze's 'today' is, of course, not the moment of now, but becomes a historically embedded reflection on the changing context of cinema. Conceptualizations of editing taken historically reveal the investments in film at a particular time and context. Eisenstein's notion of a dialectical montage breaking open the grip of the ideological mystification is of its time, was a concept wrought in the face of an ascending European fascism. Editing was put to work within a specific context. Yet the setting aside of these aspirational ideas in a museum, as Deleuze does, as objects of curiosity, reverberates differently in the 'now'. In a context in which both editing and museums have become invested with a productive curiosity and practice, the old is not so easily dismissed. The culture of film remix is not necessarily conducted with the intellectual determination for an ideological affect as Eisenstein's work, yet the practice does in a sense tear apart the clichés of classical narrative and remake perception in a manner derivative of both Eisenstein and Deleuze. How images are linked, grouped and interconnected in a process of continual transformation is a Deleuzian obsession, rewritten in the era of remix with the zeal of Eisenstein. In the realm of postproduction, there lie strange bedfellows indeed.

4

The limits of translation: transnational film

The term 'foreign' refers us to questions of context, of who is at home and who is abroad, of what is perceived as belonging and what is regarded as alien. Designating the foreign, indeed, the naturalized power in the act of identifying 'foreignness', enacts exclusions and draws complicities. Such a politics of recognition, and refusal, comes to bear not only on the human, but on the medium of film. The paths of distribution and exhibition that any film labelled as 'foreign' travels are confined by paradigms of recognition. Yet there remains a possibility that film's foreignness – that is, its alterity as an object from elsewhere, and as an affectual medium in an age of information flows – is a site of critical resource. Take, for example, the introduction to a book on subtitling by Atom Egoyan and Ian Balfour:

> Every film is a foreign film, foreign to some audience somewhere – and not simply in terms of language . . . Subtitles are only the most visible and charged markers of the way in which films engage, in direct and oblique fashion, pressing matters of difference, otherness, and translation. (Egoyan and Balfour, 2004: 21)

Could it be the case that an engagement with the foreignness of film opens up 'pressing matters of difference', and allows us to speak of the incommensurability between cultures, peoples and cultural forms? That is, could attention to foreignness fly in the face of a comfortable cosmopolitanism by reinserting the ongoing difficulty inherent to acts of recognition? In what follows, these questions are explored through a dialogue between film and theoretical texts.

Chungking Express (Wong Kar-wai, 1994), is a film of two parts, both set in Hong Kong. In the first story a man who has been rejected by his lover, May, collects tins of pineapples. Pineapples, we are told, are May's favourite food. The pineapple tins gathered are not an indiscriminate collection, but canned fruit with a specific sell-by date of 1 May. In the story, the man, who is a cop (identification number 223), resists the woman's rejection by all means possible. But his attempts at reaching her and persuading her otherwise are blocked. The cop's response is to turn to cans of fruit in the striking of a bargain: if the woman has not changed her mind by the beginning of May, the relationship is indeed over, and the cop will eat all of the cans of pineapples. The beginning of May will be the end of May. In the second story, of a different cop (identification number 633) and a waitress, the cop is oblivious to the waitress's desire for him. By foul means, she attains a set of keys to his apartment. She enters the apartment by day, without his knowledge. She cleans, rearranges furniture, plays music. The cop fails to notice. The stakes are raised as she adds more goldfish to the tank, replaces his music with her own, relabels the tins of food so that sardines become mackerel, replaces his bed linen, sticks a photograph of herself as a child on to his mirror. The cop returns unexpectedly one day, the woman screams, the cop is confused. The two sit in silence without explication of the situation.

The Hong Kong that *Chungking Express* constructs is hetero-topic, a place that Peter Brunette describes as 'non-narrative, anti-realist, hyperstylized' (2005: 57).[1] In this world of incompatible differences, objects play a critical role. If the fabric of the city, its streets, bars, bazaars, facilitate proximity without intimacy, objects become a form of relating that allows, conversely, intimacy without proximity (Gan, 2003). Objects become a critical means of communication in the absence of the other. The inanimate is made to articulate longing, to express care, and to somehow reside in a border region of negotiation.[2] Here artefacts are not part of an abstract system of exchange for profit, but the means to communicate desire, and an expression of a desire to communicate. Objects in the film become subject to purposeful play, rehearsal and performance. Objects bring human counterparts to life and animate them; it is not they who are brought to life. They allow the first cop to rehearse a process of mourning, a type of negotiation when inter-human exchange has reached an end. They enable the waitress of the second story to read the emotional state of the cop, and to express her desire for him through things. Objects come between people in the best sense. Retaining their own specific identity, they facilitate communication directed towards, but in the absence of, the other.

The presence of objects in *Chungking Express* lends itself to reflections on our relations with the non-human world, and the particular object here of film itself. As a type of 'thing', film gets between people. It is compliant with our demands for intimacy without proximity. It retains its own distinctness in the face of our expectations, projections and wily interpretations. Film is an object, like all objects, that is both with us and resistant to us. It is also, like most (post)industrial objects, a thing that comes from elsewhere, dispatched from an origin that remains mysterious no matter how hard we attempt to conjure it from the film itself. Film retains a foreignness, as Egoyan and Balfour note, in a double sense. As a medium it resists a 'translation' into the commonplace through its strange arrangement of the audio, the image and the arts of 'telling'. And as an object from elsewhere, it lures us into the state of desire that for Derrida is the condition of all desiring: 'It is necessary that I try to make the thing mine but that it remain other enough that I have some interest in making it mine, other enough that I desire it' (Derrida and Stiegler, 1996: 111).[3] The state of desiring is the crux of the matter for the characters in *Chungking Express*, of how to manage the pull towards another and yet allow their alterity to exist, without appropriating the other into a register of the same (thus losing them). A character's desire to get inside an other is made possible as the desire to be in an other's apartment, in his absence. Her appropriation of the other is in a mixing up of his things. And in the confrontation, the movement is one of retreat. In the oeuvre of Wong Kar-wai, the state of desiring is going nowhere, stuck in a loop of advance and retreat. In film studies, the question of how we negotiate the object/other is just as urgent. How do we approach, comprehend, metabolize film from elsewhere without appropriating its difference into a logic of the same? How do we resist making it the thing that we already 'know' about that other place, but convince ourselves that we are discovering?

Whilst the term 'foreign' inevitably brings with it the baggage of a colonial history, entailing misrecognition, exoticization and abuse, it articulates in the present usage a relation that comes from the outside, an alterity. Hence its usefulness in the present, a term that carries the weight of history, and underscores the ways in which the 'foreign' has become commodified (in tourism, food culture for example), made safe, consumable. Types of foreignness are at the heart of *Chungking Express*, a reflexive haunting register of alterity that works in a number of ways, or through different layers. The thematic of love within the film turns on the notion of an other as remote, irreducibly different, always slightly out of reach.[4] In the first story, the cop is chasing the woman in literal and metaphorical ways. He is constantly perplexed by the other's ability to escape him, to slip the net of his desire for contact. His ruminations concern the fantasies of proximity, but both of the women he pursues remain out of reach. In the second story, the cop attends the café regularly, encountering the woman who secretly desires him. Physically they orbit one another, but a direct advance or expression of desire is, it appears, impossible. The other is unapproachable, his alterity mediated by the objects of his apartment. In matters of love, the foreignness of the other is paramount.

Second, the space of Hong Kong is an imaginary city, produced through its complex history and relations to elsewhere (the food, music, commodities), and it retains a foreignness that resists any attempt to define an 'indigenous' culture. This is not a filmic rendition of place in which foreignness can be translated into definable differences. Nor does it lend itself to the oppositional dichotomy of traditional or modern. Rather the film presents the often paradoxical mix of influences, styles and histories through its use of music, architectural detail, clothing and naming of locations. It is a rendition of space that Wimal Dissanayake argues both references 'earlier times' and bears 'the imprint of the cosmopolitan consumer culture', underlining 'the impossibility of re-occupying an originary cultural space' (2004: 148).[5]

The third articulation of 'foreignness' is film itself, its specific language manifest as an instability of images that have given up the ghost of recording 'reality', spinning off into abstract textures. As Jean-Marc Lalanne describes Wong Kar-wai's aesthetic, it is another world, 'a land of images where cinema's mystique, as an art of registering, would cease to have any meaning, where images would seem self-engendered, deploying themselves without any reference to the real' (1997: 14). Alterity as the trademark of film is deployed in *Chungking Express* as a fracturing of vision, a slowing of pace, a redolent toning of the image. Lalanne's description of images could be applied equally to the other modes of alterity, the relationships of characters or concepts of Hong Kong, 'one forever short-circuiting the other' (1997: 11). The alterity of the image places us in a position of never quite seeing in focus, of being behind or in front of the movement, or our perspective being off at an angle. It is not only the characters who remain slightly out of reach to each other, but the relation between the image and the spectator; as Ackbar Abbas notes eloquently, the image 'misses its appointment with meaning' (1997: 45).

Chungking Express is Wong Kar-wai's fourth film, made in 1994.[6] It is shot, as we have noted, in the global city of Hong Kong. If we take Bruno Latour's definition of the global city not in terms of size and scale but in its amount of connections to elsewhere, this is the site on to which *Chungking Express* opens. The film does not offer sky-line shots of the city, the filmic tropes of aerial mastery through vision. It takes the streets, the alleyways and bazaars of Hong Kong mansions, constructing a system of cellular spaces (the food stall, the apartment, the bar) that the film moves between. There is no sense of a larger 'whole' constituted by these spaces. The film takes a different mode of operation: a city is a space to be navigated on the ground, according to a system of directions, where one cellular space gives way to another. The city is a place of proximate and relational proportions. The street is *in front of* the food stall, the bazaar appears *to the side*, the apartment *further on*, beyond as a network in which each space exists only in relation to its predecessor. The Hong Kong of *Chungking Express* is not a place whose identity is to be discovered; this is not film as tourism but a series of interrelating sites of different scales and dimensions. Principles of hierarchy, continuity and origin are absent. The opening sequences of the film feature migrant populations, black markets, Chinese restaurants, western brands, 1960s American music, and cops. This heterotopia is the location of the first story, a crushed anomaly of shops, market stalls, bars, cheap hotels and workplaces.[7] The location of the second story is central, its most memorable feature being a long stretch of escalators, moving bodies from one space to the next.

This filmic Hong Kong of *Chungking Express* offers a space without a meaningful geography. It is rather a network of endless detail. Yet the tendency in current film analysis draws back from this detail, reaching for a 'critical' distance in the socio-political context of Hong Kong. In the directory of *Fifty Contemporary Filmmakers*, Julian Stringer states, 'with Hong Kong now positioned between its existence as a postcolonial global city and its destiny as part of the Chinese nation-state, Wong's films have come to bear the burden of historical representation' (2002: 395). The term 'burden', as Stringer implies, has resonance. Such classification binds film to a sense of place, a place of origin, which leads inevitably to notions of representation of a national culture. In many accounts, the signing of the 1984 Sino-British Joint Declaration on the Future of Hong Kong announcing the return of Hong Kong to Chinese sovereignty, and the event of Tiananmen Square occurring in 1989, provide an historical context against which the film must come to 'mean'. Through a method of political analogy, Gina Marchetti reads a broader political thematic into the failure of relationships in the film: 'Under the veneer of popular optimism about the future, there is also a sense that Hong Kong has been abandoned and, worse, that, like the jilted lover, it has no power or say in this decision' (cited in Brunette, 2005: 52). Similarly, Stokes and Hoover read the story of relationships as a political analogy, this time reading the unlikely couplings as a positive symbolism; the potential unification of the pairs of potential lovers in the film 'defines a new way of uniting that has meaning for the particular time and place – Hong Kong on the verge of its return to the Mainland, as well as the couples who make a conscious decision to be together in these uncertain postmodern times' (1999: 200). Film analysis then moves by analogy between the social context of the nation and a metaphorical reading of the text. Yet this practice appears to work against the very differently textured grain of the film's language, which refutes a sense of place as a bounded knowable location.

Whilst *Chungking Express* registers the local in a particular way, it is a permeable space, fundamentally mediated by elsewhere. Music is a significant feature of spatial dislocation. Two tracks take priority, 'What a Difference a Day Makes' in the first story, and the track 'California Dreaming' by the Mamas and Papas, a soundscape looped throughout the second part of the film. It is repeated as the girl serving behind the fast-food counter routinely, compulsively and loudly plays the track as she works, with the volume so loud that she has difficulty hearing the orders of the customers. The music obfuscates communication between characters. Or rather music signals mis(sed) communication. But the particularity of the track situates a place, 'California', squarely in the narrative of the film. California dreaming is the dreaming of an imaginary elsewhere critical to the story. It is a referent doubled by the name of the bar where two characters arrange to meet, 'LA', and tripled by the airplane ticket to LA where she flies to and from in the final part of the film in her new career as a flight attendant. California dreaming is dreaming about the present context through the eyes/voice of another, dreaming as a Californian, as well as dreaming of a place that is imaginary until the character travels there in her new-found occupation. California is more readily evoked as an absent imaginary, a site of longing, than as a potential travel destination.

These two locations, and geographical referents, of Hong Kong and California, perform as oppositional poles in the film, but their instability as knowable locations blurs the distinction. The streets of Hong Kong are over-written by dreams of another place; space is the trigger for affectual experience. In the use of two cops as the main protagonists of each story, the process of meandering through streets aimlessly is common to both parts. Walking becomes a form of remembering and fantasizing; it is about the past and the future. The present, and individual psychic presence, are elusive registers, struggled toward in certain moments but usually resulting in failure.

Each character is caught in her or his emotional landscape, a place of solitary meditation and reflection, imaginary dialogue and speculation. This state of solitary affectual existence, mapped out on to the city as a series of individual emotional stories, places communication slightly out of reach. Acts of communication are either mistimed, misheard or misfiring. The cop in the first story cannot get through to his girlfriend on the phone, the cop of the second story cannot be heard above the waitress's music, the waitress is 'caught' in the cop's apartment but is unable to express anything, the letter to the cop from his ex-girlfriend is intercepted, the penultimate arrangement to meet in the bar misfires, and so forth. In the sliding sideways confrontations with otherness, the other remains elusive, slightly out of reach.

The voice-over that the film deploys does little to stabilize the narrative as a series of causal events. The ruminating thoughts of the voice-over is in fact more of a speculative voice-off, a metalingual aside (Lalanne, 1997). An apparent glossing commentary on events, it is rather a free-association, calculating distance and time as though it were to inject meaning into the transactions and encounters: 'At our closest point, we were just 0.01 cm apart from each other,' speaks the character of cop 223. 'Fifty-five hours later, I was in love with this woman.' The voice-off attempts to inject a temporal framework into experience, to create a linearity to events that are made to seem significant if arranged chronologically. The effect is the reverse, that the present is constantly invaded by the past and the future: 'two minutes from now I will be twenty-five'. Time does not offer a framing device, nor does it lend significance to experience. In the cop's obsessive organization of experience as temporal, the present appears all the more as a moment slipping away without ever being 'grasped'. Measurement of time and space hangs in the air of the commentary, impotent in its abstract relation to things.

The rendering of space as affective, polyform, palimpsestic, has a corollary in the treatment of time. Like space, time cannot be measured but only inhabited, detached from any logic of movement as progression. Time is spent, wasted, lost, used up. Individual time is out of synch with others: it speeds up and evaporates, or conversely is slowed down in Wong Kar-wai's characteristic use of

step-printing. In *Chungking Express*, moments of emotional resonance are a disjunction from others, as the cop sips his coffee outside
of the fast-food bar whilst reeling from the news that his girlfriend
has left him. The most quotidian and habitual act of drinking coffee
becomes sublimely surreal: the hand carries the coffee to the mouth
in what seems like an eternity, the girl at the counter watches, the
blink of her eye slowed to a discernible act, whilst the blur of figures
in the street cross the frame in what appears to be another world.
The step printing of the image here does not facilitate an extension
of the image in its detail, but draws attention to the disparate elements, underscored by the removal of sound. Time is broken up,
subjective and elastic, its corollary in theory expressed by Michel
Serres: 'time does not flow according to a line . . . nor according to
a plan but rather according to an extensive complex mixture, as
though it reflected stopping points, ruptures, deep wells, chimneys
of thunderous acceleration (rendings, gaps) – all sown at random,
at best in viable disorder' (1995: 57).

The experience of time involves objects and landscape ('deep
wells', 'chimneys'), and variations in speed and motion ('stopping
points', 'thunderous accelerations'). The disjunctions of time, splin-
tering experience from a shared present and forging an individual
well, occurs not only in moments of reflective reverie of *Chungking
Express*, but in the action sequences (the opening of the film, for
example). Acts of excitement and violence (the shooting that
punctuates the first story) are also out of time, another register where
the quotidian moves into a different dimension. The difficulty of
connecting to an objective time, measurable and meaningful, is
played out in the first story as the calendar (a staple of the index in
film discourse) ironically flips over into a new day. Cop 223 attempts
to make this a marker in his life, a designated end-point in his relationship. Yet even this attempt to make time 'count', an objective
measure of an emotional reality, becomes a game with objects, the
accumulation of the pineapple tins. The objects are at once a diver-
sion from the passing of time, and from the deep well of emotional
stasis into which the cop has fallen.

In the devices of disorientation, both time and space appear as
a kind of looped programme. The same streets patrolled, the same
locations visited, the same emotional experience repeated. In the

first story there is an attempt to make time a marker, 'In 48 hours, I was going to fall in love with this woman', 'May 15th 1995, I almost fell in love for the first time'. Yet time fails to progress events towards a conclusion; rather time repeats experience. The first cop reproduces his rejection by a woman in his brief encounter with the drugs trafficker. In the second story, the cop similarly reproduces his loss of a girlfriend. The solitary experience of the present condemns characters to a state of mistiming, continuously out of synch with the events in which they are caught. A lack of synchronicity in each story is retrieved by contingency rather than measured planning. In the first story, the cop chases the woman, a drug trafficker, loses her, and then coincidently finds himself next to her in a bar that evening. The sublime optimism of cop 223 is held in parenthesis, a voice-over that floats a possibility: 'We rub shoulders everyday. We may not know each other. But we could be friends some day.' As the two characters retire to a hotel room, friendship, and its further possibility, romance, is absent in the scene. The woman collapses on the bed and the cop rests in the chair, eating his way through the evening and watching old Cantonese operas. The difficulty of connection, however, is negotiated through objects. Even in this non-place of the hotel, the cop removes the woman's shoes and caringly cleans them before leaving: she later reciprocates this gesture by leaving a birthday message on his phone. This is a brief encounter or collision with its own expiry date. If the (im)possibility of human connection is a recurring theme of Wong Kar-wai's films, it is a frustrated, contorted desire to cross the threshold of subjectivity, to comprehend the space/story/imaginary of the other. And if objects mediate the desire to communicate desire, they appear to retain a calming self-presence, a world of things that can be combined any which way to serve the fantasy of the subject, yet remaining unaffected. The object-human relation provides an approach to another subject without entirely encroaching, a type of ethnography of the other relieved of the necessity of co-presence.

The effect of the split, twin-story structure is yet another manifestation of the same emotional paradigm. Denying a sense of narrative development, a refusal of the progressive sense of uncovery and attainment of knowledge that conventionally underpins film, each story circles around the other. The structure refuses to operate a dialectic of mutual inflection, the elucidation of one narrative through a cross-referencing of the other. In place of exposition, there is an echo of the first story in the second, a type of mimicry and doubling. It is as though there were one story, man mourns woman, man misses connection with second woman, resulting in solitude, played twice. In both stories a cop is the central character, but where the cop in the first story looks for signs everywhere, the second cop fails to read. Both have a difficulty with the legibility of the other. For the female characters, mimicry and performance are their modes of being. The first female character dresses in disguise, in a wig, trenchcoat and sunglasses, an appropriation of a gangster look. The second female character mimes the song, performs the rituals of a lover in the cop's apartment, and finally adopts the profession of the cop's former lover, as flight attendant. It is as though both the characters within the stories, and the stories themselves in their double structure, provide an ongoing rehearsal. Rehearsals are the event itself rather than a practice for a time when self-presence would be possible.[8] There is no designated real or original moment outside of the rehearsal, and perhaps this is a clue about film as an object. Film unwittingly rehearses our relations to others. It facilitates our movement toward and away. As an object it mediates difference and importantly resists attempts to make it the same as us. Film, as medium that is both there and not there, retains an alterity, ultimately unaffected by a desire for appropriation or containment.

In flight: anthropology's mutation

Two years before *Chungking Express* is made, the French anthropologist Marc Augé writes his treatise on supermodernity. It is also a project concerned with alterity, the palimpsestic qualities of mediatized space, and the mournful solitude of the individual, the same obsessive thematics of Wong Kar-wai (in their obsessions they are perhaps only 0.01 cm apart). Augé is also interested in flight, as an affectual experience, a metaphor, a practice of linkage or disconnection, so much so that the book opens with a fictional character on a plane:

> Somewhat dreamily, Pierre Dupont put down his magazine. The 'Fasten seat belt' notice had gone out. He adjusted his earphones, selected Channel 5 and allowed himself to be invaded by the adagio of Joseph Haydn's Concerto No. 1 in E major. For a few hours (the time it would take to fly over the Mediterranean, the Arabian Sea and the Bay of Bengal), he would be alone at last. (1992: 5)

So closes the opening prologue to *Non-places: introduction to an anthropology of supermodernity* (1992). The prologue stages for us the journey of a fictional character, Pierre Dupont, a businessman travelling to Roissy airport. We follow his journey to a cash dispenser, motorway tollbooth, the ticket machine of the car park, prefiguring the formal semi-automated routine of check-in and passport control, and the marked route through duty-free shopping, waiting lounge and terminal. We are, surreptitiously, being led by the hand through the territory of non-place, the locations of homogenized culture and the uniform processing of identities. In the intricacies of this account, Augé is presenting not only a descriptive view of non-place, but the experiential complexity of inhabiting such environments. Non-place is conferred with a particularity, a quality of experience that produces a distancing effect or, more explicitly, a disappearance of the self. In equal measure to the legitimization of his identity, Pierre Dupont is in retreat from himself, facilitated by the eclectic yet clichéd range of consumer and cultural goods on offer. Flight as a fantasy of mobility, Augé is suggestively arguing, is also a flight from the self. And the flight from self is also a fantasy of elsewhere, of alterity.[9]

The similarities and correlations between the filmic and theoretical works are uncanny. Both fashion a sense of the complex correspondences between space, alterity and the subject, both grappling with the elusive traces of the present as it becomes the past. My method here is not to elaborate the similarity, but to force the different registers of film and thought to emerge through each other: what is it that *Chungking Express* can articulate about contemporary space that Augé's work cannot? The answer takes a route through a contemporary revision of the landscape of anthropology, arriving at an ethnography of solitude. Anthropology, from the outset, is both a problem and a passion for Augé, and there are two observations about the contemporary that begin his revision of the discipline: first, the disembedding of culture from place, and second, our exposure to an overabundance of spatial and temporal artefacts. These familiar comments about the contemporary world lead to a less familiar description of a sensibility of the present where excessive referents of space fail to conform to a map of landscapes. Indeed, landscapes in Augé, as in the films of Wong Kar-wai, become emotional sites of affect, both real and imaginary, but lacking the shared or known qualities of cartography. Space becomes, in fact, imbued with the dislocations, unreliability and folded qualities associated with time and memory. Space is interrelated, stretched, extended and collapsed. What we are suffering is not a loss of spatial specificity, but an overabundance of space, an excess of the types of space we are exposed to. Spatial referents are produced through various channels: transport and travel, in the movement of the individual and of objects, and through electronic image and sound devices that bring and refract space to us. In this elaboration of the qualities and types of space we are exposed to, proximity and distance have no coordinates to distinguish them, nor is it possible to discern between events of varying scales. The foothold that Augé does offer is the distinction between two types of space, place and non-place.

The designation of space as twofold, place and non-place, should not obscure the propensity of these spatial modes to operate inside one another however, rather than existing in parallel. We might categorize *Chungking Express*, for example, as a construction of non-place within place in its disruption of the historical by referents from elsewhere. At its simplest, Augé's invocation of place and non-place refers to historical and non-historical constructions of space. Place is here given its traditional definition as the site of anthropological location, localized, connected to a lineage, tradition and identity. Non-place, by contrast, refers us to the sites of non-traditional anthropology, the areas that drop out of descriptions of the present for their anodyne quality: ATM cash dispenser lobbies, themed hotels, airports, supermarkets. These are the sites of unmediated commerce, where identity checks occur at every stage, yet paradoxically where identity is eliminated at every level except to meet a demand for legitimization. These descriptions do not identify discrete sites, but are possible manifestations of contemporary space as palimpsest: the historical town centre and the cash dispenser, the airport with the local cultural display. Place, says Augé, is never completely erased, whilst non-place is never fully completed.

Time undergoes a similar treatment. In a sense there is history and non-history, the bearing of the past on the present, and the eradication of the traces of the past in a continuous temporal present of non-place. Like spatial referents, temporal markers are also overabundant, the past increasingly collected and archived as a growing memory bank of random artefacts, reproduced as monuments, statues, memorials, in a pastiche of architectural styles. It is not that history has simply ceased to appear linear, ordered, efficient in its narrative description, but that the excess of historical materials produces a crisis of meaning. According to Augé, the present is caught in the process of becoming historical, 'history snapping at our heals', an imminent history. The present cannot be distinguished from the past or the process of historicization, as though a future perspective of the present moment is our inescapable viewpoint, and predicament. The metalingual voice-off of the film narrating the present from the future serves Augé's point well.

What we strive for in this situation of excess, he argues, is to give meaning to the world and to this moment. Yet this yearning is defeated by the weight of the world, as it were, by a proliferation of (temporal and spatial) referents. The result is a retreat into a melancholic disappointment, a melancholy for the failures of belief, set 'out there' in the context of historical narratives: 'the disappointments of all the world's disappointed: disappointment with socialism, with liberalism, and (before long) with post-communism too' (Augé, 1992: 31). In the context of a melancholic loss of faith in external narratives, the fabrication of meaning at an individual level is critical: it is only through the individualization of references that events come to signify at all. In the face of global abstract image events, such as the fall of the Berlin Wall, or Tiananmen Square, 'meaning' only becomes possible through the subject's inscription, of where and when the experience was affecting. And yet in this tracing of a movement towards an individual frame of reference, the lost world of anthropology – that is, of objects – is nowhere in sight.

The problem with a theory of the supermodern, a theory of considerable scale, is that it repeats the abstraction that is the subject of critique. Augé appeals to an individual universe, to abstract information flows, with little situated detail. The excessive references to time and space, according to Augé, produce a universe of recognition but not knowledge, familiarity without meaning. At the centre of this experience is a unidirectional flow of information, images and text, in relation to which the individual oscillates between retreat into solitude and an attempted production of meaning; but the material, for Augé, is still 'out there'. In this universe there are both excessive interconnections and a singularity of experience that remains unaffected by the world. Augé's prognoses concerning the human response include flight from complexity, revolt against traditional meaning, fear of the self and others, and performance of the self. *Supermodernity* is a text of an individual ('the' individual) in flight from an encroaching world. But paradoxically, as Monsieur Dupont makes his way through the airport, flight itself is an experience of the same encroachment, the same demarcated positions, views, scripted experiences that press in on the traveller, stripping him of identity. There is no 'outside' to supermodernity; there is only an attempted interiority. 'It is no longer possible for social analysis to dispense with individuals,' Augé asserts on the final page, 'nor for an analysis of individuals to ignore the spaces through which they are in transit' (1992: 120), but what he has dispensed with is the object world.

The limits of the thesis of non-place is that, in its desire to leave behind an 'old style' anthropology, it loses the dynamic of relationality, and discounts affect at every turn. Objects are associated, for Augé, with anthropology's excavation of another culture, focusing on its objects of performance, ritual and symbolism. This practice is retrospectively conceived as an assembling of things from which the beliefs of a community are erroneously extracted. Yet in the desire to distance anthropology from its own history, Augé dismisses the object world, its potency as an affectual realm, its co-presence and constitution of the worlds of place and non-place. In so doing, Augé gets rid of desire period. The will to an ethnography of individuals and space is an invitation into a mediatized and mobile world where objects lose their visibility and potency. Augé's emphasis is the transaction, the supermarket customer who 'gives his identity when he pays by cheque or credit card' and 'so does the autoroute driver who pays the toll' (1992: 102). Every exchange and encounter is a depletion of self, and a role-play of an internalized media identity: 'he is this well-dressed forty-year-old, apparently tasting the ineffable delight under the attentive gaze of a blonde hostess' (1992: 105). Whilst the book ends on the call for an ethnography of solitude, it is a project that Augé has already conducted if we are to extract individuals from the world of objects and place them singularly in flight.

In *Chungking Express*, the mediatized space of relations has a formidable presence in the film, yet this is not simply a conditioning factor but a context in which possibility emerges. There are perhaps two types of object in Wong Kar-wai's text, the audio-visual culture of an ephemeral object world, and the material objects of clothes, food, soap, toys. The film does not insist on the jumble of eclectic objects as simply commodities that speak for us, as a voice imposed from the outside, but conversely, they are seen to decentre the human perspective. Objects have a presence, a force, they are part of a choreography of being in which they play a part. Not simply the *mise en scène* of the film, objects are critical to the expression of desire and mourning, to movements of towards and away, the bearers of codified messages between humans who cannot articulate emotion in any other way. Shoes, a teddy bear, a napkin, a CD, goldfish, a wig, a tin of pineapple, are critical to the dynamic of relations. What the film articulates then that Augé cannot is that the life-world of objects is a critical factor in accounts of solitude.

At moments, in what we might think of as solitary asides, Augé attends to shifting emotional registers, the textures of place and non-place that appear to open momentarily the chance of emotional resonance. In the prologue, in a description of proximity with others at Roissy airport, a possibility of connection appears as a memory:

> it was in these crowded places where thousands of individual itineraries converged for a moment, unaware of one another, that there survived something of the uncertain charm of the waste lands, the yards and

building sites, the station platforms and waiting rooms where travellers break step, of all the chance meeting places where fugitive feelings occur of the possibility of continuing adventure, the feeling that all there is to do is to 'see what happens'. (1992: 3)

Here the description comes closer to a sense of the object world as affectual. And again, in an observation that is designed to show the always already scripted nature of photography, there is a ghosting of the object of the photograph: ' "This is me in front of the Parthenon," you will say later, forgetting that when the photo was taken you were wondering what on earth you were doing there' (1992: 84). The statement resonates as a voice-off from a Wong Kar-wai film, a retrospective nostalgic view of a present (back then) that was already slipping away. In these asides, there is a leakage into the text of the possibility that objects signify in a way that is not prescribed by the conditions of supermodernity. It is when theory lends itself to the particular, and to being changed by its encounter with objects, that it takes on a fuller resonance.

Disciplinary revisions and supermodernity

What is it that Augé can articulate about the study of culture and the conceptualization of space that film studies cannot say? Anthropology, as a discipline that is haunted by a past constructed around alterity, provides a useful paradigm for mapping the conceptual challenges in the study of film from other cultures. It is not a first encounter, for film and anthropology have a history. But to start with the problems faced by anthropology it is necessary briefly to retrace the footprints of the discipline and issues of methodology, as outlined in Augé's work. Historically, anthropology is a discipline concerned with the reading of other cultures, and the difficulties of encounter. Within an 'old' style anthropology, in the work of Marcel Mauss, for example, Augé identifies two central problems. The first is that the curiosity of a colonial enquiry into other cultures rested on a notion of the field as a discrete, bounded domain, an island free of the taints of modernity, a 'pure' space of 'primitive' difference. In this field work conducted in the first half of the twentieth century, other cultures are 'discovered' and found to be conveniently localized in space and time. The complexity of interrelationships (how belief systems have been influenced and changed through encounter) is therefore bracketed as the anthropologist is faced with a self-contained and endogenous culture. As many critiques have demonstrated, such an approach is predicated on a western projection of alterity and exoticism (Chow, 1995; Clifford, 1989; Pratt, 1992; Rabinow, 1977). The second methodological problem arising concerns the relationship of the individual and culture. The individual, Augé argues, is posited precisely as a representative of the group, rather than one of many conflicting definitions of individuality within the culture. Stripped of idiosyncratic qualities (in fact, individualism), the representative individual sutures the gap between systems of belief and expression (culture), and the subjects inhabiting culture. Such an elision allows the anthropologist to read continuity between subjects and systems, and to posit a generic type: 'the Melanasian', for example.

The critiques of anthropology that have ensued in the past three decades have rigorously attacked the projection of an imperial imaginary and concomitant exoticizing practices, as historical and foundational features of the discipline. The particular malady of anthropological method is this: a discovery of otherness is in fact construction, observation is projection, and interpretation is authoritative imposition. In the wake of this critique, anthropological method has followed a path of retreat from empirical practice, a withdrawal that Augé stages in three parts. First, there has been a focus on the proximate, a reconstruction of the field within local space to excavate difference. Here, the familiar terrain of 'home' is inverted to reveal the disparities, disjunctions and dissidence internal to any culture. The François Maspero and Anaik Frantz's *Roissy Express*, a journey into the suburbs of Paris, taking local trains into areas that are uncharted by tourism and national status, is a case study of this kind. Second, anthropological analysis has retreated to the texts of former anthropologists as primary material, a deconstructive approach that seeks to reveal the performativity of language in bringing the subject into being. Third, the field of study is replaced by an analysis of those conducting the work. Thus, the study of Evans-Pritchard proceeds on the understanding that the anthropologist's work is not a window onto an other world, but a mirroring of the values, assumptions and preoccupations of a colonial white male. For Augé, these critiques are poignant, yet faced with the complexity of the present, inadequate as a 'methodological reflection on the category of otherness' (1995: 24).

Film studies is not so removed from these difficulties of framing alterity. Historical discourses of film studies reveal a critical engagement with film as a mediating form; film is always already a construction rather than discovery or revelation. Yet it has at times been charged with projecting its own exoticism. In the field of documentary production, where film's indexical relation to its subject is its notable feature, the constructed nature of the image is less overt. As Stella Bruzzi argues, 'Documentary film is traditionally perceived to be the hybrid offspring of a perennial struggle between forces of objectivity (represented by the "documents" or facts that underpin it) and the forces of subjectivity (that is the translation of those facts into representational form)' (2000: 39). If we add to this struggle the prevalence in documentary for subjects that are rarely fictionalized yet emotive (working-class poverty, the housing conditions of immigrant communities), it is possible that the film's search for its subject results in discovery of otherness and authoritative interpretation. This debate is dynamically played out in discussion of the work of the film-maker Jean Rouch, where the apparatus of the production appears as a discursive two-way mirror through which the film-makers themselves become visible subjects. In the practice and analysis of documentary film, the rise of autobiographical production has created a reflexive mode of filmmaking where the film-maker is partially the subject of the film (Renov, 2004). More fundamentally, the practice of textual analysis as a discrete treatment of a film outside of socio-cultural contexts has been challenged as a fetishistic practice, isolating its subject and authorizing its own projections as analysis. Film studies has undergone a methodological revisioning in the shift from textual analysis to audience studies in the 1980s and 1990s, what we might envisage as a parallel retreat from the object to the meta-discourse of interpretation. Audience studies has invested in examining the plurality of responses to film and the multiple variables at work in any interpretative context (Staiger, 1992). This debate has had lengthy coverage elsewhere. My point here is to illustrate the parallel moments of epistemological and methodological crisis in film studies and anthropology, and similar responses: the retreat from the distant field to more local knowledges (audience studies), and the implication of the producer of the text in the generation of its meanings (documentary film).

Yet these forms of response to an epistemological crisis in approaching alterity are, for Augé, a retreat from the difficulties of approaching difference, and simultaneously a turning away in the face of new opportunities. For Augé, it is not that knowledge has foundered but that the contemporary has shifted paradigm. This is most explicitly expressed in new configurations of spatial relations, and more generally in what has been named the supermodern.

> Experience of the remote has taught us to de-centre our way of looking, and we should make use of the lesson. The world of supermodernity does not exactly match the one in which we believe we live, for we live in a world that we have not yet learnt to look at. We have to relearn to think about space. (1992: 35–6)

By implication, do we have to relearn to look at film and space? In film studies, the object of study is largely organized through its geographic origin as national or regional cinema, as troubled as that designation may be (Hjort and Mackenzie, 2000). If we begin to describe film outside of these classifications, gesturing to film's status as a mobile culture, the terminology is not promising. Terms such as transnational (like globalization) tend to appear in the domain of media and communication studies, referring to the process of cultural homogeneity and the interconnection of systems of economy and information. In film studies, where the term 'transnational' is rarely invoked, it is predominantly as a description of the global industry of Hollywood (Miller et al., 2001). And yet film, outside of what we recognize as Hollywood, is a culturally specific artefact that circulates through particular networks. It is partly linked and connected through paths of circulation and dissemination, and in turn partially produces a contemporary spatial interconnectedness. Just as film exemplified and participated in the construction of modernity's temporality at the beginning of the twentieth century, film now exemplifies and produces our experience of the present as spatial.

In this context, there is an inherent awareness in film of the conditions of mobility, that film is a travelling culture destined for multiple sites of circulation and viewing. As a result, film has evolved an awareness of its own alterity, the various prisms of foreignness through which it will be greeted, understood and incorporated. Film, it might be argued, has always been conditioned by its status as a travelling culture, a status that has given rise to claims that film provided the first global vernacular (Hansen, 2000). In this reading, it is not only the language of cinema that is at stake, but the spectator. Classical cinema's address, as Hamid Naficy argues, was to a universal spectator, a 'singular, unified but potentially universal category'. He also reminds us that American cinema was constituted by 'foreigners and émigrés', and from its origins was 'immigrant, transnational and American at the same time'. But what distinguishes contemporary film from its earlier incarnations is its retreat from the category of the universal in all but large-budget productions. The emergent forms of world cinema articulate a specificity of experience that cuts against the notion of a universal shared language or set of stories, producing a heightened sense of its 'foreignness'. The spaces into which film is dispatched, the territories that it will cross, are not simply an afterlife to production. Rather the spatial life that a film will have is anticipated in its formation, in the making or even the idea of the film itself. What form of address, then, might this cinema have?

Tropical Malady: tales of the primitive

If flight is a trope of escape, a running from, it is also a running to. In a sense, film is always in flight, emitted from a place of origin and dispatched with aplomb; it has to negotiate the risks of travel. Egoyan and Balfour (2004) provide a timely meditation on the significance of subtitling, the marks of a film's foreignness in any territory, a trace of the process of translation which is at once literal and metaphorical. Film, at its dispatch, must submit itself to translation and subtitling, but here the term 'translation' looms in all its impossibility. Walter Benjamin, musing on the dilemmas and delights of literary translation, writes: 'The traditional concepts in any discussion of translation are fidelity and licence – the freedom of faithful reproduction and, in its service, fidelity to the word.' He continues by asking critically, 'What can fidelity really do for the rendering of meaning?' (1955: 78). Benjamin's critique of faithfulness is aimed at the translation of content without attention to form. The tone, weight, flavour of a piece of literature is, for him, the essential matter in hand without which a translation remains simply an act of communication. Bringing this to bear on film, the act of translation is complicated further, by the relation of words to images and sound, of the necessity of reading the gesture of the actor's body as she speaks the line. The form of film extends the difficulty of what it means to translate the meaning of dialogue in one language into another. It is perhaps more accurate to say that the difficulty resides in the translation of one culture into another. To complete the movement of the chapter by which the last frame of reference comes to bear on the next, this is what film studies brings to bear on *Tropical Malady*, the complex articulation of cinematic languages.

The term translating 'into' already suggests a type of ingestion of the foreign element, a swallowing and incorporation into a larger body, or with Derrida in mind, an appropriation of otherness. The film *Tropical Malady*, by Thai director Apichatpong Weerasethakul, is a work that addresses and in a sense prefigures the acts of translation and incorporation that it will endure.[10] It does so by providing (again) two stories, each of which presents a different version of Thai culture, the second story echoing the first but in a different genre. The first story centres on an encounter between a forest patrol soldier (Keng) and a worker at an ice factory (Tong) who lives with his parents. The story is located in a remote rural setting, and evolves as a love story. The pace of the first story is slow, following the trope of a romantic courtship tale. The lovers' discrete meetings are characterized by hesitancy, modesty, a reticence in approaching the other, and so the tale unfolds as a series of movements away and towards. The courtship is domestic, quotidian. Keng teaches his lover to drive, accompanies him to the animal hospital when his dog falls sick, and in a curious outdoor bar scene, when a singer dedi-cates a song to Keng, Tong moves on to the stage and performs a duet. The first story of *Tropical Malady* delivers a romantic tale bordering on cultural stereotyping: gay sexuality is endearing, repressed and subtly coded, filmed as a meandering sequence of everyday scenes.

Yet the opening images of the film have already alerted us to the dangers of presumption. A group of soldiers pose in front of a camera for a group photograph. The jubilance and energy of the scene is reversed at the last moment as the camera pans down to a dead body that the soldiers have recovered. We may think that we recognize the meaning of the shot, but in its full duration, we are warned otherwise. The point is forcefully made by placing this scene at the opening of the film, at the moment of orientation for the audience. The movement then pivots again, from this 'disturb-ing' scene of death and pleasure into a story of romantic courtship. The opening scene prefigures the second story with its exploration of desire, pursuit and violence, and in between, a coy, tender por-trait of romantic love. The first story is the tale of a reticent giving of the self to the other, a reluctance rooted in fear, withholding or superstition; in one scene, Keng refuses to enter and crawl through a narrow tunnel in a cave where 'only the blessed can pass'. The story ends with Tong disappearing into the night after news that an animal is killing cattle.

The second part of the film, presented after a fade to black, pre-sents a different genre, a tale of magic realism set in the forest. The story is performed by the same actors, suggesting a doubling or mul-tiplying of identity, or a mirroring of conscious and unconscious narratives. There is minimal dialogue in this section as the sound-track gives way to ambient sounds of the jungle, of branches snap-ping, water dripping, animals calling. Sound provides the emotional tone of the film, focusing attention on the need for stealth and the danger of movement, the sense of being observed but not necessar-ily seeing, the sensation of an alien and unknowable terrain that must be navigated. The story here ceases to be a linear narrative: for example, of the pursued and the pursuer. As the soldier pursues the tiger, he is also prey to the other, and what ensues is a long choreo-graphy of movement toward and around the other. In the story there is no certainty of what the other may be ('man-beast'), possibly animal, spirit, human and all of these simultaneously.

In the spirit of magic realism and mythology, the tale of tracking is presented as an allegory, a story that evokes the darkness of fairy tales and fables, of disorientation, fear and danger. It may also function ostensibly as a reverse of the first tale: reticence is replaced by pursuit, romance flips over into predatory desire, courtship into sexual aggression. The power of the second story lies in its ability to keep opposites in play, to insist on the doubleness of expression and action. For in this story of an erotic pursuit, the soldier learns that he is both prey and companion to his lover, that desire as it roams in a landscape is both freedom and potential destruction. The soldier learns to read the forest, to trace footprints in the earth, and to listen. At one critical point, an ape speaks to him: 'The tiger trails you like a shadow, his spirit is starving and lonesome, I see you are his prey and his companion.' In the final encounter with the object of his pursuit, the tiger, the exchange of a gaze between the animal and human plays out the tension of desire without resolution. It is a gaze that defies translation as either aggression or desire. Or rather it is readable as the co-existence, the ineluctable entanglement of both.

In reading the relationship between the two parts of the film as a commentary on each other, with the second story providing a psychoanalytic subtext to the first, there is a danger of sublimating the challenge that the film presents: a replay of the primitivist imaginary directed at the film's 'others' as it circulates in territories foreign to itself. *Tropical Malady* provides two potentially clichéd representations of Thai culture, both concerning sexuality. The first story purports to a type of tourist vision of oriental passivity, a sexuality that is both latent and obliging. The second story unearths the primitivist myths of east Asian sexuality, as primal, raw and animalistic. Both stories reflect back the old-style anthropology of place, as an island culture readable in its coherent interplay of nature and symbolism. In presenting these twin accounts, the film puts into play the question of projection within interpretation. It plays with and plays back notions of alterity, a particular foreignness, within a context in which this film is to be classified and received precisely as 'foreign'. In the choice of genres, the former story borrows from documentary the feel of an unstaged, improvised structure, although clearly it is not. This is a genre that Weerasethakul has used effectively before as a lure into a seemingly haphazard journey through remote villages. Yet the practice is knowing, well rehearsed.

The juxtaposition of documentary with magical realism foregrounds two competing definitions of the real. Yet this is a context in which the real is not simply an exercise in the constructed nature of all film, but an examination of the limits of cultural translation. By posing the question of the two parts in terms of versions of realism, the film invites a further question: real to whom? In a sense, the second story is the more locatable of the two for a European audience where the discourse of magical realism is familiar. The first story remains a curious anomaly unless it is read in relation to the second, as a codified other. Yet the other here is produced in the circuit through which the film travels. In its double construction, it appears to prefigure its reception as other. It has, in a curious turning of appropriation, already appropriated the other's perception into its structure. It has predicted, courted and confounded the readings of its own foreignness, as primitive or as naive realism. What film studies can ask, in response to the film's prompting, is how to deconstruct the primitivist vision along with the film's inversion of its terms (Pratt, 1992).

Tropical Malady effectively demonstrates that film production is an act of transmission, a practice that is destined to be sent, therefore it is addressed to an other. Derrida, again, is mindful of the relation between inscription and transmission in *The Post Card* (1993). Here, the postcard serves to demonstrate the general economy of texts. It must have an address (directed at an other), an inscription (a legible message), a signature (a site of production), and a stamp (the official duty that culture pays in the service of the system that authorizes it). In Derrida's complex sense, the postcard thus, if obeying these rules, becomes a technology. Equally (albeit a reduction of Derrida's usage), film becomes a postcard. The gap that opens up between inscribing and the process of sending defers its arrival, its destination point. The postcard may not arrive at its designated destination, meaning may not arrive at its intended referent. Its message may become obscured or it may, given its dependency on the postal system, never arrive. Weerasethakul appears to have borne all of this in mind.

5

Innocent monsters: film and other media

Jack says
technology is the knack of arranging the world
so that we don't have to experience it
that the change we call progress
is just another obstacle to joy
and that stories have no point
unless they absorb our terror
Jack tells me
life swarms with innocent monsters.

Mike Hoolboom, *Imitations of Life*

Whoever fights monsters should see to it that in the process he does
not become a monster. And when you look long into an abyss, the
abyss also looks into you.

Friedrich Nietzsche, *Beyond Good and Evil*

In Mike Hoolboom's elegy to cinema, *Imitations of Life* (2003), a
host of classical, found and personal images is deployed to address
the question of what it is that cinema does with and for us. Do
images save us from the immediacy of experience in a manner of
substitution, absorbing our 'terror'? Or do they distance us from the
immediate and vicarious experience of the world, putting us at one
remove from visceral pleasure? The benign and the monstrous sit
side by side in the present context. In the film *Imitations of Life*, the
innocent monsters are the images from a film culture that has
endured and accumulated to reach its centenary. The air (and the
frame) is thick with figures, scenes and shots from the burgeoning
archive of film history. As the images are stacked and layered on top
of one another, grafted into new situations, the frame loses its

crystal focus and becomes cloudy, a hazy picture of barely discernible ghosts. The greater the volume of our filmic history, the implication seems to be, the less clearly we 'see'. If, once upon a time, films put our terror into abeyance through the comfort of stories, they now return as fragmented components, or as images alienated from their temporal context, made strange simply by the passage of time.

What happens if we reconfigure the story of the demise of cinema, and its melancholic by-line of the cessation of celluloid production, as a story of escape? What if the institution of cinema might have constrained, encased and trapped the image-stories of a century, condemning them to a predictable programme of matinees and evening performances, working the same darkened conditions in front of the same expectant and demanding audiences? What if we attribute the filmic past not with an agency of its own, but with a life-span, a materiality that undergoes its own transformative duration, without us? This thought is suggested by the work of Douglas Gordon, in the remaking of Hitchcock's *Psycho* as a 24-hour duration, projected at two frames rather than 24 frames per second. In a reported interview, Gordon speculates on how the installation might return to disrupt the thoughts of someone who had visited the gallery during the day:

> 'someone' might suddenly remember what they had seen earlier that day, later that night; perhaps at around 10 o'clock, ordering drinks in a crowded bar with friends, or somewhere else in the city, perhaps very late at night, just as the 'someone' is undressing to go to bed, they may turn their head to the pillow and start to think about what they had seen that day. He said he thought it would be interesting for that 'someone' to imagine what was happening in the gallery right then, at that moment in time when they have no access to the work. (Gordon, 1998: 83)

The speculation about the viewer unfolds another speculation, of what happens to film when no one is there. That is, how might we conceive of film in our absence, as distinct from us?

This question is not an anthropomorphism of film to create its 'character' in the manner of the human, but a question that requires us to think the possibility of how we co-exist with the object world. That is, films are not simply 'texts' to be decoded and digested, or static materials that remain constant across time and space. They are, rather, the curious objects of our fascination, with which we undergo an exploration of ourselves in relation to their changing form. This chapter is an enquiry into the strange relations we have with film now that it has escaped the cinema, now that it is dispersed across multiple sites and media platforms, now that it has, in a sense, been set loose. It is an enquiry that locates the uncanny effects of film not only at the juncture with the historical, with its hauntings of an indexical trace of time past. But the curious effects of film as a medium, a technology, as matter that produces affects rather than representations, now complicated by the various spatial contexts in which we encounter film.

An important demarcation here is in the movement from 'effect' to 'affect', a seemingly minor semantic shift that in fact refers to a paradigm shift of a conceptual order. For the notion of effect is derived from the analytical model of social constructivism, a model that had ridden high in the humanities in past decades, positing that all things, including nature, are constructed in and through discourse. Schematically, following a Lacanian reading of language as the specifically human, language in its various guises becomes the mediating grid through which an experience of the world is structured. In a paradoxical twist, the world of objects and non-humans, which are as we made them in language and not in any sense 'real', none the less return to haunt us, to leave their effects. In terms of film, such effects have been isolated in discourses such as the censorship debate, as violence and depravity, or more recently as ideological persuasions operating subliminally in the particular discourses of film language and narrative structure. 'Effects' are then both socially constructed, and paranoically those things that threaten to influence and manipulate. The problem with social constructivism is this: if the non-human world is a human construct, it has no dynamism or alterity, it is simply a series of mirror images in which we are lost.

The concept of 'affect', in contrast, works from a different foundation, where the alterity of the non-human (including film), is irreducible to human experience. Therefore, the mode of enquiry into the affectual relation between human and non-human is characterized by a search for connection, points of fleeting attachment that allow an imprint of a different order. Affect describes a very different marking to effect, in that it defies the distinction between bodily emotional response and rational comprehension, or the demarcation of unconscious and conscious processes. The affectual as a sensory apprehension, however, is not only a feature belonging to the arts, but can also be located in the illogical operations of a rampant image-based multinational capitalism, as Brian Massumi writes: 'There seems to be a growing feeling within media, literary, and art theory that affect is central to an understanding of our information- and image-based late capitalist culture, in which so-called master narratives are perceived to have foundered' (2002: 27). The ideological story has given way to the intensity of affectual appeal. He continues, 'Fredric Jameson notwithstanding, belief has waned for many, but not affect. If anything, our condition is characterized by a surfeit of it.' Massumi also notes that there is a lack of vocabulary for the affectual, and in his excavations the possibilities lead from Deleuze back through Bergson to Spinoza, to the realm of ethics.

Massumi's essay, 'The autonomy of affect', reads Spinoza and Bergson together in a productive encounter of the virtual and the actual. Affect is not simply emotion (which would reinstate a mind-body divide), but a suspension of the circuit between mind and body in a 'sink' of what Massumi names passion, 'to distinguish it from passivity and activity' (2002: 28). The affectual is the trace of an impingement, produced through an encounter that is felt as a bodily experience and doubled as an idea of the encroachment. What remains, as affect, is the memory trace of the impingement, a sensation that registers below the radar of consciousness as a type of infolding. Importantly, the virtual state of this actual encounter is characterized by the holding together of suspense and expectation, of memory and bodily sensation. The co-presence of normally mutually exclusive states produces a form of resonance, a vibration if you will, that derives from the actual only to escape capture. The dissonant or pleasurable effect Massumi links to Deleuze's concept of intensity, a potential for action, an openness to being what is commonly described as 'moved', but which in Deleuze's framing has a less metaphorical implication. For intensity is the site of emergence. And it is this sensation of movement in affect that places it always outside of the reach of a captured state, as affect moves on. What we are left with is the lingering register of emotion: 'Emotion is the most intense (most contracted) expression of that *capture* – and of the fact that something has always and again escaped.' He continues, 'That is why all emotion is more or less disorienting, and why it is classically described as being outside of oneself, at the very point at which one is most intimately and unshareably in contact with oneself and one's vitality' (2002: 35).

Through affect it is possible to apprehend the appeal of the affectual for capital's mutating purposes. For affect is at once an intensely experienced state, and a fleeting trace. Thus, it both pulls us into a deeply felt resonant state, but fails to provide that as an enduring potential. The affectual, phrased in this way, operates by capitalism's rule, as a desirable state that is in need of constant renewal.[1] We are invited, as it were, to come again. If then, in this framework, film's curious and uncanny effects are in fact affectual, film becomes an appealing prospect for a short-circuit to an affectual state. Film's uncanny jarring, of the past in the present, of the magical and hypnotic qualities of sound and image, of strange and tangential turns, constitutes the particularity of film in the present media context, a medium that resonates as an object in its own right. It is precisely because film is not information in a so-called information economy that it obtains a strangely beguiling appeal. Film remains unassimilated, in excess of factual exegesis, when compared to the information-driven economy in which it now finds itself. Film remains, as Scott Lash (2002) has noted, an auratic medium, drawing us into sacred ritual, rather than the profane realm of the everyday. For Lash, cinema presents 'something not new but old, from the past', concluding that cinema is thus a re-presentation rather than a technology (the latter defined by its informational exchanges in the present, and in the realm of the profane). It is in this comparative sense that Lash labels film an 'old' medium, a medium of cultural content against which the ephemeral and utilitarian technologies of information are cast: 'Information is not narrative, not discourse, not the novel, not cinema, not poetry, not architecture, not art, not artefact' (2002: 69).

Whilst this is an appealing distinction that imposes a division between informational and auratic media, there is, I suspect, a different shifting of ground afoot in the relation of film to informational media.[2] For film is increasingly mixed into the arenas of the profane, in the domestic space of the home and in television schedules, for example. One problem with Lash's distinction is that it reintroduces a division of film as content versus information as form. This binary overlooks film's historical entanglements of form and content, and their inseparability. This relation of film's content and form is increasingly complicated by the changing technologies of film as it is distributed across various platforms. Film in the cinema may appear substantially as auratic content, but its formatting as video and DVD loosens this arrangement. The options of an interface (the menu of choices) foreground the formal principles of film, the ways in which we access the content and arrange its matter. This is a feature that is explored in relation to viewing film below. But a second, and more substantial critique is that to arrange information and film as oppositional overlooks the curious reworkings of contingency in film, reworkings that apply to film's content and form, if indeed we can make that distinction. Lash has written about contingency elsewhere, as 'risk', one of the ways in which the contingent has mutated in recent decades.[3] The argument that I want to make here is that contingency is not only informational but part of film's particular appeal. Second, that both contingency and film are historically mutating categories, thus the ways in which film and contingency interact is in constant process and in need of elaboration.

If we take contingency to be a historically critical yet shifting concept, as Mary Ann Doane has done, the relation of film to both information and affect is rewritten in interesting ways. To recap Doane's thesis in *The Emergence of Cinematic Time*, the advent of cinema falls within the period of modernism when certain historical drives towards standardization and the management of information coalesced. This thickening of a procedure of regulation occurred, according to Doane, in the ascendancy of the field of statistics, the practice of collating heterogeneous information about populations and providing an analysis that identified standard 'norms'. The field of statistics, as it operated across the spheres of health, education, crime and work, provided a method of analysis that was productive of standard features of modern life, of consensus, and through consensus, a form of control. For, in a Foucauldian way, the production of a standard measure was simultaneously the production of an excess, modes of behaviour that failed to 'fit' the categories of recognition. Behaviours (practices, values, modes of being) that fell outside of the standard categories of recognition were matter to be excluded, yet in enacting an exclusion, the anomaly became the subversive rule, the latent trace of difference. In this context, according to Doane, the cinema served a particular function, or less pragmatically, cinema was born into a moment in which various modes of excess were in need of both recognition and management.

Early cinema met this need in several ways. Doane cites the actuality film as the staging of an excessive contingency, the selection of certain 'anomalous' events dealing with excessive subjects, such as the execution of an animal. The 'liveness' of the event is presented in the cinematic form as both present and stage-managed. Film both provided the spectacle of destruction in its vicarious occurrence, and assuaged the anxiety of the live event in its relay of a past that had been processed. Indeed, the fundamental attribute of cinema is the processing and production of time within this paradigm: time becomes, in the cinematic form, both fluid and without meaning, and crafted into a unit meaningfully designated as leisure. Cinema works through a paradox, that it recognizes the contingent as a disruptive and affectual force, whilst simultaneously harnessing contingency to a cathartic end. At its foundational moment, cinema comprises 'simultaneously the rationalization of time and an homage to contingency' (2002: 32). The contingent becomes, in cinema, the 'highly cathected' site of both pleasure and neurosis.

This management of the contingent that Doane designates as a foundation of cinematic experience under modernism is in the present played out across media forms. The relationship of media to contingency, I am suggesting, is a defining attribute of each media form. The lure of contingency as spectacle and presence characterizes the media of news and information, the liveness of events relayed immediately as catastrophe and shock. Yet without the containing trope of narrative, the contingent has literally nowhere to go, no cathecting possibility, and is thus managed through repetition of spectacular images. A more managed rendition of the spectacular contingent characterizes the media of reality television, where contingency is at once staged and stage managed. The appeal of the contingent is evident in the format of surveillance and observation, the suspense of the event unfolding. But the contingent is underpinned by the knowledge of performance and play, that reality television is a selected contingency (of location, of participants, of purpose) that is conditioned by expectations of conflict that are ultimately managed. This concept of performance and construction generates a collective anxiety about reality television, as though 'management' of a situation were to 'cheat', suggesting that an unmediated reality programme were a possibility.[4] It also disguises an anxiety of a different order: that reality television may expose the meaninglessness of the quotidian, of time wasted rather than spent in activity. In its enactment of a desire for the purely indexical, the recording of all moments from multiple angles, reality television inadvertently threatens to reduce the televisual to the pure act of recording. The stage-management of reality television thus staves off the fear that viewers may be witnesses to 'nothing'.

Film's relation to contingency is longstanding, not only in Doane's sense of the dialectical play of the unexpected and the contained. Film's affinity for the contingent is, in the writings of Siegfried Kracauer (1960), a fundamental attribute of cinema. The scale of the cinematic image as it is projected, and the juxtaposition of the close-up and the long shot, remake the visible as a realm in which vision is erratic rather than consistent. What we 'see' is an indeterminate, less than conscious selection of details from a fleeting sequence, an activity that is made all the more capricious by the shifting scale and focus of the image. The cinematic image facilitates a type of looking that falls randomly upon elements, peripheral shapes and abstract forms, and in many experimental film works, the way in which we look at the image is reconstructed. Gordon's *24 Hour Psycho*, like many other reworkings of classical films, wrenches open this desire to look at the filmic image in detail, a voracious desire to 'see it all' as well as to see it anew.[5] This and other experiments in looking at film arguably detract from what Kracauer identifies as film's contingency, its flight before the eye.

Indeed, the project of experimental film operates in a similar territory to the digital formatting of film DVD; both potentially work against the fundamental attributes of the cinematic form, or film's semiosis. Film's inexorable movement forward is rendered reversible, the narrative sequence is open to reordering, the stop function imposes rupture, and the domestic setting is littered with potential distractions. If film's contingency is historically identified as twofold, in Kracauer's assertion of film's affinity for the transient in the image, and in Doane's identification of a paradoxical staging and containment in the staging of the image, both aspects are threatened by film's exit from the cinema. Contingency mutates with film into the present in two new ways: in the indeterminate conditions of viewing film in diverse contexts, and in the disruptive potential of the digital format.

What film has lost in terms of a historically identified contingency in the setting of the cinema has resurfaced in the dispersal of film across multiple spaces. Contingency, as a historically evolving term, has shifted position, or is relocated in both the technologies of viewing film and its contextual shift out of the cinema. Yet it remains a critical affectual pull in the relationships we have to film, where the affectual imprint arises out of the unexpected. In an attempt to trace the contours of a relocated filmic contingency, there are three designated areas of exploration that I wish to elaborate. First, there is a contingency that characterizes the relation to film as it is experienced in the home. The domestic technologies of the VCR and more importantly the DVD player, have incorporated contingency as the ability to reorganize the sequence, possibly the camera position, the speed and duration of film viewing. Second, the dispersal of film, or its escape from the cinema, has facilitated a range of viewing contexts, or encounters with film, where the entry and exit points, the duration and intensity of the filmic experience is open-ended. We potentially encounter films in airplanes and art galleries and on city screens, and possibly carry them with us in portable devices. Our encounters with film may reside in indeterminate contexts.

A third point concerns changes in narrative structure, changes which have to be seen as relational responses to film's relocation outside of the cinema, in its increasing proximity to other media forms (such as the serial form of television), and the transition to a hybrid analogue-digital medium. Forms of experimental narrative appear not only in experimental art-works, but within mainstream narrative film. There are many examples of the structure of film shifting away from a classical linear model of absorption, in a reflexive turn towards fragmented, striated patterns of storytelling. Narrative film demonstrates its irreverence for the cinematic form in films such as *Irreversible*, *Run Lola Run*, *Memento* and *5x2*, which disturb the forward propulsion of cinematic time. More than in flashback, the structural challenge of these films is the twinning of epistemology with ontology: what does it feel like to move back in time, and how does retrospective knowledge inform our experience? It is not only in the reflexive play on the irreversibility of time and cinematic projection, but narrative broken into segments, delivered as discrete units in a mimicry of the digital format of scene selection. And indeed, in the viewing of these films on DVD, where the menu facilitates the rearrangement of structure, we may choose to undo experimentation and watch, for example, *5x2* in chronological order. In what follows, an emerging contingency is traced through various encounters with film in the present.

Home-view: Kiarostami's *Ten*

Out of the cinema, film comes wrapped in cellophane and contained in a plastic folder of a box. It becomes an object, an artefact in its curiously minimal form, a disc that takes the appearance of a music CD but for the printed information across one surface, a reminder of the red banner of the cinema poster. The box is larger than the square plastic box that houses music CDs; it is closer to the shape of a book. The box tells us that watching a film is somewhere between listening to music and reading a book. The DVD opens on to a menu, or a contents page listing the film, the scene selection, the director's biography, and other releases from the distribution company. I select the scene breakdown. The film, as a cinema release, is organized in ten parts, starting at ten and ending at one, ten self-contained units. I decide to start at scene six.

Shot on location in the city of Tehran, *Ten* (2002) is not a re-presentation of Iranian culture, or of this global city. It is rather the experience of a series of ten intimate encounters within the enclosure of a taxi travelling through urban landscape. Shot on DV with two micro-cameras attached to the dashboard of the car, the scene of the shoot is removed from the direct vision of the director and crew; this is, in a sense, film production unravelling at a distance, the camera mediating the scene of production for the crew (a prosthetic production?). Whilst the film is heavily scripted and rehearsed with largely non-professional actors, the mechanisms of location production are pared down to their recording devices. The cameras remain static, in contrast to the constant starts and turns of the vehicle's movement. 'We' are moving and yet still, locked into the confines of the capsule. The effect is to intensify the exchanges that take place within the space. The film becomes a distilled meditation on the spatial effects of the relational. Do characters articulate their most urgent dilemmas because of the sharing of space? And how does the transitory non-place of the taxi, a vehicle that mediates between places, become the functional centre of meaning? What type of connection is established when the face to face of encounter is removed, replaced with a side by side, a simultaneity of existence? To what extent is the fleeting journey in the car the provider of an exquisitely limited exchange? The intimacy provided by the interior of the car inverts the perspective of film. In place of the windshield screen framing the city, the camera is turned inwards. Point of view is redirected. It is not 'out there', the vista of landscape or the spectacle of the city that is deserving of attention, but the activity of driving. There is no establishing shot, no lofty vision of the location, but a focus on movement through it, with a local blindness. Tehran is to be imagined, reconstructed through and mediated by the characters. The city brushes past the window in a blur of buildings, trees, signs, with little sense of the scale or identity of place.

Story six opens with the taxi driver picking up a fare outside a mausoleum. The female fare is reticent, cautious in her statements. Of the two women, it is the driver who discloses the most information about herself, her own attendance at the mausoleum, the need to wear a chador, and the reasons for going, confiding 'I have not yet found peace'. The fare begins to disclose information about herself, that the mausoleum soothes her, that she has not yet had her prayers answered. Her prayers are for a marriage to take place, but her fiancé is full of contradiction. The taxi driver presses her but solicits no further insight as the fare says that it is down to fate. The driver then tells her story, of her son who argues against fate, who is angry with her for divorcing his father and remarrying, and who thinks that she is a bad mother. As I view the other stories in a random sequence, the mother-son story is in fact the main thread surfacing in other stories, three of which are scenes with the son himself. Another cohering factor is the cast of women who ride in the taxi. Besides the son, all other participants are female, and *Ten* provides a multifaceted fiction of femininity through women of various ages and with different preoccupations in their relationships to men, sexuality and domestic roles. Emotional life, it seems to suggest, takes place here, in the spaces in between, the transitory, haphazard encounters of the ordinary. This is boredom transformed into the tension of what can and cannot be articulated, in what kind of context and to whom. As Alberto Elena comments, Kiarostami plays on a 'predictable fatigue' with the routine, reproducing this in the cinematic audience, only to transform boredom into a game (Elena, 2005: 175).

The structure of the film, as a game of various components to be fitted together, replays the relation between contingency and narrative. The stories appear in the menu headed as iconic images, much as they would appear in the edit interface. The structure of film then is the arrangement of a series of scenes, ordered as a cata-logue, labelled and put into an inventory. How we tell the story, or rather, what the possible combination of story sequences might be, is seemingly infinite, each combination producing a variation on the overall narrative structure. In arranging the film as ten stories, in foregrounding the distinction between scenes with an intertitle of a number, Kiarostami implies that the edit is a contingent con-struction. The contingent is also present in the concept of the film, in the random meetings where encounters are unpredictable. Whilst the taxi driver is seen with various members of her family, a number of sequences feature strangers: an old woman, a prosti-tute, a young woman. The choice of the taxi as the vehicle of the film, like Kracauer's idea of the hotel lobby or the street in earlier film, serves to underscore the fleeting traces of inter-human contact that are both unpredictable and potentially transformative. We are left with the singularity of the various fares, their engagement, resistance or conflict with the driver. Each scene draws us into the intensity of the exchange, and the peculiar presentation of self in these moments of transit.

If contingency is a feature of the vehicle of the film, and of its structure as a numerically ordered sequence, it is doubled by the technology of home viewing. In effect, the DVD format deconstructs a film for us, breaks it down into component parts, if it happens to be our desire to exercise the menu options. The seams of film, its joins and cuts, are fully visible, and open to manipulation. The exposure of film's construction, and the ability to manipulate its sequencing, speed and duration, arguably affect film's potency, as Laura Mulvey notes. The viewer's relation is changed in terms of a dynamic of power, producing a new form of viewer, the possessive spectator, who 'commits an act of violence against the cohesion of a story, the aesthetic integrity that holds it together' (2006: 171). Film, in a sense, threatens to disintegrate under this deconstructive force of slowing or pausing the speed, 'actions begin to resemble mechanical, compulsive gestures'. If a 'mastery' of film suggests a form of sadistic control (the possessive spectator), it is a double-edged fantasy. For, in a sense, what is revealed is the futility of the act, and the monstrousness of film in its ability both to haunt as an index of the past, and to decompose before us. Yet the desire to remake, to reassemble the narrative order, presents a different psychic drive, one in search of the pleasures of dispersal in the multiplicity of narrative form. The contingent here, in the functions of the handset, provides the precarious relationship to the contingent as the possibility of a reconstruction or disintegration of meaning.

Kiarostami's style of directing is renowned for its use of a vocabulary of documentary mixed with fiction. *Ten* pushes this aesthetic further in the crisp images of DV, the language of televisual aesthetics and low-budget production. In the repetition of this aesthetic, the question of the veracity of the image, the notion of 'truthfulness', arises. Kiarostami pushes the question of 'meaning' through the aesthetic style, the contingency of the seemingly arbitrary events of the everyday and the performances. In the deployment of these tactics of production, the film peels away from a notion of images as representational: the aesthetics of production suggest a realist approach, and yet the repetition of this formula questions the investment in veracity, returning us to the problem of what it is we can 'know' through film. *Ten* disengages us from the sensible, from the commonplace assumptions where meaning is certain. It places us in the context of a possible disintegration of meaning, and a reconstruction of the parts available for assemblage. The situation of viewing this film, at home with a handset, pushes the conceptual into the realm of the affectual.

Station screen: Victoria, London

Walking through the concourse of a London station, a straggle of people are bunched more or less in a row, facing the same direction. Their gaze is directed towards the electronic information panels with travel details of destinations, train times and platforms. To the right a different panel attracts attention, a sizeable screen of maybe six metres wide by three metres in depth. The panel is a screen carrying an assortment of news, advertising, weather reports. But at the instant in which I look up there are the figures of Laurel and Hardy. They carry a ladder, but as Laurel shifts position, turns direction, the ladder swings haphazardly into the back of Hardy. He lurches forward in exaggerated pantomime. The gag is familiar, predictable, and yet nostalgically entrancing. Despite the surrounding soundscape of platform announcements, trains on the move, mobile phone conversations, the exchanges of commerce in nearby food outlets, the gestural language of the film effectively communicates.

I have paused for longer than I intended, although by now I am unsure of what my intentions were. I, like others around me, am captivated by the screen. For thirty seconds or so I am standing in an undemarcated space staring upwards at comic characters, at the theatre of clumsy fumbling and slapstick retorts. I am ignoring the signs of vigilance against theft and suspending my plans to travel. I am momentarily a child taking pleasure in the unexpected. And there the extract ends and the logo of an insurance company fills the screen. The invitation is implicitly to insure myself against loss and accident, and yet it is only 'by accident' that I have looked up, paused and paid attention. The accidental, it seems, cuts both ways.

In this moment I have affectually been reached, impinged upon, by the force of the strangeness of a film from the past and by the strangeness of this experience taking place out in the open, as it were, in the daylight of public exposure.[6] Here, capitalism's reliance on the affectual is prominent, explicit. It is the film, not the information, that has left its mark. Or rather, retrospectively, it is the curious combination of the film and its reframing as an advertisement for a product. In this moment, the uncanny index of a past time and cinematic culture has placed me within my personal history and effectively connected this to the current anxieties of risk and accident, the threat of disorder, loss and chaos. I am compelled to be both reassured and threatened. I am reassured by the advertisement's address to my sense of pleasure, which is not to be disrupted, and disruptions can be insured against. And I am simultaneously threatened in that my pleasure, like the film extract, can be disrupted at any moment. In this context of the concourse, contingency is an oscillation between comic caper and global risk.

It is not simply, I realize, that the old film is selected for its comedy, its theme of the accidental, or its gestural ability to communicate in an environment of sound distraction, but for its dialectical relation to the present. The past, the film suggests, is a land of bungling, foolish accidents that are comic. The corporate logo belongs to another more sinister era, of grave accidents and disasters. But images of grave disasters of ecology, exploitation and war are part of a discourse of news (which follows shortly after the advertisement). They will not reach into me in the same way because they are expected, a commonplace and impersonal language of images and subtitles that register trauma at a distance. Whilst the Laurel and Hardy film brings a past crashing in on the present, the news administrates the geopolitical anomalies as a catalogue of unrelated events. In the same way that it is more or less impossible to dance to the theme tune of a news programme, news as information is not narrative, not poetry, not architecture, not cinema.

The cinema: *My Architect*

In the space of a cinema, the boundaries around film are firm again. The ritual of the programme, the faintly illuminated auditorium, the seating arranged by height, all confer a gravity and expectation on the event that follows. *My Architect* (Nathaniel Kahn, 2004) is a documentary film in search of its subject, a man who died twenty-six years before, made by his son who was aged eleven at the time of his father's death. The narrative of a life story may seem the most scripted story to be told, conditioned by origins, events, adversity, triumph and death, a story that writes itself. Yet in reconstructing a life, the film finds itself reflexively constructing a narrative from random elements. In this sense, *My Architect* is an example of the movement between the inventory of facts, information catalogued and ordered, and the creation of a story. Indeed, one of the ways in which the film manifests the relation between the inventory and the narrative is the framing of the story under chapter headings, suggesting that this is a multi-plot, or that multiple stories are revealed and foreclosed in their potentiality.

The opening of the film posits two features to the story that arouse expectation. The father is Louis I. Khan, a significant American architect who made only a few of the buildings that he designed and yet whose work was to influence a generation of architects. The second feature is Khan's personal relations with women; whilst marrying and having a family at a young age, Khan discretely had a relationship and a child with each of the two colleagues with whom he had become lovers. The life story pivots around these two facets, a man with a public mission to change landscape and environment, and the private stories of entanglement and affection. The film circles around these two desires and their messy imbrication, selecting interviews with architects who were his contemporaries, and interviews with relatives, the two women and his children. The narrative moves haltingly between different perspectives without trying to separate the parts or arrange the interviews chronologically. Most consistent are the comments from fellow architects who distinguish Louis Khan's professional mode of being as that of the artist, the mystic, the philosopher. Khan, we learn, was unwilling to compromise his architectural visions with the consequence that he often lost commissions. It is later in life, from the age of fifty onwards, that Khan begins to receive recognition of his architectural vision, yet at the time of his death (he died of a heart attack in the public toilet at Pennsylvania Station, New York) he was bankrupt.

The son's mission in the film is a biblical one, to know his own father, and there is a strange vulnerability to his enquiry; he receives information that is, because it is about the past, incontestable. Powerless to challenge the interpretation of others, the film-maker leaves elusive gaps, the spaces of anxiety where information gleaned is presented in its difficulty and with its contradictions evident. The uncles that he visits claim to want to meet Khan's unknown son, and yet the meeting manifests a subliminal refusal to engage with him and thus recognize his identity. At one point in the film, the son receives a letter from a man claiming to have witnessed his father's death in the public toilet, twenty-six years previously. The meeting, at another station, resonates between the poles of fear and belief, openness and suspicion. The man attempts to recollect the scene, sketching a plan of the toilet, the position of the father's body, the presence of two policemen. Yet his memory falters. He cannot recall whether the police were there first or subsequent to his arrival at the scene. What he does recall is the expression on Khan's face, an expression that was not of a man at peace. The information is disturbing, brutal in its reconstruction of the moment of the father's death as deeply troubled. The moment in the film is held, a pause where the possibilities of interpretation are left in play. Possibly the man is fabricating the story, for nothing in his account provides evidence that he was incontrovertibly there. And yet what motive would he have for doing so?

At every critical point in the film where clarification is sought, the idea of 'truth' disintegrates, slips away from the moment. The 'clues' that appear to hold a key to the identity of the man never deliver their motive. At the scene of his death, Khan could not be identified as he had crossed out the address on his passport. The family could not be contacted and Khan's body remained in the state mortuary for three days, unclaimed. Khan was returning from a trip abroad working on the last of his projects, the National

Assembly building in Dhaka, Bangladesh. The detail of the crossed-out address haunts the film and fails to be situated within a coherent narrative. The film-maker's mother resolutely believes that the clue was evidence that Khan intended to leave his wife and to live with her and her son. The son remains mute, perhaps disbelieving. This is a scene of confrontation towards the end of the film, and despite the accumulation of detail about the life of this man, there is no obvious key to interpret this act. Khan remains enigmatic, a nomadic and self-enclosed character whose motives and emotional connections remain opaque. Despite the cast of commentators, the material evidence, the tracing of movements and moments, the film remains an assemblage of parts that jar, scrape and collide. 'We', the cinema audience, as an assembly of collective witnesses, are unsure of what exactly it is we are witnessing. The act of witnessing, historically a call for collective opinion, fails to achieve consensus.[7]

The range of documentation that is excavated for the film moves between the official, the private, the seemingly inconsequential. Extracts from Khan's letters to his lovers are read, a comic book he wrote for his son is summonsed, footage from lectures that he gave and television appearances are cut in. The most repeated archive imagery in the film is of Khan walking along streets and into buildings. The footage is played at various speeds, often in slow motion. The framing shifts, at times distant and at others a tight focus on the scarred face. Here, the subject of the documentary and the trope that film has become intensify in their doubling of each other. Film reproduces a past sequence, a fragment of a life, and yet it also testifies to an absence. The father is both there and not there, the ephemeral appeal of film itself, dialectically presenting us with an absence and a presence. The interleaving of the archive material exploits both the affectual pull of film, its imprint of a past moment, and its ephemeral retreat from presence; ultimately, these moments of replay fail to deliver the past, breaking up into grain, surface, texture of the image that reveal the fragile materiality of film rather than its ability to absorb and reproduce the past. These affectual moments arrest the movement of the narrative, as Laura Mulvey writes: 'When the presence of the past, the time of registration, rises to the surface, it seems to cancel the narrative flow.' The fascination of the moving image paradoxically detracts from the forward thrust of narrative. Mulvey continues, 'In almost any halt to a film, a sense of the image as document makes itself felt as the fascination of time fossilized overwhelms the fascination of narrative progression' (2006: 187). Film's perplexing mix of temporal registers haunts the medium of film, as much as it haunts this particular story.

The assemblage of the different documents that make up *My Architect* play out the fundamental tension between the inventory and the narrative, a tension that Sean Cubitt identifies as arising from the contemporary context. Cubitt asserts, 'The remarkable persistence of narrative in twentieth-century media can only be apprehended as remarkable if we apprehend the environment in which it is now performed: a landscape of other modes of documentation and dissemination' (2002: 6). According to Cubitt, narrative form has been fundamentally affected by the computer and its organizational capacities. The computer follows the procedure of classifying information in randomly (or personally and idiosyncratically) constructed categories. The information is labelled under an organizing principle that imposes its own system of likeness between artefacts or types of information. In so doing, systems of classification organize material through an arbitrary process of distinction and separation. It is the function of narrative to reconnect the elements, to draw parts into a systematized whole that functions through duration: narrative imposes a structure of journey and transportation through the inventory or indeed the archive. Narrative in a sense provides the paradigm in which a selection of artefacts are made to resonate. In *My Architect*, the strongest paradigm at work is not that of a particular love or career trajectory, it is accomplished through the objects of architecture, the buildings themselves.

If *My Architect* delivers a narrative of a life, it is articulated in relation to the catalogue of buildings that Khan designed and built. It is a film of objects, or more properly a human–object story. The buildings do not stand in for Khan, but in their presence they reveal something of the relation between the architect, the material properties of building and a conceptualization of the environment. As Khan's work is located in various parts of the world, it is a story of spatial relationships, as Khan responds to the particularity of each location, as well as a story of the evolution of an architectural style.

The first significant building, the Richards Medical Research Building, University of Pennsylvania, revels in the geometric shapes and patterns of a late modernism. The building, although considered a success at the time of its completion, appears a standard construction of the 1960s. In interviews with the residents of the building (students), we are informed of its failings: the experience of inconsistency of temperature, of birds flying into its glass panes, of the dullness of its exterior. It is in the Salk Institute in California that Khan's relation to the materials of building and to the environment first manifest themselves. Built on an edifice looking out to sea, the windows of the offices are angled towards this view. In the centre is a wide space, empty but for an incisive channel of water that leads the eye towards the water on the horizon, reflecting the sky in a shimmering line of light. The materiality of the building is both spectral and visceral: the light grey colour of the concrete reflects the light of the landscape and, in greater proximity, reveals the pitted and imperfect textures of the concrete as it has set.

In the auditorium of the cinema, the buildings take on an epic scale of magnificence. Yet the buildings, like cinema, are not simply epic but a haptic movement between the sensation of an enormous presence and the detail of its form. Cinema, like architecture, moves between the scales of the macro and micro; through the visual we are moved from the sublime experience of the 'larger than life', to the proximate and magnified detail.[8] In cinema, this is achieved through the cut, or through the movement of the camera, and in architecture, it is achieved through the body's movement in space, which may take only the smallest of steps to effect the same change as the edit. Giuliana Bruno presses this relation between cinema and architecture in *Atlas of Emotion*, and quoting the architect Jean Nouvel, the parallels are made explicit. Nouvel states,

> architecture exists, like cinema, in the dimension of time and movement. One conceives and reads a building in terms of sequences. To erect a building is to predict and seek effects of contrasts and linkage through which one passes . . . In the continuous shot/sequence that a building is, the architect works with cuts and edits, framings and openings . . . screens, planes legible from obligatory points of passage . . . (cited in Bruno, 2002: 60)

Bruno pushes this argument forcefully: 'One lives a film as one lives the space that one inhabits: as an everyday passage, tangibly' (2002: 69), figuring cinema as a space that we enter rather than work the surface of, challenging the two dimensionality of the screen.[9] In terms of *My Architect*, the project of the son amplifies the project of the father: both are engaged by the linkages, connections and vistas that fashion the parts in an experiential story.

In the imposition of intertitles, the chapter headings of the film, which appear to craft the polyform fragments of a life, are revealed in their isolation. The story, they suggest, could be viewed through this or that window ('The immigrant', 'The truth about the bastard'); the story could veer off and disappear in a certain direction. Each section, like each cut of an edit, exposes a decision taken, and simultaneously, in the momentary break, it implies all of the other possibilities available, the multitude of films and stories that could be threaded together. Each decision is also an opening on to other planes of potential. Film opens up to us the infinite range of virtual stories, images and experiences available. In the stark relation between an inventory of stock, on the one hand, and the linkage of narrative, on the other, film is revealed as a potentially indeterminate fashioning of matter. The final ordering and weaving is dependent not only on telling, but on the qualities of the materials, the angle of light, the visual matching and contrast of texture. Here, film steps away from its affectual status as document, and recasts the affectual as the potency of creating relations and new stories, surfaces and textures.

Tate Modern gallery, London: *Win, Place or Show*

In the video installation, *Win, Place or Show* (Stan Douglas, 1998–9), a six-minute film is projected on to two screens arranged next to each other, one screen contiguous with the other. The film, which is composed of two separate films, shows two men in combative form, arguing about a number of subjects, from news stories and radio, to horse racing and conspiracy theories. The banter rises in tone to reach an aggressive high in a physical confrontation, and the two men wrestle each other, and at moments cross into each other's screen space. The sequence is repeated every six minutes, but the version each time is different. A computer randomly selects the sequence of scenes; each time is a version, but a version without an original. The potency of the random is evident here, as the possibility of repeating the same sequence, the programme notes inform, occurs only once in every twenty thousand hours.

The presence of contingency is figured in the relation between the computer and the film, in the meeting of these two media. What the computer adds to or exacerbates about film is the relationship to chance, troping the mathematical relation to probability and numerology, bringing together rational calculation and mystical belief. The installation plays on the contingency of film's assemblage, and doubles this with the context. For the gallery is a space of viewing that facilitates a certain contingent relation to the works: the moment that we happen to enter the space (the building, the room, the installation) is unprogrammed. We may enter the installation half way through a sequence, we may choose to leave at any point, we may watch as many or as few versions as we choose. Not only a contingency of entrance and duration of viewing, the installation also facilitates a bodily contingency of how and where we place ourselves in relation to the film. How we situate our bodies, whether we choose to sit or stand, or indeed to move in front of the moving image, brings a more intuitive embodiment into the viewing context. I choose to sit on the floor and lean against a wall, which angles the image sideways. I am also aware of others stumbling into the darkened space, attempting to orientate themselves by the light of the screens. The context literally trips us up in its possibilities of encounter and collision. In the recreation of the cinema in the gallery (the darkened room, the enclosure of image and sound), the furniture that stages our relation to the image is missing.

There is something stark about the difference between the bodily stumblings in the dark and the clinical repetition of the computer. Douglas has commented, in relation to another of his works, *Pursuit, Fear, Catastrophe: Ruskin, BC,* on the difference between the time of the machine and the time of the human: 'Mechanical time is about endless repetition, whereas human time is about transformation and

change, with the processes of growth, ageing and death' (1998: 18).
Here the mechanical time of the machine is a computer that is
capable of greater variation than the modernist machines of late
industrialization. Yet the question of what it achieves, of whether
the random play of shots is a productive extension of the work, or
a meaningless exercise in redundancy, is unclear. Is a loop still a loop
when it varies slightly? Or does it suggest, like Nietzsche's eternal
return, that repetition is never a pure form but changed by the possibilities of the moment in which it is repeated?[10] The structure of
the circuit is both an entrapment and an invitation to start all over
again and produce a difference to the outcome of events. In this
sense, Douglas creates in each version a moment within narrative, a
potential turning point, and suspends its outcome.

The *mise en scène* of the film, and nature of filming, provide the
specificity to the project, clues about the type of narrative moment
that is put in suspension. The *mise en scène* references two types of
genre, or aesthetic: modernism and television drama. The location
of the story is a modern apartment replete with modernist furniture. The reference to modernism is made more explicit by the programme notes, which assert that the setting is constructed from the
design plans for a building drawn up in 1950, in Vancouver. The
building was intended to house low-income tenants, an extension
of the modernist aspirations for mass housing developed in the
work of Le Corbusier and others in the first half of the twentieth
century. The planned building in Vancouver, however, never mate-
rialized, suggesting a cleaving between the ideals of modernism and
the delivery of those ideals. In providing this information, the
gallery paradoxically reduces radically the interpretative possibilities
of the work, the contingency of its semiosis. The 'history' of the
production is filled in for us, in a similar way to the behind-the-
scenes information on DVD 'extra' features: both are footnotes to
the work. The particular fate of a modernist scheme, however, is
not the only history evoked. There is also a collision of styles in the
modernist feel of the apartment and the mass cultural genre of the
dialogue, dress and action, which appropriate a televisual aesthetic,
perhaps a police drama. This disjunction between generic forms
resonates more powerfully through the style of shooting and presentation. Despite the appearance of a dialogue of exchange and

response, the two men never appear to be face to face, delivering lines to no one in particular. In this sense, the popular appeal of the televisual form fails to deliver its goal of connecting us to a collective drama, repeating the failure of modernism's utopian aspirations for collective housing. Or is it modernism and mass culture that are set in an eternal stand-off?

In this experience of a gallery-work as film, we are offered a cross-section of film production, narrative in the making. A moment of dramatic tension is isolated from what we might struggle to construct as a bigger picture. The longer we watch, the more the narrative fails to accumulate meaning; the desire for narrative development and resolution is thwarted. In its place, we are returned to the moment of expectation, and confronted with our desire for the narrative to take a particular direction. In this sense, *Win, Place or Show* discloses the possibilities of narrative as an open system, liable to change direction, to misfire expectation. The film delivers us to this point of narrating, of the relation between the stock of characters and situations available, and the multiple possibilities of their configuration. And in the space of the gallery, we may choose to linger here, or move on. The mobile spectator of the gallery is also weaving a narrative between the range of works, the various rooms and spaces constructed as a pathway yet open to our meandering reinvention. Is the installation in competition with other works to 'win' our attention in this place or artists' show, or is it the characters on screen that are trapped between these terms?

Contingent affect

To walk through a gallery, a shopping mall or a station concourse and happen upon a film has a quality of ghosting, at once a return of something from the past and a potential following or haunting. The historical sense of film as a phantasmagoric medium, bringing alive dead things, is doubled by the surprise of context; it is not only the past that haunts, but film itself, rising in sites where we least expect to find it. Such an experience of ghosting recalls Benjamin's description of the commodity world of the arcades, where walking pivots on a sense of aimless meandering and a surreal stumbling into other worlds:

> The dread of doors that won't close is something everyone knows from dreams. Stated more precisely: these are doors that appear closed without being so. It was with heightened senses that I learned of this phenomenon in a dream in which, while I was in the company of a friend, a ghost appeared to me in the window of the ground floor of a house to our right. And as we walked on, the ghost accompanied us from inside all the houses. It passed through all the walls and always remained at the same height with us. I saw this, though I was blind. The path we travel through arcades is fundamentally just such a ghost walk, on which doors give way and walls yield. [L2,7] (Benjamin, 1972: 409)

In this passage it is unclear who exactly is doing the ghosting. The dreamer is pursued by a ghost that moves through walls, yet by the final line, it appears to be the *flâneur* of the arcades who has become ghostly. For Benjamin, the commodity relations set out so seductively in the arcades as a suspension of the laws of gravity and mortality deliver us to a world of charmed objects and surfaces that yield and flex as we move through them. In Benjamin's writings, the cinema effected a severance of images from contexts in a way that echoed the dislocation of commodities from sites of production. Yet the cinema remained discrete, a haunting that ran parallel to the experience of the arcades. Film now pursues us outside of the discrete housing of the cinema, offering us a new sense of walls that open up and doors that will not close.

In its release from the confines of the cinema, film has come to haunt us in many locations and some surprising contexts. Like a ghost, film will not disappear into the ether, nor will it announce itself as a concrete 'thing', but in its multiple sightings, film convinces us that walls indeed yield as the flat screen opens up on to other worlds. If film's escape from the cinema is characterized by a spatial dispersal, we might imagine that the distilled experience of cinematic affect has become diluted. In its meanderings, film has made new affiliations, conversing with the narrative forms of television, the spectacle of news, the branding of advertising (McCarthy, 2001). Yet it would appear that film's affectual qualities have not suffered in the strength of their appeal, but rather, the contingent element of film has intensified its affectual distinctiveness. Film's curious imprint, or affectual trace, is pronounced by its difference from the media of the environments in which it is relocated. Almost in spite of its dislocation from the institution of cinema, film remains recognizable in its particularity, a particularity however that is in constant revision over time and in context. The question remains of how, from these examples, to critically identify film's current affectual potency.

There are, I would suggest, three qualities of film that affectually 'capture' in these different circumstances. First, the conditions of affectual relating can be located in film's relation to the past, to the ongoing indexicality of film. As Godard has illustrated in his work, *Histoire(s) du Cinéma* (1998), film fascinates as a record of what was, but a history that is shaped, framed, fictionalized, cut about and distorted.[11] Film's phantasmagoric state accrues over time. Second, the changing materiality of film, the uncertain relations of analogue with the digital, imposes an interruption in the history of film which is not yet worked through. Bernard Stiegler comments, 'Great moments of technical innovation are moments of suspension', and in this suspended state, the force of the contingent is felt (1996: 149). Film could, it seems, move in a number of directions, and this trope of the indeterminate and the accidental is thematized by many films in disparate contexts of viewing. This sensation of suspense is a component of the affectual imprint that film leaves on us. Third, the specific dynamic through which contingency is mobilized and contained in film is in an interplay of narrative and inventory. Whilst the project of arranging matter and information into files directs us to the computer interface, and a very contemporary process, the project of classification derives from the epoch of modernism. As both Cubitt and Doane point out in different ways, modernism's drive to create taxonomies served the demands of a growing bureaucracy, whose foundations in the arbitrary were disguised.[12] In the present, the oscillation between inventory and narrative produces an anxious dynamic, both potent in its creativity and without foundation. These three conditions of affectual relating are not discrete areas, but often overlap in the contexts in which we encounter film, in the station concourse, the gallery, the home and cinema, and in many other locations besides.

What is clear from this enquiry into the changing nature of film is that a search for film's ontology, the characteristics of its fundamental mode of being, is a futile exercise. Whilst there remain many links between earlier film scholarship and the present analytical moment of film theory, film's mutations escape the clutches of a grounding ontology. To borrow Siegfried Kracauer's terminology, film's 'affinities' are transient, always at a point of emergence and reinvention.[13] The method of enquiry for film studies can no longer be a method of deduction, of a measured movement that extracts what film is from what film has been. In the present moment, the method has to be one of addition, of an 'also' and an 'and', elaborating the paradigm of what it is that film does.[14] In a sense, we are in the realm of supplementation, a project of ongoing evolution that incorporates the supplement as the thing itself. This is the supplement in Derrida's sense, not as an addition to an 'original' which until this point has appeared complete (Derrida, 1973). But in the logic of supplementation, the original can never have been complete if it is open to addition. In deconstructive terms, the supplement reveals the lack or the hole that has always been there in any object or text. The addition of the supplement reveals the fluid boundaries between an interior and an exterior. Film, in the logic of the supplement, has then always been open to addition, and it is only in the present moment of digital suspension that 'film' may appear retrospectively to have been a stable designation.

A final question remains concerning film's relation to affect: if film derives much of its potency and particularity from its affectual pull, is this different from the general affectual economy identified by Massumi? How is filmic affect to be distinguished from the other sites of its emergence? Massumi offers an example of the functioning of affect at the heart of capitalism's machinations, in the stock market. In his reading, the stock market is a mechanism responding with immediacy to affectual states (induced by rumour and 'feeling') rather than 'facts'. The price of shares is conditioned by the rumours that circulate and their attendant 'feelings', an affectual response to a situation in which economic fluctuation is the outcome. Massumi writes, 'The ability of affect to produce an economic effect more swiftly and surely than economics itself means that affect is a real condition, an intrinsic variable of the late capitalist system, as instrumental as a factory' (2002: 45). The unpredictable outcome of rumour and speculation produces a system that surfs the instability of a situation, fluctuating and consolidating its management of stock. Like film, the stock market operates both axes of narrative and inventory, of a story unfolding (the fate of a company as it rises, plummets, suffers adverse conditions and so on), and of an inventory of stock, characters and contexts. But there the analogy ends, for the stock market aims to nail down the value of a resource, and it does so in stabilizing the 'meaning' of a brand. The semiosis of the stock market is intended to be as consistent and legible as possible to ensure the widespread desirability of a product: its circuit of referentiality tends towards closure. Film, conversely, in a postclassical context, opens up the repertoire of references, and composes a fragile synthesis of parts.

In 'these times', in which the present has infamously and lengthily been designated as a context of declining belief, the affectual makes sense of the investments that we do make and the ways in which we make them. In place of theories of 'post' belief/ ideology/modernism, and indeed, of post-cinema, the project is perhaps to identify where and how our engagements take place. Film, whether in or out of the cinema, creates a threshold of the past and the present, of the proximate and the distant, of the known and unknown. How this threshold is worked is the particularity of film's appeal, a particularity that I have argued here is deeply embedded in forms of contingency. And curiously, in the etymology of the term 'contingent', we find an affectual root: contingent, from the Latin *contingere*, derives from *tangere*, to touch.

6

Inertia: on energy and film

Energy is the unifying concept of all physical science, pertaining to bodies, technologies and systems. Indeed, it is the relation between human bodies, the technologies of film and the systems of capital circulation that this chapter hopes to elucidate. In short, it is my belief that film as a medium is sensitive to the flow of energy, implicit in its characteristic tooling of rhythms, repetitions and cuts in a circuit of meaning. Film is a radar, at its most abstract, of the freedoms and constraints that condition flows of energy. Picture, to begin with, a body, your body, going about its daily quotidian tasks:

> When you walk, each step is the body's movement against falling – each movement is felt in our potential for freedom as we move with the earth's gravitational pull. When we navigate our way through the world, there are different pulls, constraints and freedoms that move us forward and propel us into life. But in the changing face of capitalism, media information and technologies – which circulate the globe in more virtual and less obvious ways – how do the constraints on freedom involve our affective and embodied dimensions of experience? (Zournazi, 2003: 1)

How a body moves, within what paradigms of constraint and enhancement, draws our attention to questions of energy and flow, force and resistance. And even in its most fundamental, or indeed its most accomplished act, in walking, it is unclear whether gravity is the body's obstacle to movement or its enabling factor. We move both with and against gravity. Whilst a fascination with the body in movement appears to focus very contemporary concerns, this description of action broken down to a minimal unit such as a step might have been an account of a short sequence of a film or photographic experimentation from the end of the nineteenth century. It recalls the obsession with which the photographic, as recording device, explored the body in time and through movement, evident in the experiments of Eadweard Muybridge: the lean, naked body of *Man Running* (1887), both mechanical in its coordinated effort and astoundingly fragile in its mastery of balance. Yet in this series of co-ordinated frames, movement eludes the image; movement and the static shot as record emerge as antagonists in this enterprise, and it is only in Étienne-Jules Marey's attempts to represent movement graphically by dressing his models in black and attaching luminous fabric to their joints, that a sense of mobility emerges.[1] *Jump from a Height with Knees Bent* (1884) is an image of a string of lights, closer to an astronomer's chart than a human body.[2] An earlier attempt, *Demeney Walking* (1883), where Marey had lengthened the exposure, captures a ghostly trace of bodies sliding into one another, a kind of staccato human trail. Movement as a graph of illuminated points, or movement as fudged trace; in either example, the legibility of movement depends on the disappearance of the body.

How do we get hold of movement, how do we figure the body in the force field of tensions in a way that grasps the possibilities, freedoms and obstacles? These questions of how a body moves, with what degree of energy and resource, and in what kind of matrix of resistance and constraint, have returned in the present. If, in the era of modernism, the human body and the machine (machines of industry and representation) are poised in opposition, the implication of photographic experiments is that human and machine might also be analogous. The question appears to be, does the body function like a machine, its anatomy comparable to the components of engineering? Or does the body remain illusive, that which resists mechanical quantification and empirical knowledge?

Film, in part, contains this paradox in that movement, when it is strung together in a sequence of frames, appears to record the animated form of human energy. Yet as we know it is a cheat, its effects produced through a conspiracy of the eye and the still image: the body in film is both movement and stasis, creating a disjunction between what we know (film is a composition of stills) and what we experience to be the case (film is movement). Yet the paradigm of body and machine over a hundred years ago provided a set of antagonisms that were clearly laid out, in literature, film, medicine and social analysis. How does the human body operate in an increasingly mechanical age, and what are its conscious and unconscious modes of being, are questions revisited across the disciplines.

Against a backdrop of increasingly mechanical production replacing the labour of bodies, the body versus the machine provided a containing framework for thinking movement, constraint and energy. The present moment denies us such analytical clarity for, as Mary Zournazi points out in her address to Brian Massumi, the present is characterized by an increasingly virtual matrix in which we operate. Unlike the early twentieth century, where the machines of industry posited a physical presence for production, in the early twenty-first century production has either been removed from the centres of global organization and relocated to a series of transient labour camps, or become virtual, a dematerialized culture of contracts, exchanges and communication (Virilio, 1986; 1994). Production, like movement in early photographic experiments, is difficult to trace, to locate, to identify. The productivity of capital in the present is both virtual and mobile, its legibility as obscure as the elliptical trace of the moving body, and attempts to pin it down or rationally engage with its operations are as readily defeated. As Michael Hardt and Antonio Negri argue in *Empire* (2000), their attempt to analyse capital in the present, accelerated processes of deterritorialization by which empire operates render it centreless, transient and invisible. At moments of its appearance, or materialization, in trade negotiations for example, its presence flares momentarily. The stealth of empire defines the terms of human engagement with the mutations of capital as similarly opportunistic, sprung into a momentary opposition before it again evades the eye.

It is my belief that film offers a different conceptualization of the contemporary as a condition of uneven flows and mutations of capital, as a force field of energies. An unlikely contender perhaps in the explications of the present, film has since its inception contained the paradoxes of vision and knowledge, energy and stasis. To see is not to know, film has been telling us for some time; vision is not to be trusted as the guarantor of truth. Yet in an age in which vision is not only unreliable but ineffectual in the face of the virtual, and its fellow traveller, rationality, is revealed as a less than useful tool, film moves us towards the diverse and diffuse *experiences* of the conditions of capital rather than *knowledge* of it. Film does not operate as a trustworthy representation of cultures, places or people; what it can offer is the sense of energy as it flows into and animates space and bodies, or conversely eddies and falters. As a medium trading in movement, film is sensitive to what it is that animates and sets alive, and what acts as a blockage. Central to this argument is a concept of differential energies, and this is a point made as a critique of the current fascination with 'intensity'. Like affect, intensity identifies an imprint but one that sets the subject in motion. Yet filmic affect also identifies the conditions of stasis, immobility and blockage.

As a quality, intensity summons a particular notion of energy, as forceful and condensed. It articulates a quality of experience produced by a convergence of effects, and so is useful in a theoretical account of our exposure to multiple affects. As a philosophical concept drawn from the work of Deleuze and Guattari (1972, 1980, 1997) (itself a reworking of Bergson's formulation), its currency is as a description of the deterritorialized body in its relations with others (human, animal and object). The body ceases to be a foundation of identity or interiority, and is reformulated as the site of various intersections of energy. Becoming temporarily stable, such intersections form a plane of consistency. The term gestures to a model of the body in the present moment as a site of connection and disconnection, a point on a surface through which various energies gather and coalesce. Intensity refers us to a temporary gathering of investments that take meaning by being intensive, and in so doing, it provides a way of imagining the mobile virtual energies of the present in their abstract form. Intensity has become theory's way of grasping the affectual.

Yet the focus on intensity has itself become an intensive trope, and what this focus excludes is other modes of affectual experience, and by implication, other modes of being conditioned by forms of deterritorialization. Film is often a highly affectual experience but one that delivers us to various states. One of the most interesting of these, perhaps precisely because it is critically unfashionable, is the state of inertia, the condition in which energies are curtailed, short-circuited or simply impossible to summon. Films of this kind mark out a space that is external to the paradigm of the action-image, for they are not structured by progression, linearity or outcome. They offer a challenge to the sense of time as purposeful. Moreover, they disturb the neat divisions between productive and wasteful time upon which capitalism wholeheartedly depends, and through which cinema as a narrative form and cultural experience was finely honed. If, as Mary Ann Doane suggests, early cinema rides a cusp between productive and unproductive time, this is a legacy of cinema that has largely been lost to the dominance of narrative film where every sequence needs to 'pay off' in the progression of a chain of causal events. Unproductive time, in the history of film, is relegated to the fringes of avant-garde experimentation. Yet the question of productivity and energy, of where productivity takes place and through which networks, channels and bodies energy flows, has circled back in the present order of global instability and contingency, as a pressing issue. It has also circled back to disrupt the causal structure of narrative film. In order to muster this illusive matter of energy as a marker of productive and unproductive spaces in the contemporary, it is necessary to summon a few of the appearances it makes in the history of film/production.

The tiredness of a century

> Power . . . fears and despises a vacuum.
>
>   Michael Hardt and Antonio Negri, *Empire*

> Nature abhors a vacuum.
>
>   Leo Charney, *Empty Moments*

In the period of early film, questions of productivity are in the ether. In an era in which decentred agrarian forms of existence are displaced by an urban industrial centralization of production, the nature of productivity is the conscious political concern, in the foreground of thought. At the periphery of socio-political discourse, in the work of writers, film-makers and critics, the experiential underbelly of production emerges in a number of ways. The experience of time, now divided, fragmented and organized into periods of productivity and leisure, reveals the opposite: the disintegration of linear time and the collapse of temporal boundaries. Famously, Proust's work discloses the experience of modernity in its fractured rather than seamless totality. In Simmel's analysis, the urban environment of collective city culture is turned inside out to reveal anonymous alienation. And the displacement of the human by the machine in the process of production emerges as a central concern in a range of work, in relation to film particularly in the writings of Kracauer, Benjamin and Epstein. The swift, efficient free-flow of assembly line factory production gives rise to a frayed set of discourses concerned with the transformation of experience for the machine's human counterpart.

The cinema retains a specific significance in this moment, not only for its slapstick carking representation of life inside the factory, but as a result of its own ambiguous status as a mechanical culture. Kracauer's reading of the synchronized legs of the dancing girls on stage identifies the abstract patterning of the human as machine, facilitating for the viewer a distracted mode of apprehension, distraction allowing the spectator to perceive the abstract shapes, objects and textures of the everyday in a new type of optical relation. Benjamin's essay on the artwork in the mechanical age has come to be regarded as the defining response to modernity's shift of modes of perception, from a concentrated engagement with the image to a revelation of objects through an optical unconscious. Their writings detect in different ways new modes of perception produced through or most evident in the encounter with cinema. Cinema facilitates a decentred form of reception, where the mobility of the gaze as it traverses the screen, or the shifting points of mimetic identification, gesture towards an evacuation of interiority, the sovereign subject of being. Leo Charney, writing modernism's tropes from the contemporary, identifies in cinema a dialectic of presence and absence (the image is both here and not here), a dialectic that is at play in the experience of the viewer. For Charney, the cinema is an important cultural resource in its ability to replay the absence of being to the subject. The subject/spectator is not present in the moment, but subject to 'drift', an ontological category of non-presence. 'In the common sense of directionless passivity, drift provided the background for modernity's shocking moments, surprising distractions, and overwhelming stimuli' (1998: 8), he writes, embedding drift in a dialectic with modernity's energetic impulses of spectacle.

In each of these accounts, distraction is both a new mode of apprehension and a draining of concentration and energy. But what is less clearly settled is the question of whether the cinema is complicit with capital's new modes of production, as a mode of organized leisure, or itself a relief from or even reversal of the demand to annihilate dead time. The elegiac tone of Charney's work reproduces the languorous sensation of meandering through a series of images or thoughts in any order: 'The present goes away and leaves behind an empty space. Why do people assume it stays vacant. Nature abhors a vacuum' (p. 13). Drift for Charney is the reverse ontology of modernity's rush and excitation, a hole in the fabric revealing boredom and emptiness that opens up within the culture of attractions. The empty space or boredom is invested with the release from organized productivity. Both image and spectator are caught in the dilemma of apparent presence and actual absence. Charney's reading retrospectively invests the early cinematic moment with a poststructural refusal of presence, insisting on the impossibility of the positive sense of self in time. In contrast, Doane claims for boredom a type of ontological presence, drawing on a more phenomenological framework for a description of the subject's relation to mass culture: 'Boredom ensures one's presence, one's refusal to be absorbed into and overcome by the regulated temporality of mass culture' (2002: 162).

For Benjamin, the question is not whether boredom is a productive state, but whether it is attainable under the aegis of modernism's structured ordering of labour. In an essay on the arts of storytelling, he posits the case negatively. As Rachel Moore writes, 'The nature of mechanical labor, the noise of its machines and the rapid repetitive tasks, had made not only storytelling but also the state of boredom, which had filled the idle mind, impossible. The tasks of the industrial laborer and office worker alike render boredom a thing of the past' (2000: 98). In Moore's reading, boredom is closely aligned to the further state of fatigue, celebrated in the work of film-maker and writer Jean Epstein (1921). For Epstein, fatigue, engendered by the relentless motion of machinic production, is a potential route into the obscure semi-conscious states necessary for creative production. 'In the light of this dispersion of cognitive capabilities,' Moore writes, 'Epstein saw his opening' (p. 97). The opening was a type of free-association, contingent on modernity's insistence on production and reproduction of 'the same'. From a bodily exhaustion to a trance-like state of reverie, the encounter of human and mechanical culture fermented various unexpected outcomes.[3]

If the cinema in its earliest incarnations purports to both the rationalization of time (as programmes of organized leisure), and the inducement of a distracted state potentially open to boredom's tangential meanderings, this ambiguity takes root in a particular way. Mary Ann Doane argues that the shock and surprise of cinema, its ability to capture the contingent, doubles back to threaten the organized structure of cinematic time. Contingency has a specific meaning in the era of modernism, as the oppositional force to an increased systematization of matter evidenced in the proliferation of statistical information (Doane, 2002: 17). She sites the social sciences as the disciplines where statistical knowledge on the very individual life events of births, marriages, suicides and crime led to the identification of certain common patterns. The feats of an individual life are transformed into facts of a general nature. Statistical information, like the grids of Marey's luminous body parts, manage to plot human activity as a map, a list, a taxonomy that appears to erase the random. Through statistics, the contingent appears to be harnessed, or at least minimized, disorder contained. The cinema, for Doane, manages a similar taming of the contingent through its staging of a 'live' event.

It is not simply that the cinema captures an event, and contingency remains in the realm of the event itself. Rather, the argument is that cinema produces the event as it both constructs or stage-manages the happening, and produces its effects as contingent 'surprise'. Doane illustrates this with the early sub-genre of the actuality film, a film of compellingly shocking events such as the recording of death. In *Electrocuting an Elephant* (1903), the event is planned and recorded, the moment of death captured as the elephant is lashed by its feet to an electrical apparatus and electrocuted.[4] The fascination with the immediacy of the live event of death provides the shock of pure presence, the witnessing of something unassimilable. Shadowy figures pass in front of the camera, the movement of the scene is not choreographed but open to unexpected rupture. The contingent, argues Doane, is both threat and lure: 'The embarrassment of contingency is that it is everywhere and that it everywhere poses the threat of an evacuation of meaning' (2002: 144). If the threat of contingency to cinema is the possibility of an occurrence that will destabilize the story, in the actuality film the contingent is made present, yet harnessed to a meaningful structure as an event. Just as the threat of contingency to the socio-political order is managed through administrative techniques such as statistical collation, it is managed in the cinema by the staging of the contingent as event. It becomes further harnessed into the structure of cinema as narrative form premised on progression, linear clarity and closure.

The thread between boredom and contingency is that they both exist at the edges of the social infrastructure of modernism, both threatening to invert productive time and a rationalized meaningful order. Both boredom and the contingent escape the net of socially mandated time, and they are further related: the associative state of boredom creates an opening where the contingent may surface. Yet, whilst the present continues to be haunted by contingency, the paradigm in which it exists is markedly different from that of modernism. In the present moment, contingency is not that which capital struggles to control, but that which it seeks to assess as risk, or use to its own advantage. The contingent is no longer opposed to capital's mechanical productivity, for capital no longer bears the hallmarks of rationalized operations within structured universal time. As Paul Virilio argues, the accident is now built into the instability of the present as a component of capital's mutations, whether as ecological damage, terrorism or war (Virilio and Lotringer, 2005). Chernobyl is the contingent event that spectacularly emerges in real time, addressing us collectively in its disaster, and the medium of contingency becomes the live television relay rather than film.

Arguably, film drops out of the paradigm of boredom-creativity, contingency-event. Contingency has largely been lost to film as it has evolved as a highly structured narrative form, the lure of the contingent devolved to the genre of documentary film as the site of the 'real' (and again, relocated to television). Yet film presents us with the underbelly of this scenario, not an inversion of spectacular event and intensity, but an extension of what we might come to recognize as the experiential present. In the margins of film culture, in productions created in what I want to name inert zones, areas where conflict is present but movement lacking, the paradigm of the present is extended, if not challenged. Indeed, these films suggest that we may be looking in the wrong direction by focusing on time, intensity and event. If there is a category that can be summoned as a cinema of inertia, it is drawn from a scattered array of pockets where the energy of the present has become blocked or short-circuited, areas that capital has ceased to find productive as a result of socio-political conflict. Space, rather than time, is the axis through which the tensions of contingency and mobility are played out. Boredom as the wasting of time is replaced by inertia as the wasting of space.

The characteristics of a cinema of inertia are not simply circling the absence of energy and a lack of action. Inertia may, like boredom, have its productive capacities; inertia as the continuation of a uniform motion, lacking resistance or motivation, gives rise to a form of absurdism. Repetition is a characteristic feature of inertia, actions carried out with minimal energy or with frenetic energy and within confined spatial limits. Inertia is a play on predictability produced through blockage: there is literally nowhere to go to escape this cycle. In this sense, inertia evokes part of cinema's lost heritage, of the cyclical looped structure of early film, where the loop itself flies in the face of progression and teleology. The loop toys with the idea of progress and movement; what appears to be 'going somewhere' arrives back at the starting point. This structure of the loop patterns the film *Divine Intervention* (Elia Suleiman, 2002), a film set in the uncompromising context of the Palestinian–Israeli conflict. A man sits at a table, smokes a cigarette, his mail spread out in front of him unopened. He gets up, picks up a garbage bag, carries it across his front courtyard and throws it into a neighbour's garden. A second man on a roof, watched by two others on an adjacent roof, carries a bag of bottles up a ladder and arranges them neatly in rows. A third man stands at a bus stop, waiting. A neighbour emerges from the house behind and tells him that the bus isn't coming. A fourth man drives to a road checkpoint policed by army attendants. He waits. A car pulls in, a woman gets out and climbs into the passenger seat of the other car. They hold hands, staring ahead. Each scene is repeated several times. We are caught in a loop, in the semi-comic, certainly absurd drama of the loop, a parody of early film's appeal to the ridiculous. The distant, still camera observes in a manner that is both detached and ridiculing. We are observing a fetishization of action, a repetitious re-enactment of the quotidian. Yet here, the everyday is a series of violations, futile actions, blocked attempts at connection. The series is devoid of progress, and here, time ceases to mean, it is out of joint. The film is set in Ramallah and Jerusalem, or rather, the intertitles require us to connect these place names with this series of events.

The structure of *Divine Intervention* is a series of disconnected episodic sequences with a loose thread of characters that reappear rather than connect in the duration of the film. In the first part is an older man, a father, who becomes bankrupt and has a heart attack. In the middle and last sections, his son visits him in hospital and meets with a woman at an Israeli army checkpoint. There is no progression, development or resolution, only reproduction of sequences and actions. The arbitrary construction of the narrative is reflexively featured in the film as the protagonist (played by director Elia Suleiman) stands in front of two walls covered by yellow Post-it notes. The notes are a description of each scene of the film. The character takes one note from the wall and replaces it on the wall opposite. It is the scene instruction 'father falls sick'. The removal of the scene from one wall and its relocation elsewhere in the narrative gestures to a reworking of the story. Yet it is precisely the ineffectual nature of this gesture that is apparent. The contingent here is not an openness to the possibility of change, but a foregrounding of the meaninglessness of the action. Events do not 'add up' or lead anywhere, they simply accumulate. Order and disorder sit side by side. For each day is predictable in its routine events, a ritual of order, yet the order has no meaning in its accumulated state. Each event can be shuffled, placed randomly in a set of predictable actions. Action as repetition, repetition as inertia.

In a similar mode to the random series of events that replays a loop, *Divine Intervention* is in many ways a film of reversals, a play of action and reverse action. This is not the convention of filmic grammar in the pattern of shot–reverse shot, where the emotional register of a statement is traced back and forth. What we take to be the meaning of an event flips over into its opposite. This rhythm is set up in the opening sequence: some children chase a character dressed in a Father Christmas outfit across a landscape. Presents spill from the basket on his back. The iconic figure of paternal giving is cornered, fearful, chased from the city. The opening sequence sets the note of the film, where any expectation of care, reciprocity or compassion is met with its opposite. A boy kicks a ball from foot to foot. When it lands on the roof of a neighbouring house, a man punctures it with a knife and throws it back. Not only is expectation reversed, but an action conducted in one sequence will be overturned in another. Road workers arrive to repair a road in the neighbourhood. Subsequently a neighbour appears and takes a sledge-hammer to the repair. Progression has no currency here, there is only action and reversal, an endless dialectic of aggression and response, where victim becomes aggressor and vice versa. If this can indeed be described as a dialectic, an exchange of positions, it is a movement without negotiation. In a film of virtually no dialogue, where actions are injuries, the construction of scenes avoids the convention of shot–reverse shot. This would gesture to a dynamism of exchange. In *Divine Intervention*, acts occur in isolation, producing greater acts of irrational violence at other moments.

The lack of progression within the narrative form recalls Deleuze's consideration of the ethical dimensions of cinema in the *Time-Image*. Here he notes 'Narration always refers to a *system of judgment*' (1985: 37), whereby the revelatory acts of narrative, bent on exposing error and reasserting a moral order, appeal to a rational orthodoxy. This is the structure of normative cinema, which implicitly stages a higher moral authority, a transcendental legislation.

And it is precisely this notion of a greater or absolute truth that he finds addled and in decline by the postwar period. Some twenty years later, the concept of a transcendental legislation is significantly further collapsed, appearing as the hyperbolic in normative narrative cinema, absent in cinema cultures of the margins. In *Divine Intervention* there is no narrative structure to perform a revelation or exposure of 'truth' that suggests an appeal to justice. There is simply repetition, accumulation of acts and no 'greater' meaning. The structure of accumulation (of indifference and violence), we might expect to break, to collapse into a greater violence and a moment of breakthrough. Yet contingency is the element that is absent. Contingency has been appropriated by the chaotic mechanisms of empire, now a characteristic of capital rather than an external aberrant force. Chance, the random, the arbitrary operate elsewhere, across other spaces; in Ramallah and Jerusalem, the spatial relations create a tight circuit of energy that deny contingent forces as far as possible. For contingency to appear, it is a forced extreme act that thematizes the contingent.

The contingent becomes, in *Divine Intervention*, an act of the imagination, an opening of thought on to the unthinkable. The imaginative opening occurs in relation to space; spatial barriers, routes, demarcated territories lose their defining power to contain energy. There are three moments in the film when movement across rather than through prescribed space is allowed to happen, and each is a moment bordering on the trope of what has become known as magical realism, but what might be thought of as a mixing of filmic registers. The first moment is the punctuation of the first act of the film: the female lover queues at the checkpoint, the soldiers turn back all cars, and the road is cleared except for her vehicle. She steps out of her car, walks towards the checkpoint and straight past the armed guards. As she does so, the tower of the checkpoint magically collapses. It is a moment of absolute confrontation, of a body asserting a right to act in the face of anonymous military uniforms and weapons, luxuriating in the power of female sexual prowess as an unchallengeable force. The second moment takes place when the lovers continue their ritual of meeting in a car park by a checkpoint, to sit and observe the activities of policing, and to inhabit the only common ground available to them. The lover takes a balloon from his pocket and breathes into it, attaches it to a helium gas canister and properly inflates it. A balloon, with an image of Yaser Arafat printed on the side, is released through the sunroof of the car, rising up over the check-point, and into the forbidden territory of the old city.

The third moment of breakthrough, the most extended and con-troversial, is when Israeli soldiers are training to shoot, firing at targets in the image of a Palestinian woman. During the sequence, the figure of a woman emerges behind the two-dimensional target. She rises into the air, her head encircled by bullets, an image that echoes the Christian crucifix. With a shield, in the shape of Palestine as it was defined before the creation of the state of Israel, she returns the gun fire. As she spins in the air, she hurls an object and brings down an Israeli helicopter. The 'rising up' is of course a political uprising, and the product of the former part of the film: in a situation of spatial blockage (in curfews and checkpoint control), the air is the only space to occupy. The sequence is a momentary acceleration of pace in the structure of the film, not only breaking with the quotidian inertia that dominates the film but mixing cinematic traditions. What we might think of as national and transnational cinematic influences are compressed here. The action sequence of a human figure rising magically into aerial combat recalls the martial arts set pieces of recent transnational films, the potency of the body matched with special effects, a par-ticular configuration of technology and the body from popular film. This is mixed with the symbols of a Palestinian nation state, and the Christian reference as a reminder of the history of this space as a 'Holy land'. In the moment of magical breakthrough, the thick effects of space-time are in condensed form, as though the past and present appear together, hovering in this site as a visionary, out-of-time apprehension. Suleiman's magical realism is an entry into another dimension in which a form of 'total' perception is matched by a potential for acting.

Divine Intervention is, of course, a film that emanates from a specific place, and a particular conflict. Yet what it achieves is not a 're-presentation' of a situation, but the production of time and space through the curtailment of energy and its effects. The roads travelled, the neighbourhoods inhabited, the interiors walked through are spaces of containment, and in the looped structure, appear as temporal stasis: the film re-enacts this on the audience. It is only in a shift of filmic register that change occurs, that time and space open up and energy is released, breaking the cycle. Location is not produced in its clichéd form, as one of the contemporaneous conflicts of global news coverage. It is produced as a fragmented series of images that exist without order, reason, connection or progression. The particularities of the Palestinian-Israeli conflict as filmic experience are manifest as an experience of space as a matrix of energies. In contrast to the borderless transactions of an inter-connected empire, this film discloses the reverse, that space, like time, can be looped, folded and fractured. In the contemporary readings of geo-politics, to recover space from its empirical conser-vatism is to pull theory back into an engagement with the diversity of space-time, and the specificity of experience.

Unproductive expenditure

Space can also be looped, folded and fractured, and space is pro-duced through the movement of energy in an 'unproductive' circuit. Yet to assert such a proposition is to work against a history of thought about film, movement and time. Even at the point at which a dominant narrative cinema is seen to be running out of energy, exhausted by the recycling of its own clichés, it is the appre-hension of time that emerges as the new force of cinema. This is most clearly demonstrated in the two books on cinema, published in 1983 and 1985 respectively, by Gilles Deleuze.[5] The works do not belong to traditional film theory; the books are more con-cerned with explicating Bergson's concept of the image to undo classical philosophy than with the development of ideas about film. Yet they offer at some level a survey of the development of cine-matic forms from early cinema through to the postwar European new waves, viewed through the question of how concepts are created, and how thought is propelled into movement. At the end of *The Movement-Image*, Deleuze launches his attack on the clichéd state of cinema by the time of the Second World War. Cinema's fascination with, and dependency on, the action image has become a crisis, a 'crisis of both the action-image and the American Dream' (1983: 210). He elaborates:

> In fact, what gave the American cinema its advantage, the fact of being born without a previous tradition to suffocate it, now rebounded against it. For the cinema of the action-image had itself engendered a tradition from which it could now only, in the majority of cases, extricate itself negatively. The great genres of this cinema, the psycho-social film, the film noir, the Western, the American comedy, collapse and yet maintain their empty frame. (p. 211)

The 'traps' of American cinema, for Deleuze, become replayed as the familiar, and in the process begin to weaken the hold of given thought, familiar cinema. 'Nothing but clichés, clichés everywhere . . .', he rails (p. 208).

The negativity of the 'empty frame' is a reference to the parody of American ideals in the work of Altman and Scorsese, a turning of clichés against themselves which gains momentum in the American cinema of postmodern reflexivity, subsequent to Deleuze's two cinema volumes. Noting these emergent forms of self-critique in American cinema at the end of the movement image, Deleuze turns to European cinema as the site of new energy in the postwar period. The response to the 'empty frame' of American cinema is formulated by Deleuze as a set of five cinematic characteristics: the dispersive situation, the deliberately weak links, the voyage form, the consciousness of clichés and the condemnation of the plot. It is in Europe that the cinema comes to break properly from the given, and find new modes of production that are distinctly different from the action image. Here, the timing is explicit: it is in Italy in 1948, France in 1958, and Germany in 1968. In the new energies of the postwar European film movements, Deleuze identifies a mutation of cinema. Emancipated from action, images become aberrant, lack coherence, turn the destroyed fabric of postwar cities into 'any-space-whatever'. And if Deleuze cites neo-realism as a key movement in a new wave of cinematic form, it is without any concept of representational realism. The postwar world and the modern cinema are incommensurate, broken away from each other. There is a cleavage here in the opening between the movement image and the time image (classical cinema and modern cinema). It is not that classical cinema achieved a representation of an external world, but in its strategic form it facilitated a mode of thinking driven by causal logic, chains of action that were threaded together, edits that bridged the relation between parts. In the postwar cinema, the paradigm has mutated; the potential of cinema is now to produce an image of time itself, of its constant becoming.

In Deleuze's work on the cinema, time and space are read through the prism of a philosophical tradition, where space is the conservative force and time the radical becoming. As Rodowick notes, 'We perceive in space, but we think in time' (1997: 124). Time is subordinated to space; space materializes time as measurement, quantity, thus space drags at the heels of time, roots it in calibration. Classical cinema, for Deleuze, reproduces this subordination in a particular way, by situating us within the motor-sensory schema of perception, where the action is constructed between space and protagonist as a continuum of sensation and movement. Modern cinema breaks from this in a liberation of what Deleuze regards as cinema's full potential, to perceive time itself. Modern cinema is suffused with a self-consciousness, subjectivity and fantasy, which move away from the commonsensical connections and representations of classical cinema. The relationship between images retains an importance here: as the causal chain of narrative events disappears in modern cinema, a gap opens, a void appears in the midst of the thinkable. Here cinema portends to the unthought, or brings us to an encounter with the limits of the thinkable. In such a way, cinema dislodges us from the known territory of clichéd comprehension and propels us into the outside of thought, where thought appears to itself.

In cinema's new form, exhaustion, wandering, drifting and aimlessness are the characteristic terms, yet, perhaps paradoxically, these are a force of life in that they suggest the question, how can one act, and what can one do? (Flaxman, 2000: 104). Deleuze names this the *bal(l)ade*, the translation of which doubles as both a story/journey and a type of movement that is staggering towards the unknown. The known constituents of the world, of time measured by the

clock, of travel cartographically organized, of a world set out as recognizable, are lost to this disjuncture, 'the cinema becoming, no
longer an undertaking of recognition [reconnaissance], but of
knowledge [connaisance], "a science of visual impressions, forcing
us to forget our own logic and retinal habitus"' (1985: 18–19). In
this wandering, the self is set in motion to experience images and
thought anew. This is a cinema of disintegration, of the 'intolerable'
and 'unbearable', yet Deleuze assures us, 'The important thing is
always that the character or the viewer, and the two together,
become visionaries' (p. 19). The visionary refuses what the cliché
suggests is interesting, and is open to perceiving something from the
outside, which may be 'to make holes, to introduce voids and white
spaces, to rarefy the image' (p. 21).

Yet when Deleuze is speaking about the action image of classical
cinema and the shift to the meandering movement of the *bal(l)ade*,
he is articulating the production of space through movement. One
might ask, why does space have to mean this for Deleuze? Why
does space have to submit to the significance of time when surely
the new energy of postwar European cinema, as he defines it, is a
conjunction of space-time? In the positing of time as the creative
force of cinema, as thought, and as the force that puts truth into
crisis, space becomes the conservative dimension of the pairing,
space as knowable, measured, empirical. Yet this in itself is to accept
the clichés of thinking about space: it represses the relationship of
space to energy and productivity. Unlike *A Thousand Plateaus*,
where Deleuze, with Guattari, writes space as a multidimensional
phenomenon produced through the figure of the nomad, the
cinema books clamp down on space. More suggestive for a cinema
of space-time produced through movement is the work of Michel
Serres, credited along with Bruno Latour as the originators of
actor-network theory.[6] For Serres, the division between space and
time is a convenience, and worse, a lazy form of thought. Their
reconnection, conversely, inconveniences the neatness of categories, revealing states of movement, process and a constant
recombining of elements as forms that resist conventional
classification. Of this division of space from time, Latour writes,
'We are not forced to choose forever between losing either the feel
of time or the structural features of the world. Processes are no

more in time than in space. Process is a third term' (1997: 172).

Process suggests instead that space can be thought as a product of movement, rather than a frame within which action takes place. Space, according to Serres (1994), is where a body travels, a weaving of elements that are multiple, unruly, ill-mannered. To travel in space is also to travel in thought, confusing the question of what the world is, with what can be known about the world. Epistemology cannot be separated from ontology. Latour's notion of process is significant for the analysis of film, for it shifts attention away from action towards movement as an emotional state. Serres extends this idea of process into the grammatical, identifying the redundancy of thinking with verbs, with actions and activities, suggesting rather that process draws attention to the movement between things, the prepositional terms that situate relations (Bingham and Thrift, 2000: 290). Within this paradigm, movement within space, or what Serres names the topological, describes the mobile relations between things. Of topology, Serres writes: 'To do this it employs the closed (*within*), the open (*out of*), intervals (*between*), orientation and directionality (*toward, in front of, behind*), proximity and adherence (*near, on, against, following, touching*), immersion (*among*), dimension . . . and so on, all realities outside of measurement but within relations' (1994: 71). The articulation of spatial relations in terms of prepositions facilitates a reading of how the particular energies in any context, or text, are operating. Space is not a container for action, but itself a landscape produced through the relational contracts of things. In terms of the analysis of film, this provides a terminology for articulating space as something other than setting, a static backdrop to events. It opens analysis on to an affectual understanding of filmic space.

The title of the Turkish film, *Uzak* (Nuri Bilge Ceylan, 2002), translates as 'distant'. Its thematic is signified in the title as a complex analysis of the relations of space. The opening scene of the film tracks the path of a man across a snow-covered rural landscape, a figure moving with difficulty across the terrain, the sound of his feet compacting the snow underfoot. He reaches a road and waits for a car to approach in order to hitch a ride. This is the pre-title sequence, which is followed by the interior of an apartment, in the foreground a figure of a man and in the background the outline of a woman.

They are undressing in separate parts of the room. The scenes are shot without dialogue. The sounds of the man's breathing and sighs gesture to a reticence. A wind chime sounds, bird song and a low drumming like a heating system. The building and the outside space have greater presence than the characters. Here, the contrasting sense of a man on a journey is set against a man largely static, moving with reserve, whose rasping breath creates a sense of difficulty.

Uzak is a film of an encounter of two individuals, cousins, one (Yusuf) from the country in search of work in the city of Istanbul, and the other (Mahmut) an established photographer living in the city. Yet the city is inhabited by Mahmut as a place not of possibility, but of withdrawal from its potential sites of contact. Here, energy is expended with great reluctance, channelled into ritual and routine of a quotidian life pared down to 'essential' practices: eating, sleeping, perfunctory sex, watching television, setting a mouse trap, work. The organization of life involves minimal contact with others and the utmost control of the environment. The way that space is produced is through well-honed practices, clichéd signatures of an individual who can no longer conceive of himself in the world as a purposeful individual. The production of inertia is created in this exercise of a body in space. Mahmut uses each room functionally. There are rules of how to use which toilet (there are two), where to smoke (the kitchen), how to relax (in the single chair in front of the television), how to move (avoiding the sticky mouse tape along the hall), how to work (the photographic studio along the corridor). The apartment is not the *mise en scène* which gives the film its affective dimension. The apartment is produced as bodies move through and in it, towards objects, enclosures, away from other bodies, its contours traced through a vectorization of space.

If Mahmut's actions are characterized by the preposition 'away from', Yusuf's actions are a movement towards, a drama of approach which is never allowed to develop into intimacy or arrival. Yusuf's movement through the city in search of work mirrors the relations set out in the apartment: the space of Istanbul is a landscape where energy is blocked and intimate contact an impossibility. The path of his journeys moves through the industrial area of the shipyard, yet there is little industry. A marooned ship lies on its side, tipped off balance, static. The shipyard where some activity is evident remains a place out of bounds. The city provides few openings, few spaces to inhabit. The offices he calls at in search of work barely allow him over the threshold, and it is only in a cheap bar that he finds a place to be. His preoccupation, other then finding work, is to have some contact with women, yet he remains an observer. He stands at the side of the road and watches them pass, he follows a woman into a park and observes her from behind a tree, he stands uncomfortably in the entrance of the apartment watching a cleaner. His movements towards an other are halted, arrested in the path of movement, so that he too becomes static, rigid, fixed at a distance.

Within the walls of the apartment, interior space is not intimate but the demarcation of territory, boundary, fixity. Whilst Yusuf is in search of intimacy, Mahmut creates demarcations to eliminate intimacy. His affair with a married woman is conducted in an apparently functional manner: he wipes bodily fluids from the bed cover, erasing traces of what has occurred, and a second encounter ends with the woman crying alone in the bathroom. The rhythms of daily life are monitored and controlled to avoid flux, accident, contingency. The arrival of the cousin breaks into this cycle, yet the encounter fails to break through. The other is required to enter this space and inhabit it in the same way, in a form of mimicry. This form of existence is almost a contagion, as the cousin's experience of the outside world mirrors that of life in the apartment. There are pathways, routes, practices that are reproduced but never offer an opening on to a state of energized activity. Space is produced as the travelled, the worn, the unaffectual journey of the everyday that signifies an ongoing inertia.

This is a film of unexplained drama, enacted in relation to things rather than people. Characterized by long takes and moments of tableau, the stillness at the heart of the film reverberates with the questions of still-life photography, of what can be 'read' into this moment. Photographer Philip DiCorcia describes the exigencies of the still tableau image, here a man looking into an opened refrigerator: 'The inexorable description of the static tableau is a psychological vice that tightens our attention on the unexplained drama. Looking at a man searching for a snack, we see a man confronting his failure and longings' (DiCorcia 1995: 5).

Watching Mahmut, we are forced to 'read his mind', to find all of the suggestive possibilities that could be the cause of such a distance from his own life. The camera's pausing on acts of seeming banality, observing with a meticulously steady eye, provokes this search for reasons, to fill the gaps in the void of explanation. If explanation is not forthcoming, it is possibly due to the lush tableau that characterizes most shots, a detailed frame of coloured interiors that distracts from the narrative exegesis. It seems that we are witness to something like still-life painting as well as the photographic image. Yet, the tableau in film is, as Deleuze notes, set apart from the still-life photograph: 'At the point where the cinematographic image most directly confronts the photo, it also becomes most radically distinct from it' (1985: 17). Where photography posits not a stillness but an instant extracted from the flow of time, the stillness of film creates a tension in the discomfort of a lack of movement, of *durée* held in frozen form yet still breathing. It suggests, at the edges of this moment, the possibility that time passes yet nothing has changed. It gestures to an internal world that remains out of sight, unknowable, unreadable. Mahmut pauses at the window to look at the snow-filled cityscape, the stillness of the external world a mirror of his own immobility.

If the thematic of inertia is foregrounded in the pace of the film itself, in scenes of staged stillness, it is a theme extended within the film in relation to photography. Mahmut's inertia, his profound disaffection for the world, is manifest in his working life as a photographer. In an early scene in the film, we witness him mechanically shooting boards in his studio, supposedly the space constructed for creative endeavour. We see him in conversation with a group of middle-aged male friends decrying the usefulness of the medium. Disaffection is played out more poignantly when he embarks on a shoot that takes him outside of the space of the city, reluctantly taking his cousin as an assistant. The job is executed with little attention to the process other than utter functionality, but on the return journey, Mahmut pauses the car in a landscape that momentarily, or potentially, inspires him. The scene is a rural landscape with a sun low in the sky. The car stops, pauses, the scene literally arrests Mahmut, bursts into his interiority momentarily as an affectual experience. He stops or is stopped in this place, yet as he looks the energy drains away, despite the cousin's offer to set up the equipment, and he drives on. In this scene, the potential of photography to grasp the moment, its history as a medium able to select the significant detail in the flow of time and 'capture' that experience, is a belief without substance. Photography, it appears, has failed expectation. And in the slow pace of the film, the question of utility, of purpose, of what film can offer, is a question residing at the edges of a larger disappointment.

The medium of film does not escape the question of purpose presented most squarely in relation to photography, a dilemma posed in terms of its ability to affect. Film is also a metatext in *Uzak*, a medium present in the domestic interior as the possibility of a shared culture. In a scene where the two men sit in front of the television screen, the film they are watching is clearly Tarkovsky's *Stalker*, a film devoted to the question of what desire is and whether it is attainable. In the extract viewed, the characters travel from the 'real' world towards the unknown zone of desire, into a landscape utterly alien and full of traps. In this interval of domestic proximity, as the two men watch, the pace of *Stalker* is unbearably slow; a train carriage rhythmically propels the characters along a track for what seems like an eternity. The length of the scene and the pace of *Stalker* reproduce the energy of *Uzak*. The two men watch, uncomfortable in each other's presence and visibly bored, but with a boredom that cannot be sustained and transformed into a creative enterprise. The search to locate desire, to arrive at a place of actively wanting, is a journey not worth taking. Yusuf retires to bed, and Mahmut changes the screen to pornography, a genre most renowned for its scripted and predictable sequences. In contrast to the premise of *Stalker*, that desire is to be discovered, the choice of pornography suggests that desire can only be figured as the already known. Boredom as the possible opening on to a state of distraction, or the chance openings of contingency, is eradicated. The presence of the cousin is the only contingent factor burst into the world of Mahmut, and he does his utmost to contain any form of affect on himself.

What animates us is a question that resonates here. Yet the response might be to reframe the question: what is it that becomes animated? Is it the space itself, produced through the arrangement of objects, that is as animated as any individual? In a scene that blurs the states of dreaming and waking life, the character of Mahmut reclines in his chair in front of the television screen. Yet it is not the screen that takes on life, or the individual character, but the lamp in the corner of the room. Shot from the point of view of the character, the lamp tilts forward, towards, and elegantly falls to the ground in slow frame sequence. Objects, in addition to humans, have a life-force, and here the life-force of the object throws into relief the fixed existence of the individual. It is a moment in which the stasis of character, the profound inertia of his existence, is fundamentally challenged. The world around him is alive, approaches him, moves towards him, and yet he is fixed, seated, sedated. This is a moment in which animation becomes a magical element. Yet there is something of a different order afoot in *Uzak*.

In the everyday banality that the film appears to register, and that the character manufactures meticulously, the opposite effect of 'banality' is achieved. The rituals of smoking in a demarcated area, viewing television in the solitary chair, the ordering of shelves of music, the signs of a supposedly temperate life are over-invested. Where routine produces what Deleuze calls the sensory-motor schema (a type of automatic response), we are prevented from 'seeing', we are merely acting in the world that we presume to be there in the way that we wish it to be. The project of *Uzak* is the conflict between the investment in the supposed 'comfort' of familiar perceptions and an acknowledged breakdown of this structure. The slightest change to his world (the arrival of the cousin, the presence of a mouse), produces a disequilibrium, a disturbance. In the scene with the lamp there is perhaps a pivot in perception, whereby the quotidian takes on a quality of its own, and the *mise en scène* breaks into optical images and sounds. The object world of the *mise en scène* has become unfamiliar. This moment in which the object moves, and moves out of place in the over-organized space of the apartment, is the moment in which 'seeing' becomes a question.

With the earth's gravitational pull

If the concerns of early forms of photographic experiment were to capture the movement of a body, to deploy the mechanical apparatus in order to understand the body's mobility, it is a desire that inspired a fascination with film as a moving image. And yet movement, within the discourses of film theory, becomes fixated with time, most clearly demonstrated in Deleuze's two-part analysis of film as a movement image and a time image. Film appears to puncture a hole in the fabric of sealed uniform time, in its ability to sculpt, to craft the temporal by cutting it up, stretching it, rearranging its components in any which way. Yet such a fixation with time neglects the second axis of space, or rather, has reproduced space as the inert backdrop against which a body moves. Film theory has been culpable in its replay of this perspective, wielding space as the setting for action, or as the representation of an existing material world. Within these terms, space becomes representations of a city, a nation or a culture, against which human figures move. Space attaches film to the real whilst time detaches it from the empiricism of the material world, or so the legacy of film theory would lead us to believe.

Yet space, perhaps more than time or certainly equal to it, allows us to conceive of the body in motion, and not simply as movement but as an entity through which differential forms of energy flow. In the examples of films in this chapter, these are particular bodies operating in and producing particular spaces. This is not 'Palestine' or 'Istanbul' as knowable, mapped terrain, but the experience of the possibilities and constraints of space. There is no stabilizing shot of a city, an overview to reassure that vision is indeed knowledge. Rather we move blindly, from frame to frame, from sequence to sequence, in a searching attempt to locate where expenditure of energy may occur or to recognize its limited confines and blockages. Film here is more a science of the inequities of the particular than a complete journey, the joins of each shot setting sequences of movement in relation to each other. It is worth paying attention to the grammar that film utilizes here, a grammar quite removed from the verb, more fittingly the prepositional: the description of a sequence in relation to another sequence. The prepositions of *Divine Intervention* suggest to us an endless 'and', the layering of more sequences of the same, whilst the prepositions of *Uzak* propose the tensions of away and towards. These are the specific languages of a particular energy that film, perhaps more than other media, is able to convey.

The particular grammar of these films is not representative of 'contemporary film', but rather, it is an instance in which an understanding of energy and movement is opened out to reveal differential states. If there is a broader claim to be made, it resides in the comparison with previous conceptualizations of energy, historically embedded in concerns with productivity. If I have suggested that the filmic texts cited here are concerned with unproductive expenditure, the paradigm of productivity is of a different order from that of earlier theoretical usages. The concept of unproductive expenditure emerges in the work of Bataille, writing in the mid-twentieth century, furiously scribing the antidote to capital's utilitarian demand to be productive. The sacred, writes Bataille, is the use made of productivity's excess, the cause of disturbances, changes of structure, rents in the fabric of reason. For Bataille, the split between the useful and the useless, the sacred and profane, the necessary and the superfluous, is a division worth reversing, up-ending to topple the system of rationalized production. In a similar vein, early film scholars grappled with a reversal of concentration and distraction, boredom and animation, in relation to cinema. In a discursive turn that pivoted on oppositional concepts, it required us to question whether cinema is a mechanical culture of reproduction, structuring leisure time outside of productivity and softening the human-mechanical interface, or whether cinema is a spanner in the works, as it were, of the general utilitarian vision, a portal into the realm of the unthinkable. Early cinema played these oppositions through the body and the unnerving energy of machines, the machines of cinema and the mechanical world: bodies were summoned and disappeared, tied up and undone, flattened and resuscitated.

In contemporary film, the body and the machine no longer stand in opposition. In what appears to have been for Bataille an unforeseeable turn, capital has appropriated the discourse of excess, and the machine has largely disappeared from view, relocated out of sight. The body now moves against invisible forces, the energies of capital that have become virtual. 'When we navigate our way through the world, there are different pulls, constraints and freedoms that move us forward and propel us into life. But in the changing face of capitalism, media information and technologies – which circulate the globe in more virtual and less obvious ways – how do the constraints on freedom involve our affective and embodied dimensions of experience?' (Zournazi, 2003: 1). Film goes some way to exploring the affective dimensions of experience. Capital, like gravity, pulls at bodies, weighs them down or enables their propulsion. Capital, in this present moment, seeks to assure us that its products provide intensity, compulsion, propulsion, the ever-ascending rise to stronger feeling and greater vitality. What remains invisible in the discourses of capital are the pockets of other affectual and economic states, delinked from the flows of circulation and energized states of being. These are the conditions in which walking feels more like falling and where standing still may be a useful compromise.

These questions of mobility, energy and space provoked by the film texts are, of course, equally prescient for the spectator. In each of the films discussed here there are moments in which characters are observed witnessing events. At the close of *Divine Intervention*, the main character and his mother sit watching a pressure cooker steam menacingly. In *Uzak*, the characters sit silently in front of a range of moving images on the television screen. These moments mimic our own activity in viewing, throwing back in parodic fashion the question of who is mobile and who gets to act. Is film viewing an activity or another state of inertia is a question we are taunted with in film studies. And yet states of inertia are also the conditions in which perception becomes enhanced, as both compelled and detached. This strange relation is one of film's most potent affects, a relation of encounter and distance, an exposure that leaves an imprint and a sense of absence. This may be how film involves 'our affective and embodied dimensions of experience', not as a question of 'active' or 'passive' response, but the ability to discern various conditions of energy. In this there is continuity of tradition, for film has always rendered legible the secret life of things.

Notes

Introduction

1   Vertigo in the field is addressed in recent editions of journals: for example, *Screen* (2004) vol. 45, no. 2, and *Cinema Journal* (2004) vol. 43, no. 3. That this sense of crisis may not be shared across different regions is apparent in *Wasafari* (2004) special issue, vol. 43. The editorial announces, 'counter to critical orthodoxy', that international cinema (largely non-western film) is increasingly characterized by complexity, aesthetic experimentation and socio-political engagement.

2   The term 'singularity' is used by Doane, and in this text, to describe an exception rather than specificity. Jean-Luc Nancy (2004: 41) provides a succinct definition: 'What is a singularity? It is that which occurs only once, at a single point (out of time and out of place, in short), that which is an exception. Not a particular, which comes to belong to a genre, but a unique property that escapes appropriation – an exclusive touch – and that, as such, is neither extracted or removed from, nor opposed to, a common ground'. See also the definition of affect in Chapter 5.

Chapter 1   One hundred years of film theory

1   André Bazin's self-description as a journalist rather than a theorist is a case in point.

2   Sam Rohdie takes issue with the 'narrow' appropriation of other histories by film history: 'In film histories, the intersection of other histories are refashioned to become subordinate to the history of cinema. For example, the significance of Marey becomes nothing more than a precursor to the Lumières, which belittles an achievement and impoverishes the history of the cinema' (2001: 31).

3   In addition to Flaxman and Rodowick, recent scholarship on Deleuze includes Ronald Bogue, *Deleuze on Cinema* (2003), Claire Colebrook, *Gilles Deleuze* (2002), Barbara M. Kennedy, *Deleuze and Cinema: the aesthetics of sensation* (2002) Patricia Pisters, *The Matrix of Visual Culture: working with Deleuze in film theory* (2003), and Steven Shaviro *The cinematic Body* (1993).

4   See Marcus A. Doel, 'Un-gluncking geography: spatial science after Dr Seuss and Gilles Deleuze' (2000) for an entertaining tour of Deleuze's geophilosophy.

5   This term is used by David Rodowick in *Gilles Deleuze's Time Machine* (1997), a reference to and play on Benjamin's 'Short history of photography' (1980).

6   Periodization is an effect of the cinema books rather than a framework. For a discussion of this, see Alain Ménil, 'The time(s) of the cinema' (1999).

7   In a discussion of Deleuze's relation to history, Rodowick comments, 'one can also trace the emergence of a kind of "postmodern" mentality – the faltering belief in totality, either from the point of view of the grand "organic" ideologies (universal democracy or socialism), or from a belief in the image as anything other than a partial and contingent description of reality' (1997: 75). Indeed, some of the passages in *The Time-Image* are imbued with a pathos for this faltering belief: for example, when Deleuze asks, 'how does cinema restore our belief in the world?' (1985: 181–2).

8   The scene recalls Spinoza's assertion, that we do not yet know what a body can do: that is, the intelligibility of a thing (human or otherwise) is determined not by an essence or a history of what it has been, but in its emergence.

9   The cinema books lend themselves to a type of toolkit enterprise where concepts may be selected and deployed at will, yet the accumulative structure of the books makes this possibility difficult to enact. This type of reading is more successfully invited by *A Thousand Plateaus* (Deleuze and Guattari, 1980), where the reader is encouraged to enter the book at any point, to approach it as a manual, an index to ideas to be accessed in any way whatever.

Chapter 2   Hollywood's last decade

1   Gaines argues that the contradictory pull of the terms 'dream/factory' produces a historical faultline in film which is identifiable as far back as the 1920s, when product placement was an overt irritation, and 'the commodity stuffed screen was in danger of being seen by spectators as "just advertising"' (2000: 101).

2   The melodramatic structure of *Blue Velvet* and the 'star' quality of the lead characters in *Wild at Heart* refer us back to this earlier filmic era. The performance of miming to period songs appears in these films, as well as *Mulholland Drive*, as a type of excessive homage to melodrama. For an extensive exploration of melodrama and performance, see Jan Campbell, *Film and Cinema Spectatorship: melodrama and mimesis* (2005).

3   The particular discussion is of Eisenstein's flirtation with Hollywood, and his notion of a radical animation that would reveal, for example, in the human-animal relation, that 'these animals live in us as our past – as species and as embryo – though also as our unfurled possibilities' (Leslie, 2002: 243).

4   Jameson's famous essay extracted from this book uses the rather odd example of *Bodyheat*, and the remake of *The Postman Always Rings Twice*.

5   In terms of expanding archives, a recent industry accession has been the appropriation of the copyright of dead celebrities. The facility to recompose and reanimate digitally, literally to bring back to life in digital film mode, opens the future to another historical schism, where old stars appear in new contexts. Among the most highly valued are Elvis Presley, Marilyn Monroe, James Dean, John Wayne and Fred Astaire. CMG Worldwide is at the head of the licensing field, whilst Corbis, owned by Bill Gates, is set to enter the market.

6 *Archive Fever* (1995) is another manifestation of Derrida's thesis on a paradoxical impulse to move towards and away from death. Derrida draws on Freud in *Beyond the Pleasure Principle*, where 'life' is to be understood as the number of detours that an organism takes on its way to its destination and goal, which is death. Partial drives guard the journey and storm ahead, whilst others delay, detract from the project by returning to repeat life over again.

7 Christopher Williams provides a history of how the concept 'classical Hollywood cinema' appears and travels through the work of Bordwell, observing that this formulation is replayed obsessively with little conceptual development. A taste of his appraisal reads: 'By the time of the 1993 edition of *Film Art*, chapter three has been rejigged. After an interesting new section called "Narration the flow of story information" (pp. 75–81), there follows a further new section, "Narrative conventions" (p. 81), the second subheading of which, on the very next page, turns out to be – "The Classic Hollywood Cinema", much the same as it was in 1979, apart from one new paragraph about objectivity' (Williams, 2000: 212–13).

8 This metaphor of following rather than orchestrating echoes across the practice of film-making: for example, in the methods of Kiarostami and Figgis.

Chapter 3   Assemblage: editing space-time

1 The theme of insomnia as an ongoing response to the political situation in the first part of the twentieth century is explored by Jani Scandura. In 'Cinematic insomnia' (2004: 104) she writes, 'For sleeplessness seems a survivor's tactic, a model of and impetus for artistic and intellectual work that becomes visible only belatedly, *in* the wake and *at* the wake of a modernity gone awry – a modernity that is anxious, hunted, on perpetual red alert and that is, simultaneously, haunted by the reign of Fascist spectacle, by the irrational dream world put to totalitarian use.'

2 On the question of cinematic scale and its relationship to the study of biological forms, see Hannah Landecker, 'Cellular features: microcinematography and film theory' (2005). Her argument suggests that the scientific study of minute life-forms influenced early film-makers and theoreticians: 'From Jean Epstein's book *Magnification* to Béla Baláz's

notion of the close-up, one can read what seems a fanciful metaphorical connection between seeing life at a microscopic level and seeing through a camera' (p. 903). Landecker states that biology was not simply the provider of metaphorical associations, but that scientific films themselves resonated in other spheres of thought.

3 The case made by Ropars includes sound as a dimension that creates further instability and rupture between the figurative image and the linguistic network (Rodowick, 2001: 91).

4 Eisenstein's plans for the adaptation are set out in 'Notes for a film', 1928 (Kepley, 1997: 43).

5 For an enlightening reading of Eisenstein's relations with Disney and Hollywood, see Esther Leslie *Hollywood Flatlands: animation, critical theory and the avant-garde* (2002).

6 Kahn points out that Vertov in fact trained in sound and that this remained his primary passion. Frustrated by the technology of the time, Vertov turned to film as a secondary medium: 'he spoke of his transition to film in terms of the inadequacy of phonographic technology . . . Since determinations of sound quality usually prove to be creatures of the historical moment, not of some timeless measure of sonic realism, it is likely that other limitations of acoustic phonographs, primarily the difficulty of manipulating the inscribed sound materially, sent him packing into the kino-eye' (1999: 140).

7 Bazin writes retrospectively of the effect of sound, confirming Eisenstein's fears: 'It is understandable, as a matter of fact, that the sound image, far less flexible than the visual image, would carry montage in the direction of realism, increasingly eliminating both plastic impressionism and the symbolic relation between images' (Bazin, 1967, vol. 1: 33).

8 It is interesting to recall here Gunning's (1991a) observation about the prevalence of telephones in early film: as a 'new' technology, the telephone and telegraph connected across space. Telephones appear in early film to link disparate locations in real time, and become an icon of connectivity. Continuity between spaces is assured in featuring this technology, allowing a manoeuvrability between locations and an assertion of a standard time. This figuring of 'new' technology, as assurance and connectivity, I would argue, no longer holds for contemporary film. Technology, having failed to become the assurance of communication, clarity and connectivity that it was once invested

with, is distrusted. Editing, as assemblage, functions within the same framework as the computer terminal, with its ability to bring together unrelated, obscure, distant information.

9 Michael Haneke, born in Munich, is known as an Austrian film-maker.

10 Haneke (1992: 89) has commented on distance and proximity: 'My films are intended as polemical statements against the American "barrel down" cinema and its disempowerment of the spectator. They are an appeal for a cinema of insistent questions instead of false (because too quick) answers, for clarifying distance in place of violating closeness, for provocation and dialogue instead of consumption and consensus.'

11 The currency of this concept of editing as relational is not contemporary in film theory or practice. Kracauer, for example, touts the widely known example by Kuleshov: 'That [a] reduction of meanings falls to editing was demonstrated by Kuleshov in the experiment he conducted together with Pudovkin. In order to prove the impact of editing on the significance of shots, he inserted one and the same shot of Musjuhin's otherwise noncommittal face in different story contexts; the result was that the actor's face appeared to express grief on a sad occasion and smiling satisfaction in a pleasant environment' (Kracauer, 1960: 69).

12 Haneke uses this tactic more forcefully still in the opening sequence of *The Piano Teacher* (2001). The sublime sounds of a piano being played are radically cut to the silent, black screen of the film titles, then returning to the music. The effect is to prefigure the theme of sadism which is at the centre of the film.

13 Miller remixed *Birth of a Nation* at the London Imax cinema, September 2005.

Chapter 4   The limits of translation: transnational film

1 The aesthetic of Wong Kar-wai's films has been compared to the geographically slippery, referent-less global image culture of MTV. Yet the heterotopic sensibility of *Chungking Express* is less a mimicry of contemporary image-flows, and more a disorientation that operates across time and space. If, in the film, time is stretched and contracted to produce chronological disorientation, the spatial experiences a similar treatment. Space suffers a lack of correspondence between parts,

surfaces and routes, dissolving into pockets that are not stitched into a larger fabric.

2 The transitional role that objects seem to play is reminiscent of Winnicott's work on the object as a primary playing out of separation and difference between mother and child.

3 This quote is taken from Derrida's recorded conversation with Bernard Stiegler (transcribed and published in 1996 and translated into English in 2002) on teletechnologies and their effect on the philosophical and political moment, in which he draws on many of the foundational ideas in his body of work.

4 The connections between national and ethnic foreignness and the foreignness experienced in the context of love are explored again by Wong Kar-wai in the film *Happy Together* (1997). Here, a gay relationship between two men from Hong Kong is set in Buenos Aires. The foreignness of the territory reverberates the tensions of the relationship: the context is at times a fantasy of happiness (the imagined trip to the Iguazu Falls, for example), and at others an experience of isolation and outsiderness (the street scenes outside of the bar). The location is a space of desire in all of its manifestations of expectation, frustration and disappointment.

5 Dissanayake's illustrations in this article are from Bollywood film, but his more central thesis is that the 'complex and multifaceted relationship between the global and the local is most vividly represented in cinema' (2004: 145).

6 *Chungking Express* was made in down-time, hurriedly in two months between shooting the epic *Ashes of Time*.

7 Heterotopia, as the compatibility of incompatible or dissonant parts, is explored conversely (in terms of *Chungking Express*, where LA is a coherent other and Hong Kong is the heterotopia) in relation to LA in Charles Jencks, *Los Angeles, the Riots and the Strange Beauty of Hetero-Architecture* (1993), and Edward W. Soja, *Thirdspace: journeys to Los Angeles and other real and imagined places* (1996).

8 The significance of rehearsals is played out most fully in *In the Mood for Love* (2002), in which the main characters rehearse lines to each other in preparation for an encounter between the female protagonist and her husband. Yet the main rehearsal in the film is the performance of a relationship between these characters.

9 That flight tempts us to believe that we have escaped not only gravity

but the demarcations of territory is noted by Nitvin Govil in an essay on in-flight entertainment and the back-of-the-seat screen. In a description of the flight map's representation of space, Govil comments: 'The affective reassurance of the moving map and the construction of a world cleansed of geopolitical borders is part of the airplane's historical role in modern cartographic technology' (2004: 247). In flying, he argues, we are encouraged to imagine moving across landscape (nature) but not territory (culture); 'to fly is to travel unencumbered by the details of national borders, territorial demarcations, political entities.'

10 For further discussion of foreignness in East Asian film, see Chris Berry, 'Ballad or bazooka: tropical maladies and iron pussies' (2005) and Kent Jones, 'Here and there: the films of Tsai Ming Liang' (2003).

Chapter 5   Innocent monsters: film and other media

1 The movement of film from the cinema into the gallery creates different questions of the medium's object hood, explored here by Gordon. The fact that the 24-hour version of *Psycho* prevents us from viewing the film in its totality (with the exception of special night-long screenings), the fragment of the film available to view suggests that a complete film exists in our absence. Thus, film's status as an object independent of a human gaze is part of the work's accomplishment. The suggestiveness of *24-hour Psycho* is that film exists as a thing in its own right, as it were, displacing the centrality of human agency.

2 Deleuze approaches the distinction between information and cinema towards the end of *The Time-Image*, arguing that the belief in access to information as empowering, or even liberating, is a fallacy. 'Syberberg's powerful idea is that no information, whatever it might be, is sufficient to defeat Hitler. All the documents could be shown, all the testimonies could be heard, but in vain: what makes information all-powerful (the newspapers, and then the radio, and then the television), is its very nullity, its radical ineffectiveness' (1985: 268).

3 See Beck, Giddens and Lash (1994).

4 This anxiety about the constructedness of reality television appears, for example, in discussions about participants' levels of performance for the camera, and in debates about how far the programme makers can

manipulate participants. Such discussions appear in websites about the programme, and more generally in journalistic coverage.

5 Hitchcock's work alone has inspired John Baldessari's *Tetral Series* (1994) which incorporates scenes from *North by Northwest*, David Reed's replay of *Vertigo* in *Scottie's Bedroom* (1994), Pierre Huyghe's use of *Rear Window* in *Remake* (1995), and Stan Douglas's reworking of *Marnie* in *Subject to a Film: Marnie* (1989).

6 The unexpected encounter with film echoes Victor Burgin's involuntary memory of *The Canterbury Tales* whilst on a train journey. Film arises out of the blue, as it were, in Burgin's account an internal process, here an external screen, but both an affect of film's sudden imposition (see Burgin, 2004).

7 On acts of witnessing and the establishment of 'facts', see Bruno Latour's reading of the invention of witnessing as scientific method, in the practice of natural philosopher Robert Boyle in the mid-seventeenth century. Latour writes, 'Instead of seeking to ground his work in logic, mathematics or rhetoric, Boyle relied on a parajuridical metaphor: credible, trustworthy, well-to-do witnesses gathered at the scene of the action can attest to the existence of a fact, the matter of fact, even if they do not know its true nature' (Latour, 1993: 18).

8 For an extensive treatment of the relations between film and architecture, see Anthony Vidler, *Warped Space: art, architecture and anxiety in modern culture* (2001). Vidler writes 'Of all the arts . . . it is architecture that has had the most privileged and difficult relation to film. An obvious role model for spatial experimentation, film has also been criticized for its deleterious effects on the architectural image' (2001: 100).

9 Implicit to Bruno's argument is the work of Walter Benjamin in *The Arcades Project*, where the relation between the *flâneur* and the cinema spectator is conceived as a distracted experience. But where Benjamin emphasized the relation of architecture, image culture and walking as dreamwork, Bruno develops the concept of a haptic relation.

10 If we wish to take account of Douglas's interpretation of the loop, he states in an interview: 'Even when you're seeing the same film loop again and again your perception of it changes, because you have changed even though it has remained the same. It's like listening to recorded polyphonic music: on a second listening, you can hear things that you missed the first time around' (1998: 19).

11 See Jacques Rancière's analysis of Godard's project in 'A fable without a moral: Godard, cinema, (h)istories', in *Film Fables* (2001).

12 Cubitt traces the relations between modernist classification and the origins of the computer systems of data storage and retrieval: 'Parallel with the demands of bureaucracy, the accumulation of knowledge in books began to demand a radical overhaul of library design. The introduction of classified catalogues led directly to the first designs in the 1930s for taxonomies based on semantic principles, origin of the familiar key-word search' (2002: 7).

13 Kracauer's conceptualization of film posits certain affinities that remain constant over time. Yet, in *Theory of Film*, written over a period of fifteen years, there is a sense of the gradual shift in affinities according to the historical context in which they are located. Kracauer may also be read, then, as working a situated notion of film's affinities.

14 For an elaboration of the significance of a logic of addition in critical thought, see Bruno Latour 'Why has critique run out of steam?' (2004).

Chapter 6   Inertia: on energy and film

1 The consequent cross-fertilization of art and the represented body appears some years later in Duchamp's *Nude Descending a Staircase*, which might have taken Marey's graphs as its primary material rather than a body.

2 Marey's image of the body as series of lights also draws on the magical effects of electricity, the ability to illuminate as both a practical effect in households and cities, and simultaneously the 'fact' of illumination as a metaphorical opening up to knowledge.

3 Jani Scandura, in an essay entitled 'Cinematic insomnia' (2004), argues that the anxiety of the effects of cinema on un/conscious life is the concern not only of critical thinkers, but also of official institutions. In her account of research conducted in the USA between 1929 and 1932, the Payne Foundation financed the study of the effects of cinema on the behaviour and health of children, which itself threaded together concerns with sleep, restfulness and productivity. Part of the research focused on the sleep patterns of children, half of whom were taken to the cinema every evening, half of whom saw no films. The children who watched films were observed to be restless at night, either in their waking or sleeping states, their productive states com-

promised. Here the anxieties of a modernist demand for productivity are played out in the clearest empirical light.

4   The death of the elephant was deemed a necessary act as the animal had killed three people. Again, the fascination with immediacy as energy is evidenced in the form of execution; the passing of electrical currents through the body of the animal.

5   As Gregory Flaxman notes, the cinema books received uneven treatment. In France, the reading public was prepared for Deleuze's work, a context where the philosopher was known as a cinephile producing a lengthy reflection on film. The books emerged out of the intellectual climate in which structuralism and psychoanalytic models were losing explicatory power. In Anglo-American contexts, the books met with a greater scepticism about Deleuze himself (a philosopher taking on cinema) and the vast sweep of the project. Part of the controversy surrounding the cinema books and their 'place' in film theory has been generated by a debate on the merits of early translations. The English translations are 'notorious for botched film titles, fumbled footnotes, and even an occasionally distorted plotline' (Flaxman, 2000: 2).

6   Bruno Latour is credited with being the disciple of Michel Serres and the disseminator of his ideas. For an introduction to their work, see Bingham and Thrift (2000). Citing Donald Wesling, they concur that 'Serres' many conceptual inventions . . . must now seem secondary to his invention of Bruno Latour' (p. 296).

References

Abbas, Ackbar (1997) 'The erotics of disappointment', in Martinez Lalanne and Ngai Abbas (eds), *Wong Kar-wai*, Paris: Disvoir.

Agamben, Giorgio (2002) 'Difference and repetition: on Guy Debord's films', in Tom McDonough (ed.), *Guy Debord and the Situationist International: texts and documents*, Cambridge, Mass. and London: *October* with MIT Press.

Anderson, Perry (2004) 'Renewals', *New Left Review*, second series, vol. 1.

Andrew, Dudley (1984) *Film in the Aura of Art*, Princeton: Princeton University Press.

Augé, Marc (1992/1995) *Non-places: introduction to an anthropology of supermodernity*, translated by John Howe, London and New York: Verso.

Balázs, Béla (1952) *Theory of the Film: character and growth of a new art*, translated by Edith Bone, London: Dennis Dobson.

Batailles, Georges (2001) 'The method of meditation', in *The Unfinished System of Nonknowledge*, edited by Stuart Kendall, translated by Michelle Kendall and Stuart Kendall, Minneapolis: University of Minnesota Press.

Bazin, André (1967) *What is Cinema?* vol. 1, translated and edited by Hugh Gray, Berkeley: University of California Press.

Bazin, André (1971) *What is Cinema?* vol. 2, translated and edited by Hugh Gray, Berkeley: University of California Press.

Beck, Ulrich, Giddens, Anthony and Lash, Scott (1994) *Reflexive Modernization*, Cambridge: Polity.

Benjamin, Walter (1955/1999) *Illuminations*, translated by Harry Zorn, London: Pimlico.

Benjamin, Walter (1972/2002) *The Arcades Project*, translated by Howard Eiland and Kevin McLaughlin, Cambridge, Mass. and London: Belknap Press of Harvard University Press.

Benjamin, Walter (1980) 'A short history of photography', in Alan Trachtenberg (ed.), *Classic Essays on Photography*, translated by P. Patton, New Haven: Leete's Island Books.

Bergson, Henri (1889/1919) *Time and Free Will*, translated by F. L. Pogson, New York: Macmillan.

Bergson, Henri (1896/1991) *Matter and Memory*, translated by Nancy Margaret Paul and W. Scott Palmer, New York: Zone.

Bergson, Henri (1907/1911) *Creative Evolution*, translated by Arthur Mitchell, New York: Henry Holt.

Berry, Chris (2005) 'Ballad or bazooka: tropical maladies and iron pussies', *Cinemaya: Asian Film Quarterly*, vols 18/19, pp. 63–4.

Beugnet, Martine (2004) *Claire Denis*, Manchester and New York: Manchester University Press.

Bingham, Nick and Thrift, Nigel (2000) 'Some new instructions for travellers: the geography of Bruno Latour and Michel Serres', in Mike Crang and Nigel Thrift (eds), *Thinking Space*, London and New York: Routledge.

Bogue, Ronald (2003) *Deleuze on Cinema*, London and New York: Routledge.

Bordwell, David (1989) *Making Meaning: Inference and Rhetoric in the Interpretation of Cinema*, Cambridge, Mass.: Harvard University Press.

Bordwell, David and Carroll, Noel (eds) (1996) *Post-theory: reconstructing film studies*, Madison: University of Wisconsin Press.

Bordwell, David and Thompson, Kristin (1993) *Film Art: an introduction*, 5th edition, New York: McGraw-Hill.

Bordwell, David, Staiger, Janet and Thompson, Kristin (1985) *The Classical Hollywood Cinema: film style and mode of production to 1960*, London: Routledge.

Bourriaud, Nicolas (1998/2002) *Relational Aesthetics*, translated by Simon

Pleasance and Fronza Woods with Mathieu Copeland, Dijon: Presses du réel.

Bourriaud, Nicolas (2000/2005) *Postproduction: culture as screenplay – how art reprograms the world*, translated by Jeanine Herman, New York: Lukas and Sternberg.

Brown, Bill (ed.) (2004) *Things*, Chicago and London: University of Chicago Press.

Brunette, Peter (2005) *Wong Kar-wai*, Urbana and Chicago: University of Illinois Press.

Bruno, Giuliana (2002) *Atlas of Emotion: journeys in art, architecture, and film*, London: Verso.

Bruzzi, Stella (2000) *New Documentary: a critical introduction*, London and New York: Routledge.

Burgin, Victor (2004) *The Remembered Film*, London: Reaktion.

Campbell, Jan (2005) *Film and Cinema Spectatorship: melodrama and mimesis*, Cambridge: Polity.

Casetti, Francesco (1999) *Theories of Cinema 1945–1990*, translated by Francesca Chiostri and Elizabeth Gard Bartolini-Salimboni with Thomas Kelso, Austin, Texas: University of Texas Press.

Cavell, Stanley (1981) *Pursuits of Happiness: Hollywood's comedies of remarriage*, Cambridge, Mass.: Harvard University Press.

Chanan, Michael (1980) *The Dream that Kicks: the prehistory and early years of cinema in Britain*, London: Routledge and Kegan Paul.

Charney, Leo (1998) *Empty Moments: cinema, modernity and drift*, Durham, NC: Duke University Press.

Chion, Michel (1990/1994) *Audio-Vision: sound on screen*, translated and edited by Claudia Gorbman New York: Columbia University Press.

Chow, Rey (1995) *Primitive Passions: visibility, ethnography and contemporary Chinese cinema*, New York: Columbia University Press.

Clifford, James (1989) 'Notes on theory and travel', *Inscriptions*, vol. 5, pp. 177–88.

Colebrook, Claire (2002) *Gilles Deleuze*, London and New York: Routledge.

Coombe, Rosemary J. (1998) *The Cultural Life of Intellectual Properties: authorship, appropriation and the law*, Durham and London: Duke University Press.

Crary, Jonathan (1991) *Techniques of the Observer: on vision and modernity in the nineteenth century*, Cambridge, Mass.: MIT Press.

Crary, Jonathan (1999) *Suspensions of Perception: attention, spectacle, and modern culture*, Cambridge, Mass.: MIT Press.

Cubitt, Sean (2002) 'Spreadsheets, sitemaps and search engines: why narrative is marginal to multimedia and networked communication, and why marginality is more vital than universality', in Martin Rieser and Andrea Zapp (eds), *New Screen Media: cinema/art/narrative*, London: BFI.

Cubitt, Sean (2004) *The Cinema Effect*, Cambridge, Mass. and London: MIT Press.

Debord, Guy (1978/2003) 'Howls for Sade', in *Guy Debord: complete cinematic works: scripts, stills, documents*, translated and edited by Ken Knabb, Oakland and Edinburgh: AK Press.

De Landa, Manuel (1999) 'Immanence and transcendence in the genesis of form', in Ian Buchanan (ed.), *A Deleuzian Century?*, Durham and London: Duke University Press.

De Landa, Manuel (2000) *A Thousand Years of Nonlinear History*, New York: Swerve Editions.

Deleuze, Gilles (1983/1986) *Cinema 1: the movement-image*, translated by Hugh Tomlinson and Barbara Habberjam, Minneapolis: University of Minnesota Press.

Deleuze, Gilles (1985/1989) *Cinema 2: the time-image*, translated by Hugh Tomlinson and Robert Galeta, Minneapolis: University of Minnesota Press.

Deleuze, Giles and Guattari, Felix (1972/1983) *Anti-Oedipus: capitalism and schizophrenia*, vol. 1, translated by Robert Hurley et al., Minneapolis: University of Minnesota Press.

Deleuze, Gilles and Guattari, Felix (1980/1987) *A Thousand Plateaus: capitalism and schizophrenia*, translated by Brian Massumi, Minneapolis: University of Minnesota Press.

Deleuze, Gilles and Guattari, Felix (1991/1994) *What is Philosophy?*, translated by Hugh Tomlinson and Graham Burchell, London: Verso.

Derrida, Jacques (1973) *Speech and Phenomena, and Other Essays on Husserl's Theory of Signs*, translated by David B. Allison, Evanston: Northwestern University Press.

Derrida, Jacques (1993) *The Post Card: From Socrates to Freud and Beyond*, translated by Alan Bass, Chicago: University of Chicago Press.

Derrida, Jacques (1995) *Archive Fever: a Freudian impression*, translated by Erie Prenowitz, Chicago and London: University of Chicago Press.

Derrida, Jacques and Stiegler, Bernard (1996/2002) *Echographies of Television*, translated by Jennifer Bajorek, Cambridge: Polity.

DiCorcia, Philip-Lorca (1995) *Contemporaries*, New York: MOMA/ Thames and Hudson.

Dissanayake, Wimal (2004) 'Globalization and cultural narcissism: note on Bollywood cinema', *Journal of Asian Cinema*, spring/summer, pp. 143–50.

Doane, Mary Ann (2002) *The Emergence of Cinematic Time: modernity, contingency, the archive*, Cambridge, Mass. and London: Harvard University Press.

Doel, Marcus A. (2000) 'Un-glunking geography: spatial science after Dr Seuss and Gilles Deleuze', in Mike Crang and Nigel Thrift (eds), *Thinking Space*, London and New York: Routledge.

Douglas, Stan (1998) 'Interview', in Scott Watson, Diana Thater and Carol J. Clover (eds), *Stan Douglas*, London: Phaidon.

Duras, Marguerite (1980) *Green Eyes*, translated by Carol Barko, New York: Columbia University Press.

Egoyan, Atom and Balfour, Ian (eds) (2004) *Subtitles: on the foreignness of film*, Cambridge, Mass. and London: Alphabet City Media and MIT Press.

Eisenstein, Sergei (1988) *S. M. Eisenstein: selected works, volume 1: writings 1922–34*, translated by Richard Taylor, London: BFI, and Bloomington and Indianapolis: Indiana University Press.

Eisenstein, Sergei (1991) *S. M. Eisenstein: selected works, volume 2: towards a theory of montage*, edited and translated by Michael Glenny and Richard Taylor, London: BFI, and Bloomington and Indianapolis: Indiana University Press.

Elena, Alberto (2005) *The Cinema of Abbas Kiarostami*, London: SAQI in association with Iran Heritage Foundation.

Epstein, Jean (1921/1984) 'Cine-Mystique', translated by Stuart Liebman, *Millennium Film Journal*, vols 10–11, pp. 191–3.

Epstein, Jean (1981) 'Bonjour cinema and other writings by Jean Epstein', translated by Tom Milne, *Afterimage*, vol. 10, pp. 2–39.

Flaxman, Gregory (ed.) (2000) *The Brain is the Screen: Deleuze and the philosophy of cinema*, Minneapolis and London: University of Minnesota Press.

Foucault, Michel (1966) *The Order of Things*, Routledge: London and New York.

Friedberg, Anne (1993) *Window Shopping: cinema and the postmodern*,

Berkeley: University of California Press.

Freud, Sigmund (1920/1961) *Beyond the Pleasure Principle*, translated by James Strachey, London: Penguin.

Gaines, Jane M. (2000) 'Dream/Factory', in Christine Gledhill and Linda Williams (eds), *Reinventing Film Studies*, London: Arnold.

Gan, Wendy (2003) '0.01cm: affectivity and urban space in *Chungking Express*', *Scope* online journal.

Godard, Jean-Luc (1998) *Histoire(s) du Cinéma*, Paris: Gallimard.

Gordon, Douglas (1998) 'By way of a statement on the artist's behalf', in David Gordon, (ed.), *Douglas Gordon*, Eindhoven: kidnapping.

Govil, Nitin (2004) 'Something spatial in the air: in-flight entertainment and the topographies of modern air travel', in Nick Couldry and Anna McCarthy (eds), *Mediaspace: place, scale and culture in a media age*, London and New York: Routledge.

Gunning, Tom (1991a) 'Heard over the phone: the lonely villa and the deLorde tradition of the terrors of technology', *Screen*, vol. 32, no. 2, pp. 184–96.

Gunning, Tom (1991b) *D.W. Griffiths and the Origins of American Narrative Film: the early years at biograph*, Urbana: University of Illinois Press.

Gunning, Tom (2000) ' "Animated Pictures": tales of cinema's forgotten future, after 100 years of films', in Christine Gledhill and Linda Williams (eds), *Reinventing Film Studies*, London: Arnold.

Haneke, Michael (1992) 'Film als Katharsis', in Francesco Bono (ed.), *Austria (in)felix: zum österreichischem Film der 80er Jahre*, Graz: Blimp.

Hansen, Miriam Bratu (1991) *Babel and Babylon: spectatorship in American silent film*, Cambridge, Mass.: Harvard University Press.

Hansen, Miriam Bratu (1993) ' "With skin and hair": Kracauer's theory of film, Marseille 1940', *Critical Inquiry*, vol. 19, pp. 437–69.

Hansen, Miriam Bratu (1997) 'Introduction', in Siegfried Kracauer, *Theory of Film: the redemption of physical reality*, Princeton: Princeton University Press.

Hansen, Miriam (2000) 'The mass production of the senses: classical cinema as vernacular modernism', in Christine Gledhill and Linda Williams (eds), *Reinventing Film Studies*, London and New York: Arnold.

Haraway, Donna J. (2000) *How Like a Leaf*, New York and London: Routledge.

Hardt, Michael and Negri, Antonio (2000) *Empire*, Cambridge, Mass.: Harvard University Press.

Hebdige, Dick (2003) 'Dis-gnosis: Disney and the re-tooling of knowledge, art, culture, life etc.', *Cultural Studies*, vol. 17, no. 2, pp. 150–67.

Hjort, Mette and MacKenzie, Scott (2000) *Cinema and Nation*, London and New York: Routledge.

Hoolboom, Mike (dir. and writer) (2003) Transcript from *Imitations of Life* (film), independent distribution.

Jameson, Fredric (1991) *Postmodernism, or the Cultural Logic of Late Capitalism*, London: Verso.

Jencks, Charles (1993) *Los Angeles, the Riots and the Strange Beauty of Hetero-Architecture*, London: Academy Editions.

Jones, Kent (2003) 'Here and there: the films of Tsai Ming Liang', in Jonathan Rosenbaum and Adrian Martin (eds), *Movie Mutations: the changing face of world cinephilia*, London: BFI.

Kahn, Douglas (1999) *Noise, Water, Meat: a history of sound in the arts*, Cambridge, Mass. and London: MIT Press.

Kaplan, E. Ann (2004) 'The state of the field: notes toward an article', in *Cinema Journal*, vol. 43, no. 3, pp. 85–8.

Kennedy, Barbara M. (2002) *Deleuze and Cinema: the aesthetics of sensation*, Edinburgh: Edinburgh University Press.

Kepley, Vance (1997) 'Eisenstein and Soviet cinema', in Peter Lehman (ed.), *Defining Cinema*, London: Athlone.

Kittler, Friedrich A. (1986) *Gramophone, Film, Typewriter*, translated by Geoffrey Winthrop-Young and Michael Wutz, Stanford, Calif.: Stanford University Press.

Klinger, Barbara (1997) 'Film history terminable and interminable: recovering the past in reception studies', *Screen* vol. 38, no. 1, pp. 107–28.

Kracauer, Siegfried (1960) *Theory of Film: the redemption of physical reality*, Princeton: Princeton University Press.

Lalanne, Jean-Marc (1997) 'Images from the inside', in Martinez Lalanne and Ngai Abbas (eds), *Wong Kar-wai*, Paris: Disvoir.

Landecker, Hannah (2005) 'Cellular features: microcinematography and film theory', *Critical Inquiry*, vol. 31, no. 4, pp. 903–37.

Lash, Scott (2002) *Critique of Information*, London, Thousand Oaks, New Delhi: Sage.

Latour, Bruno (1993) *We Have Never Been Modern*, translated by Catherine Porter, Cambridge, Mass.: Harvard University Press.

Latour, Bruno (1997) 'Trains of thought: Piaget, formalism, and the fifth dimension', *Common Knowledge*, vol. 6, no. 3, pp. 170–91.

Latour, Bruno (2004) 'Why has critique run out of steam? From matters of fact to matters of concern', in Bill Brown (ed.), *Things*, Chicago and London: University of Chicago Press.

Leslie, Esther (2002) *Hollywood Flatlands: animation, critical theory and the avant-garde*, London and New York: Verso.

Lury, Celia (1993) *Cultural Rights: technology, legality and personality*, London and New York: Routledge.

Lury, Celia (2004) *Brands: the logos of the global economy*, London and New York: Routledge.

McCarthy, Anna (2001) *Ambient Television*, Durham, NC and London: Duke University Press.

Manovich, Lev (2001) *The Language of New Media*, Cambridge, Mass. and London: MIT Press.

Marchetti, Gina (2000) 'Buying American, consuming Hong Kong: cultural commerce, fantasies of identity, and the cinema', in Poshek Fu and David Desser (eds), *The Cinema of Hong Kong: history, arts, identity*, New York: Cambridge University Press.

Marcus, George E. (1994) 'The modernist sensibility in recent ethnographic writing and the cinematic metaphor of montage', in Lucien Taylor (ed.), *Visualising Theory: selected essays from VAR 1990–94*, New York and London: Routledge.

Marey, Étienne-Jules (1895) *Movement*, translated by Eric Pritchard, New York: D. Appleton.

Massumi, Brian (2002) *Parables for the Virtual: movement, affect, sensation*, Durham, NC and London: Duke University Press.

Ménil, Alain (1999) 'The time(s) of the cinema', in Jean Khalfa (ed), *An Introduction to the Philosophy of Gilles Deleuze*, London: Continuum.

Miller, Paul D. (2004) *Rhythm Science*, Amsterdam/New York: Mediawork and MIT Press.

Miller, Toby, Govil, Nitin, McMurria, John and Maxwell, Richard (2001) *Global Hollywood*, London: BFI.

Moore, Rachel O. (2000) 'The tired lens', in *Savage Theory: cinema as modern magic*, Durham, NC and London: Duke University Press.

Morrison, Bill (2002) *Decasia*, DVD notes, London: BFI.

Mulvey, Laura (2004) 'Passing time: reflections on cinema from a new technological age', *Screen*, vol. 45, no. 2, pp. 142–57.

Mulvey, Laura (2006) *Death 24x a Second: stillness and the moving image*, London: Reaktion.

Musser, Charles (1990) *History of the American Cinema: the emergence of cinema – the American screen to 1907*, New York: Charles Scribner's Sons.

Naficy, Hamid (2001) *An Accented Cinema: exilic and diasporic filmmaking*, Princeton and Oxford: Princeton University Press.

Nancy, Jean-Luc (2004) 'Banks, edges, limits (of singularity)', translated by Gil Anidjar, *Angelaki*, vol. 9, no. 2, pp. 41–9.

Nietzsche, Friedrich (1971) *Beyond Good and Evil: prelude to a philosophy of the future*, translated by R. J. Hollingdale, London: Penguin.

Pasolini, Pier Paolo (1972) *Heretical Empiricism*, edited by Louise K. Barnett, translated by Ben Lawton and Louise K. Barnett, Bloomington and Indianapolis: Indiana University Press.

Pisters, Patricia (2003) *The Matrix of Visual Culture: working with Deleuze in film theory*, Stanford: Stanford University Press.

Pratt, Marie-Louise (1992) *Imperial Eyes: travel writing and transculturation*, London: Routledge.

Prigogine, Ilya and Stengers, Isabelle (1984) *Order Out of Chaos: man's dialogue with nature*, New York: Bantam.

Prigogine, Ilya and Stengers, Isabelle (1997) *The End of Certainty: time, chaos, and the laws of nature*, New York: Free Press.

Rabinow, Paul (1977) *Reflections on Fieldwork in Morocco*, Berkeley: University of California Press.

Rancière, Jacques (2001/2006) *Film Fables*, translated by Emiliano Battista, Oxford and New York: Berg.

Renov, Michael (2004) *The Subject of Documentary*, Minneapolis: University of Minnesota Press.

Rodowick, D. N. (1997) *Gilles Deleuze's Time Machine*, Durham, NC and London: Duke University Press.

Rodowick, D. N. (2001) *Reading the Figural, or, Philosophy After the New Media*, Durham, NC, and London: Duke University Press.

Rohdie, Sam (2001) *Promised Lands: cinema, geography, modernism*, London: BFI.

Ropars-Wuilleumier, Marie-Claire (1982) 'The graphic in filmic writing: *A Bout de Souffle*, or The Erratic Alphabet', *Enclitic*, vol. 5.2–6.1 (spring), pp. 147–61.

Russell, Catherine (2004) 'New media and film history: Walter Benjamin and the awakening of cinema', *Cinema Journal*, vol. 43, no. 3, pp. 81–5.

Scandura, Jani (2004) 'Cinematic insomnia', *New Formations*, vol. 53, pp. 103–14.

Serres, Michel (1994) *Atlas*, Paris: Julliard.

Serres, Michel (1995) *Genesis*, translated by Genevieve James and James Nielson, Ann Arbor: University of Michigan Press.

Shaviro, Steven (1993) *The Cinematic Body*, Minneapolis: University of Minnesota Press.

Sobchack, Vivian (2000) 'What is film history? Or, the riddle of the sphinxes', in Christine Gledhill and Linda Williams (eds), *Reinventing Film Studies*, London: Arnold.

Soja, Edward W. (1996) *Thirdspace: journeys to Los Angeles and other real and imagined places*, Oxford: Blackwell.

Staiger, Janet (1992) *Interpreting Films: studies in the historical reception of American cinema*, Princeton: Princeton University Press.

Stam, Robert (2003) 'Beyond Third Cinema: the aesthetics of hybridity', in Anthony R. Guneratne and Wimal Dissanayake (eds), *Rethinking Third Cinema*, London and New York: Routledge.

Stiegler, Bernard (1996/2002) 'The discrete image', in Bernard Stiegler and Jacques Derrida, *Echographies of Television*, translated by Jennifer Bajorek, Cambridge: Polity.

Stokes, Lisa and Hoover, Michael (1999) *City on Fire: Hong Kong cinema*, New York: Verso.

Stringer, Julian (2002) 'Wong Kar-wai', in Yvonne Tasker (ed.), *Fifty Contemporary Filmmakers*, London and New York: Routledge.

Stringer, Julian (2003) 'Boat people: second thoughts on text and context', in Chris Berry (ed.), *Chinese Films in Focus: 25 new takes*, London: BFI.

Tarkovsky, Andrey (1986) *Sculpting in Time: reflections on the cinema*, translated by Kitty Hunter-Blair, London: The Bodley Head.

Usai, Paolo Cherchi (2001) *The Death of Cinema: history, cultural memory and the digital dark age*, London: BFI.

Vidler, Anthony (2001) *Warped Space: art, architecture and anxiety in modern culture*, Cambridge, Mass.: MIT Press.

Virilio, Paul (1986) *Speed and Politics*, New York: Semiotext(e).

Virilio, Paul (1994) *The Vision Machine*, London: BFI.

Virilio, Paul and Lotringer, Sylvère (2005) *The Accident of Art*, translated by Michael Taormina, New York and Los Angeles: Semiotext(e).

Vitali, Valenta and Willeman, Paul (eds) (2006) *Theorising National Cinema*, London: BFI.

Wasafari (2004) 'Introduction', special issue, vol. 43, winter.

Williams, Christopher (2000) 'After the classic, the classical and ideology: the differences of realism', in Christine Gledhill and Linda Williams (eds), *Reinventing Film Studies*, London: Arnold.

Wim, Wenders (2001) *On Film*, London: Faber and Faber.

Winston, Brian (1993) 'The documentary film as scientific inscription', in Michael Renov (ed.), *Theorizing Documentary*, New York: Routledge.

Žižek, Slavoj (2001) *The Fright of Real Tears: Krzysztof Kieslowski between theory and post-theory*, London: BFI

Zournazi, Mary (2003) 'Navigating movements: an interview with Brian Massumi', *21C Magazine*, issue 2: p. 1.

Index